10/13/12

EVERY PERSON IS WORTH UNDERSTANDING

DR. CLYDE M. NARRAMORE

CROSSBOOKS
PUBLISHING

CrossBooks™
A Division of LifeWay
1663 Liberty Drive
Bloomington, IN 47403
www.crossbooks.com
Phone: 1-866-879-0502

Scripture taken from the New King James Version. Copyright 1979, 1980, 1982 by Thomas Nelson, inc. Used by permission. All rights reserved.

First published by CrossBooks 06/07/2011

ISBN: 978-1-6150-7693-2 (sc)
ISBN: 978-1-6150-7694-9 (dj)

Library of Congress Control Number: 2010942565

Printed in the United States of America

This book is printed on acid-free paper.

Any people depicted in stock imagery provided by Thinkstock are models, and such images are being used for illustrative purposes only.

Certain stock imagery © Thinkstock.

INTRODUCTION

The conviction that *Every Person Is Worth Understanding* is based on the fact that God has designed each person, and that person is responsible to God and is facing eternity. It is also based on the fact that relating well to people is pleasing to God and creates personal happiness.

Feeling understood has many implications. From early childhood, a person needs to feel that someone understands him. When we believe that *Every Person Is Worth Understanding*, we are meeting a basic emotional need in the life of everyone with whom we associate.

Realizing that *Every Person Is Worth Understanding* does not necessarily mean you approve of some of his behavior or that you want to pattern your life after his.

But if you believe *Every Person Is Worth Understanding*, you will more likely be less judgmental and instead focus on his potential and the causes of his behavior.

In other words, it helps you as much as it does the other person.

CONTENTS

CHAPTER ONE

THE WHITE HOUSE

Dr. Kenneth Markley, Psychologist

On a nippy spring morning in Washington, DC, Dr. Clyde Narramore and I walked down Pennsylvania Avenue approaching the White House. As a psychologist, I had been serving as the East Coast representative for the California-based Narramore Christian Foundation for a number of years. In fact, I had made the arrangements for him to speak, as he had before, to the president's staff.

I have always gotten a super lift from these special assignments. I had been with Dr. Narramore numerous times as he had spoken at the Pentagon, the State Department, the Treasury Department, the CIA, the Justice Department, the Agricultural Department, the US Army War College, as well as Annapolis and West Point. So we were both looking forward to the meeting this morning.

The president's staff had been notified of the meeting, which was to be held in an auditorium-type room inside the White House. We were checked by the guards and then ushered into an attractive auditorium. I suppose forty or more people were present. *Wow!* I thought. *It doesn't get much better than this.*

I didn't know just what topic he would speak on, but I was quite sure he would devote some time to questions and answers. This gave him an opportunity to better understand the individuals in the audience. In other words, he really believes his lifetime slogan, *Every Person Is Worth Understanding!*

"Handling Stress and Pressure" was Dr. Narramore's topic. And of course, if there's any place where stress and pressure are compounded, it's undoubtedly the nation's capitol. Pressure comes from the very nature of the activities, since the White House is, in a sense, the brain or nerve center of the world, but also because many of the people working at the White House may be newcomers. Perhaps they've said good-bye to old friends back home or where the president hailed from. So there's the stress of a new job, new ways of working, new people, new living arrangements, and a host of other challenges.

Dr. Narramore was introduced as a psychologist, author, and frequent speaker in Washington, as well as a pioneer in the field of Christian psychology. In his usual gracious manner, he thanked all for being there. He expressed not only his personal thanks but also the gratitude of many people across America who appreciate the fine work our government people were doing.

Yes, he began with a brief period of questions and answers, although he knew his time was limited to about thirty-five or forty minutes. Questions came one right after the other, and Dr. Narramore's answers provided insights as well as some humor. So we were off to a good start.

"Stress and pressure: we all have some, and perhaps a little is helpful at times. But too much is harmful. Let's consider it," he said.

In his first point, Dr. Narramore spoke about *physiological* conditions that may cause stress. "Many people," he said, "are vulnerable to undue stress and pressure because they are not in good health. But some medical conditions may be subtle. For example, I have seen people go for years before finding they had a significant chemical imbalance or some other physical problem. My point is this: if you or a friend are sensing undue stress, don't overlook the possibility of a medical cause. When we're not feeling well, we're vulnerable to stress and pressure." Then he gave several examples.

Dr. Narramore's second point centered on the *psychological* aspects of pressure. He emphasized that we may have been raised in a negative, abusive, or neglectful environment throughout childhood. We may have grown up feeling unloved or unimportant. He told of a person who said she never had a childhood because it felt as though no one knew she was there. He also mentioned another person saying his childhood was "full of holes."

He estimated that many children, perhaps a majority, grow up in homes where basic emotional needs are not well met. They reach adulthood with personality deficits, such as severe insecurity, anger, fear, feeling withdrawn, non-trusting, and the like. He indicated that unless these negative feelings (which we may not know we have) are discovered and resolved, we become "sitting ducks" for undue stress. Then he gave an illustration. Several in the audience raised specific questions. I think some would have liked to discuss the psychological factors all morning.

Dr. Narramore's third point highlighted the *spiritual* aspects of stress and pressure. He pointed out that all humans are spiritual beings; we are different from plants and animals. People are created in the image of God. "So God created man in His own image: in the image of God He created him; male or female He created them" (Gen. 1:27). As such, we all have a capacity for God; we can each know God personally. He went into this briefly, pointing out that all of us can have an intimate encounter with God because God's Son, Jesus Christ, had died on the cross to pay the penalty for our sins. Dr. Narramore then showed that this "born-again" spiritual transaction would change a person's nature and cause him to develop and grow spiritually. This thorough life change brings understanding, a new nature, peace, and love rather than stress and pressure. The room was quiet, and people seemed to be extremely interested.

He then discussed practical points of living that could reduce stress and pressure. "And don't forget to talk," he said. "The more you talk, the less pressure you'll feel. One of the major ways God has given people to rid themselves of stress, fear, anger, and other emotional baggage is through talking. So try to find someone who will listen. It may be wise to see a professional counselor."

"And of course," Dr. Narramore continued, "we must take inventory of our suitability to our profession. Many people tend to slip or slide into a vocation and then stay there. Simply because we have a college degree in a certain field doesn't mean that it's the best career fit for us, and it may be producing undue stress and pressure."

He then suggested steps a person can take to be certain he is in the right vocation or profession. I sat there like most of the others, completely engrossed. Here was an "Ivy League" man with a doctorate from Columbia

University, a licensed psychologist and a well-known author and speaker putting all this together succinctly and clearly. And it made good sense. As one attorney said to me after the meeting, "This is the most helpful seminar we've had in the years I've been here."

In closing, Dr. Narramore mentioned that we only had two or three minutes left, and if anyone wanted to make a lifetime decision and trust Christ as his personal Savior, he or she could do so right then. As he briefly challenged the group to consider the claims of Christ, I remember him saying, "Here at the White House, you make many decisions that may influence many parts of the world. But there has never been a decision made in the White House more important to you personally than the one you're considering this moment, because it will affect your life not only here on earth but for all eternity." Then he asked everyone to bow his or her head as he led in a prayer of confession of sin and acceptance of Christ.

At the close of the prayer, and as the audience looked up, he asked, "How many of you this morning have just now made this decision, and the best you know how, you'll serve Christ for the rest of your life?" Immediately eight of the forty-some people raised their hands!

Afterward, we had an opportunity to speak briefly to several of these eight. At that point, one of the officials in the White House walked up to me and said, "Would you and Dr. Narramore like to have a private tour of the White House?"

We said we would be delighted. So our host started us on the tour.

However, we had only entered the first room when a man stepped up to our guide and said there was another small private party there and asked if they could join our tour. "Of course!" we said. They were introduced as the Jackson Five! They ranged in age from young adults to little Michael, who was about twelve or so. He was cute and very polite. What a pleasant and delightful group.

An hour later, Dr. Narramore and I went back to our hotel and got ready for our next meeting, which would be at the State Department.

As I bring this opening chapter to a close, I want to express my delight in having had this privilege. This book shares much about a great movement in counseling and Christian psychology. And it is about a deeply devoted and talented man who, along with his wife, Ruth, God has chosen to give the movement leadership. Due at least in part to his influence, today there are thousands of licensed Christian psychologists, counselors, plus many pastors who are ministering to people around the world, taking into consideration the *physical, emotional,* and *spiritual* aspects of human behavior!

Occasionally someone asks why Dr. Narramore includes spiritual matters in his lectures and writings. He says that when you think about human beings, you cannot be scientific in your consideration of them unless you realize that human beings are spiritual beings, created by God, and are responsible to Him. To ignore this fact would be as unreasonable as saying human beings do not have physical bodies.

May I add that having traveled with Dr. Narramore for many years, and having visited in their home on numerous occasions, I have learned so much, especially since they have consistently lived what they taught. They have lived by their slogan, *Every Person Is Worth Understanding,* and it has affected nearly everything they have done.

On the Ranch

CHAPTER TWO

GROWING UP ON THE RANCH

When people ask me where I come from, they're often surprised as I tell them I was raised on a ranch in Arizona. I suppose they think cowboys and psychology don't go together. But perhaps there are few places better than a ranch where a kid has an opportunity to see things in a practical way and time to think about people and life while riding horses.

There were seven of us children—six boys and one girl. My sister, Lela, was the oldest and I, the youngest. My pioneer parents represented families from both the North and the South. My father's mother came from Pennsylvania. My father was born and raised in Crossville, Tennessee, formerly called Narramore.

In time, my father's family of eight brothers and sisters began their migration west to Arizona. On their way, they settled for a short time in Arkansas where my father met and married my mother, a close relative of Mrs. Jefferson Davis.

At that time, the U. S. government was offering free desert land in the Arizona Territory as homesteads to those who would build and live there for a period of time. My parents settled a 160-acre desert homestead adjacent to the Gila River about ten miles from Gila Bend. There, all the children except the last two (my brother Earl and I), were born. A few years later, the family moved to Palo Verde, Arizona, a small ranching community about forty-two miles west of Phoenix.

A SEVERE LOSS

Two years after I was born, my father, along with millions of others, died from the World War I flu epidemic. He had gone a few miles away to help his brother who had come down with the flu, and they both died within a week of each other. So, I grew up not knowing a father. Mom never remarried, but dedicated her life to raising her one girl and us six boys!

> *We know that the pre-talking months of human development are especially important whether we remember them or not.*

As a child, I rarely ever thought about not having a father. It seldom crossed my mind; I had no memory of him. I just knew it was that way. I never felt disadvantaged. Also, I had five older brothers and my mother was one of the most encouraging persons I could imagine!

Did I miss out by not having both parents? Of course! I'm sure my life would have been different and better if I had known a father. However, my family told me that during those first two years when I did have him, I was the apple of his eye, and he showed me much love and affection. So, that period undoubtedly left a positive impact. *We know that the pre-talking months of human development are especially important whether we remember them or not.* All of us benefit by having loving, encouraging, and godly moms and dads. It's a definite loss to have only one parent. God has intended that fathers and mothers both contribute significantly to a child's best development. And these influences last a lifetime.

THE RANCH

People sometimes ask, "Did you ride horses?" Yes, quite a lot.

We had beef cattle, dairy cattle, work horses, and riding horses. In the early days, most machinery had not yet reached American farms and ranches. Electricity had not come to our little community—no electric lights, appliances, or radios. Television didn't arrive until nearly thirty years later. But we did have a small church, a school, a tiny country store, and plenty of space! Model T cars were just beginning to appear. Horses played an important role. If I wanted to go somewhere or do something, I'd jump on a horse and go!

Like other teenagers, we ranch kids had our occasional fantasies. One time we thought we could put on a local rodeo and charge twenty-five cents so we could make some money. Six or seven of us got together and decided who'd do the roping and who'd do the bulldogging and all the rest of it. But eventually, the idea got lost because we had to get busy and work. Cattle and crops were calling!

We got up early to milk cows, and we milked again in the evening. On top of that, as teenagers we had to walk (or run) half a mile each morning to the main road where we caught the school bus to ride seven miles to the nearest high school. So we were busy, with no time to get into trouble.

My interests seemed to follow those of my brothers. Besides ranching, we were all interested in sports, music, and people. Our family was musical, and four of us boys became tenor soloists. One brother, Earl, was an exceptionally good pianist, even as a child. He accompanied all of us as we gathered around the piano to sing. This was an important part of our development. It introduced an artistic element into our lives that was a contrast to ranch work.

Did I like cattle? They were okay; that's how we made a living. But I was much more interested in people, and I knew *I could never influence a cow!* My brothers taught me about ranch life—raising and harvesting crops, breeding and butchering cattle, treating sick animals, breaking horses, repairing harnesses and farm machinery, milking cows, raising pigs, and whatever. Since there were no "consultants" or "resources," we had to do it all ourselves! Naturally, I absorbed a lot. But I'm afraid I was a rather disinterested learner. My mind seemed to focus on people and why they felt and acted the way they did.

I enjoyed growing up on the ranch. My brothers treated me fairly, and church and school (our two meeting places) were a delight. We lived in a productive, irrigated valley just a mile from the desert. In fact, I felt sorry for kids who didn't live near a desert. I often wondered how they could have much fun!

There weren't many people in our little community, perhaps a hundred or so including the children. I knew them all and they knew me. In a sense, we were accountable to one another. So between them and my family, plus dynamic faith in Christ, I managed to grow up behaving myself with a heart filled with hope and excitement about the future!

BUTTERMILK AND KISSES

In our community there was no kindergarten, so a child could not enter school until he was about six. Was that so bad? No, not especially—at least not in my case. I was learning a lot around our farm and since my five brothers and one sister were older and in school, my mom was able to show me much love and attention.

One day when I was about four or five, I came into the kitchen where my mother was standing at the table, hand-churning cream so we could have fresh butter.

"Here, stand on this chair," Mom said, "and you can see butter. This is like a miracle. We're churning this cream, and in just a few minutes, it will separate and we'll have both butter and buttermilk." That was exciting to me. Surely enough, the butter began to gather, and soon a big yellow ball appeared in the churn. Then my mother took the buttermilk, strained it, put some in a glass with a little salt, and drank it, saying, "Oh, this is so good."

"I want some too, Mommy," I said.

"Well, this is not like regular milk," she explained. "It's a little sour and you have to learn to like it. So I'll give you just a little taste." Then she poured a small amount in a glass, and as I drank it, she gave me a sweet kiss on the forehead.

"I want more!" I said.

"Okay, you can have more," she said. So she gave me just a little, and as I drank it, she gave me another kiss. Then she hugged me and said, "You know something? You're such a wonderful little boy that I wish I had forty more just like you!"

Long-forgotten experiences can remain tucked away and have an influence on our behavior, positive or negative, for years to come.

I thought, *Forty brothers! That would be wonderful; we could have lots of teams and play lots of games.* I never doubted her statement. I felt that she was really in earnest. I suppose I heard that in my childhood a hundred times: "I'd like to have forty more just like you."

And even today, years later, whenever I drink buttermilk I seem to feel my mother's kisses! You know how it is: you taste, smell, or see something, and suddenly it takes you back ten, twenty, or even fifty years ago to a certain experience. *Long-forgotten experiences can remain tucked away and have an influence on our behavior, positive or negative, for years to come.*

We may be unaware of these forgotten but influential childhood experiences. In fact, professional counselors spend much of their time uncovering some of these forgotten episodes. Eventually, the client may suddenly recall a traumatic experience of childhood or perhaps a whole series of them. As he examines them carefully, he can see how they have caused him to have severe feelings of hostility, insecurity, jealousy, or some other negative trait. With careful guidance by the Christian counselor, these unhealthy feelings can be changed so that the client is able to feel and act differently. A Christian psychologist can help the client to replace negative feelings about oneself with positive feelings based on the eternal Word of God. The result: new, improved ways of thinking and acting!

A few years ago, I was driving down a freeway in southern California and I began to think: *I wonder if Mom really meant it when she used to say she wished she had forty boys just like me.* But by that time, it really didn't matter because I had assimilated all those wonderful feelings inside; feelings that helped me know that I was worthwhile, that I was loved and accepted.

A basic emotional need of every person is to be loved and accepted! Undoubtedly, *one of the most serious tragedies in childhood is to grow up not feeling loved and not having anyone to love. Kids can do without most "things," but they don't develop well without love.*

> *One of the most serious tragedies in childhood is to grow up not feeling loved and not having anyone to love. Kids can do without most "things," but they don't develop well without love.*

As adults, we should also realize that many of our friends and associates have never had much love and affection during their growing-up years. When we recognize this, it can help us understand their behavior and we will be more likely to reach out and encourage them.

In short, they've never had buttermilk mixed with kisses!

THE OLD PLANK ROAD

One summer when I was about nine, our family decided to get out of the oppressive heat of the Arizona desert. So with my mother and two brothers, we made plans to go over to Southern California for a couple of weeks.

The shortest route for us was west to Yuma, Arizona, located at the California border, then onto the coast.

Our vehicle was a Ford touring car. We had four isinglass covers, which we could button onto the window openings to keep the hot wind out. They didn't work very well, but they were "state of the art" in those days.

The narrow highway to Yuma was bad enough, but when we arrived there, people warned us about traveling on west to California. There was a stretch of desert between Yuma and Holtville, California, that was nothing but desolate shifting sand. They called this seven-mile trek the Imperial Sand Dunes.

How could we cross the shifting sands in our Ford? Well, we soon found out. First, when leaving Yuma, we hung canvas water bags on the sides of our car. The hot wind blowing against the canvas covers cooled the water a little so we could have something to drink as we crossed the scorching desert.

A few miles west of Yuma, we came to the shifting sand dunes. And there was the road! It was made of wooden planks about eight feet wide that were joined together—just wide enough for one car to travel on. Every so often there was a double-width turnout about thirty feet long. Consequently, when we saw another car coming toward us, one car would have to go forward or back up until the driver could find a spot where the road was wider. Then we would maneuver our car onto this wider section. I've heard of an occasional driver who refused to back up to a turnout area. In such cases, men from the tied-up passersby would lift the offending car partly off the plank road. Then the two or three cars would drive through. When the cars had passed, they got the car back onto the road, and everyone went on his way.

An old sign along the road said the official speed was ten miles an hour. I doubt if anyone exceeded that! As we drove on the Old Plank Road, there was nothing but sand all around us. Occasionally, we'd notice the carcass of a cow or mule that had evidently died of thirst or hunger. Their white bones gleamed in the burning hot sun.

My brothers were good drivers, and I don't remember our car slipping off the eight-foot-wide plank road. We made it across.

Today, all that's left of the Old Plank Road is a crumbling section just east of Holtville. It has been well-designated as a historic landmark.

After we had crossed the sand dunes and arrived in the Imperial Valley, our road turned north alongside the Salton Sea located on the desert. It was about thirty-five miles long.

As a kid, this interested me because my mother had told me about the formation of this large, salty body of water. Between 1905 and 1907, the unbridled Colorado River went on a rampage for more than a year and flooded this below-sea-level desert area, covering communities, farms, and the main line of the Southern Pacific Railroad. It continued to fill until 1907, when a line of protective levies was built by Southern Pacific boxcars, which dumped boulders into the breach. By then this inland lake was about forty miles long and fifteen miles wide, covering an area of four hundred square miles.

Mom had told us that during the time of the flooding in 1905, my father, along with other men from the Gila Bend area, was asked to come and help stop the flooding. They went but were almost powerless to hold back the raging river.

Today the Salton Sea has no outlet. It is so salty that most species of birds and fish cannot live there.

Finally we arrived in Indio, Beaumont, and Banning, about eighty miles east of Los Angeles. From there, we headed toward Long Beach, where our family rented a little house a block from the beach. The rent? About $20 a month!

This was like the vestibule to heaven to us. We saw the orange trees, felt the Pacific breezes, and spent much of the day swimming in the ocean. Then, on a wooden walkway along the beach, we would ride on a tram into town and see the amusement park. At the park, I especially remember riding the scary "Jack Rabbit Racer" rollercoaster.

These few weeks in California introduced us to a whole new culture. We met people from many places and saw how they did things.

I remember my mother doing a very wise thing. She took us to big tent meetings in Long Beach where an evangelist, John Brown from Siloam Springs, Arkansas, was speaking. He was a college president. It seemed to me that half of the world's population was crowded into that big tent. There was an enormous choir, so different from the choirs with eight or nine people that I was accustomed to back home. I was amazed at the large number of people walking down the aisles and surrendering their lives to Christ. The preaching and music made a lasting impression on my life. I had never attended such meetings. I felt like we were in the spiritual majority. My life was expanding, and God was working in my heart!

STOVEPIPE AND CONVERSION

I came from a family where we had a basic belief in God and a reverence for the Bible and Christian teachings. My mother encouraged the children spiritually. Our one little church was attended by thirty or forty people most of the time. Our family made up six or seven of the congregation.

One of my earliest encounters with spiritual conversion involved two farm workers in our community. These men were known for their filthy, foul mouths and their sinfulness. As a boy working on the ranch, I knew these men, and I heard them talk about almost everything. Then one day I was told that on Sunday night they "went forward" in an evangelistic meeting and were "saved."

My, I thought, *I wonder how they're going to act now—and how long the change (if any) will last.*

So I observed them as we worked in the fields. Indeed, a great change had come into their lives! Their talk was different, their attitudes improved, and their actions were different. This was proof to me that spiritual conversion was real!

As I attended Sunday school, my teachers often emphasized the memorization of Scripture. Sometimes they gave little prizes to those who learned the most verses. Since I memorized rather easily and liked prizes, I committed many Bible verses to memory. Little did I realize that those Scriptures imbedded in my mind and heart would influence me profoundly all through my life.

Even as a child, I knew I was a sinner. No one had to draw a picture to explain that. And on Sundays when I went to our little church, it seemed that no matter where I sat, the preacher was looking right at me; I felt certain he had my number. I really don't suppose he even knew I was there, but I sure knew he was!

Finally I decided that the best place to sit was on the bench in back of the stovepipe of the church's potbellied wood-burning stove. When the pastor moved to his left, I would scoot to my left. When he moved to his right, I would scoot to my right, always keeping the stovepipe between us.

The Bible says there are three kinds of stovepipes—three things that can keep people from a personal relationship with God. The first is the *lust of the flesh*, the second is *the lust of the eyes*, and the third is *the pride of life (1 John 2:16)*. I suppose the third may be the most common.

One day at home, I had a little scare when I overheard by brother, just older than I, talking with my mother. He was complaining because I always sat in the same place when we went to church. Finally my mother said, "We live in America, a free country, and when we go to church, we should be able to sit where we want. So leave him alone."

Thank God for a smart mother! I thought.

So I continued to sit behind the stovepipe. But although I could hide from the pastor's gaze, I always heard his messages. In addition, my Sunday school teacher reinforced the things the pastor preached. In time, I became convinced that John 14:6 was true: "I [Jesus] am the way, the truth, and the life: No man comes to the Father, but by me."

I knew that the only way to God was through Christ. Yet during the years when I sat there behind the stovepipe, I wanted to do my own thing. Then one day when I was about eleven, a wonderful thing happened. I was riding a horse bringing some cattle into the corral when I thought to myself, *I've been hiding behind that stovepipe long enough. When I get these cattle in the corral, I think I'll get off my horse, kneel down, and ask Christ to come into my heart and save me.* And I did just that! Kneeling there beside a ditch bank, I told God something I will never forget: "I'll serve You as long as I live!"

You may wonder what kind of feeling I got. Frankly, I wasn't looking for a feeling; I was looking for Jesus. No tingles down my spine? No, but I did have the assurance that if I died at that moment, I would be in the presence of God. The Bible says when you're saved, you can know it. "Most assuredly, I say to you, he who hears My word and believes in Him who sent Me has everlasting life and shall not come into judgment, but is passed from death unto life" (John 5:24).

One fault that soon left me was my temper. God seemed to replace it with a more kindly spirit. Other things I'm still working on! The Bible says we are made conformable to the image of Christ, and indeed, this is true.

Being saved and indwelt by God's Holy Spirit put a whole host of dynamics into motion. It was now possible in the future, as I dedicated my life to Christ, to accomplish important things. Someday I would be able to choose a Christian wife and stand in the White House encouraging the president's staff to choose eternal life. I would be interested in founding a Christian graduate school of psychology, speak to millions on Christian radio, serve the Lord, and enjoy the blessings to God all the days of my life—all this, plus eternity with Him. What a decision!

From that day on, I have never doubted my salvation. Christ lives in my heart, and He is my best friend. I suppose, in a sense, He also took the place of my father who had died when I was a baby.

Being born again has helped me put things in proper perspective. I believe I have avoided a rollercoaster, up-and-down secular life by being saved at an early age, studying the Bible, associating with godly people, and committing each day to Him! Indeed, it pays to stop hiding behind our "stovepipes!"

DISAPPOINTMENT

I liked going to our church because it was where the people gathered to hear preaching, Bible teaching, and music. It was also the meeting place for dinners and various social occasions.

Our Sunday school class at the church was a little different. An irrigation ditch ran near the church where shady trees protected us from the sun. We'd often have our Sunday school class outside, kids sitting on the ditch bank with their feet dangling in the dry ditch while the teacher sat on the opposite side telling us about Paul, Moses, and Jesus. When water was in the ditch, we moved away and sat on the grass under the tree. We had no fancy classrooms, but somehow we got by! It was there that I memorized many portions of Scripture.

> *It's amazing how many things you do "incorrectly" that turn out so well.*

Years later, when I studied Christian education, I learned that we had made a big mistake: when I was a kid, boys and girls were in classes together! There was none of this divided bifurcation stuff. Today, Sunday school specialists may say that boys should be in one classroom and girls in another. So I guess we had it all wrong! We sat together, and somehow it seemed just right. In fact, I liked it a lot better. *It's amazing how many things you do "incorrectly" that turn out so well.*

But as a child, I learned that even in the church things weren't always perfect. When I was about thirteen, I was very disappointed when I learned that our pastor had done something very wrong. Evidently he had become infatuated with a young lady about nineteen or twenty years of age, and he had run away with her, leaving his wife and family.

This really disturbed me, of course, but somehow God gave me some understanding. As the weeks went by, I thought I had it all figured out. It seemed to me that our pastor, although he was a believer in Christ, had a lot of hang-ups (some of which I had noticed), which left him vulnerable to doing the sinful thing he chose to do.

So I never blamed God for our pastor's sin, because I didn't think God made him do it. Nor did I blame the church, because the people there were good, decent people. I knew what they thought and talked about.

Perhaps God permitted me to have this experience in preparation for when, later on as a psychologist, many serious problems would be brought to my attention for counseling. One of the greatest joys of my life has been to know so many outstanding Christian leaders who are godly through and through. At the same time, I have known other Christian leaders who have been such disappointments. Many have come to me for counseling about their sinful problems. It's been a rather conflicting experience for me to be exalting Christ in public while privately counseling with fallen believers.

But I always remember what seemed to be impressed upon me as a child—that God does not cause the downfalls. Most problems have long root systems. *Serious problems seldom begin suddenly. They often start years earlier.* Today when I counsel with a Christian leader who has fallen into sin, I can usually trace the causes, at least in part, to the early years of

> *Serious problems seldom begin suddenly. They often start years earlier.*

his life. At that time, there was probably no one to help him work through and solve his problems. So he eventually grew up and entered adulthood with personality deficits, along with spiritual lacks.

There are many causes for people's problems. But of this you can be sure: *people who have pronounced personality deficits are "sitting ducks" for all kinds of evil things that come down the pike!* I learned that as a kid.

VOTE FOR ME

I began to get my first insight into politics when I was about twelve years old. It happened on a hot August evening in our small ranching community. I was surprised at the "large" crowd of eighty or so that had gathered. Everybody in the area seemed to know about it.

State and county elections were coming up shortly, so the candidates came to tell us why we should vote for them. The rally was held on our local school grounds. A flatbed truck was the stage! I remember how it was decorated all around with red, white, and blue bunting.

One at a time, the candidates stepped up a short ladder to the bed of the truck, and there they talked to us. Each tried to convince us he was the best candidate. Their speeches seemed to follow a similar pattern. Each would usually crack a joke, mention the summer heat, and then say something nice about our community before starting his spiel. We gathered around the truck sitting on the ground or on benches listening as though we could hardly wait for the next words of wisdom to fall from their anointed lips! After all, this was a big event for our small community. However, we kids had another interest—we kept one eye glued to a big box near the truck. That's where the ice cream and cold drinks were kept!

There was clearly a "pecking order" for the speakers. Local candidates spoke first. Those for county offices came second on the program, and so on. I especially liked the one running for the U. S. Senate. I liked the way he looked and spoke. In fact, the thought crossed my mind: *maybe someday I can be a Senator. He probably gets to travel and makes lots of money.* Interestingly, nine years later I had the privilege of working part-time for a U. S. senator.

Finally, the candidate for governor spoke. The weather was hot, as much as 110 to 120 degrees, but he slipped on his white coat just before getting up to speak. That impressed me. No one in our family wore a white coat, or seldom a coat of any kind. The weather dictated that!

After all the speaking had run down, the candidates milled around the people shaking hands and "working the crowd." But we kids made a beeline for the big box filled with ice cream bars and soft drinks. It was kept frozen with dry ice, which was like magic to us. In fact, we got a big kick out of playing with the ice, which was both cold and hot. I'm sure we were more interested in the dry ice and refreshments than we were in the election!

Time passes, and changes come. Little did I realize as a kid that someday I would be invited to the White House myself, speaking to the staffs of several presidents!

Looking back at it now, I wonder why those politicians would bother coming to our little community where there were only a handful of people. I suppose one reason they did was because there weren't many more people in other places in Arizona! But I think there is an important lesson here. The politicians knew that if they could touch a few people at a time, they could eventually be elected and make a difference. Today most of us won't influence millions or even thousands. *But if each of us reaches out to the people around us, together we can make a tremendous difference.*

These childhood experiences with elections were important. They showed democracy in action, and they were proof that each one of us as an American is important and can be proud of our country.

> *But if each of us reaches out to the people around us, together we can make a tremendous difference.*

Today in the twenty-first century, politicians are still telling us why we should vote for them, not on flatbed trucks but on television. Kids are no longer looking for the soft drinks and ice cream. But some large corporations and special interest groups are very interested in their own sweet deals. But praise God, we live in America!

THE SHEEP ARE COMING

Our little farming community didn't produce many spectacular or earthshaking events, but we did have a few occasional highlights. One was the arrival of the sheep! Each fall, sheep companies gathered their enormous flocks from the mountains and high grasslands ready to move them south for the winter. These massive carpets of wool would come from northern Arizona.

The object was not only to get the valuable herds of ewes to warmer climates, but also to give them the best green fields and a place where they could give birth to their little lambs. The transportation was a feat in itself. After herding the sheep from the mountain pasturelands, the experienced sheepherders with their expertly trained dogs ran the sheep through narrow chutes to load them onto the waiting railroad cars designed for such travel.

Then the trains rushed their precious wooly cargo to the unloading depot just a mile and a half north of our Palo Verde ranch. Our train station area was far from pretentious. In fact, most trains passing through didn't even know it was there! It was simply a single room built of lumber and painted a typical railroad yellow. But I don't suppose the sheep knew the difference—-or even cared. They were all busy jumping off the boxcars and blindly following each other.

As thousands of sheep touched the warm earth of their new location, the sheepherders and their cunning dogs guided them down the country dirt road, which local ranchers called the Palo Verde Road. It was a straight mile and a half shot, due south to our ranch. As a kid, I got my first glimpse of this tightly packed herd when I stood by the dusty road in front of our house.

These newcomers looked like a three-foot-deep carpet of dirty white wool slowly drifting forward toward the fields of green alfalfa that surrounded our home.

How exciting! This migration of white wooly creatures signaled a new season. The oppressive heat of the summer had escaped, and the pleasant weeks of November had arrived. But the coming of the sheep signaled a lot more. We were in for many exciting experiences as the enormous flocks shared our community, giving birth to their young. To our family, it also meant that we would be paid for the pasturing and that the much-needed checks would help us to make it through another winter when there was no harvesting—-only the milking of cows and the occasional butchering of a steer or pig.

After a few weeks when the sheep had eaten all the alfalfa and had nibbled every remaining blade of grass, the sheepherders moved them to an adjacent new field. These pasture areas were fenced, which helped keep the sneaky coyotes out. To make sure the gentle, unsuspecting sheep were safe, the vigilant sheepherders and their dogs made their rounds by the fences several times during the day and night. Each day, perhaps fifty or more fuzzy little lambs were born. This was the biggest population increase our community had ever seen!

But what seemed to interest me most were the sheepherders. Only two were needed to handle a whole field of sheep. They were usually Basque from northern Spain or southern France. They appeared to be in their thirties or forties, and along with other languages, they spoke some Spanish and a smattering of English. They were camped in a little folding canvas tent on the edge of the field near the sheep. They often cooked in a small iron Dutch oven pan. They slept on a folding canvas cot, using a sheepskin for a pillow. They moved around quietly and seemed to know everything that was going on with their thousands of sheep. They used their whistling to signal what they wanted their dogs and sheep to do. They all seemed to understand his blowing of the lips.

Some of the sheepherders were artistic and spent part of their lonely hours carving walking sticks, which they had found as limbs around the mesquite trees. Their carvings on the sticks were remarkably detailed and artistic. I was reminded of them many years later when I was given one of Harry Lauder's walking sticks.

I got personally involved when occasionally a tiny lamb was orphaned. The sheepherders would give it to our family, so we built a little pen for it and gave the newborn leppie (a motherless lamb) nippled bottles of milk several times a day.

When winter had passed and spring arrived, the sheep left our community, heading again for the high country. Now there were twice as many as before because all the ewes had given birth to a lamb, and often twins. They were strong, frisky, and ready for the trip to their mountain pasture home.

But they left lots of memories and a great deal of understanding of the ways and importance of sheep and the men who patiently cared for them.

THE GREAT DEPRESSION

If you should go on the Internet or turn to an encyclopedia to learn about the Great Depression, it might carry the heading, "The Great Depression of 1929." This could lead you to believe that the times were hard only during that particular year, but not so. The Great Depression began in 1929 and lasted for about ten years. It was triggered by a serious crash in the stock market in "Black October, 1929." The Great Depression not only strangled the United States, but it also spread its hungry claws over many nations of the world.

I was in junior high when the crash came. Since there was no television and very little radio, we received most of our information from a newspaper which was usually delivered one day late to the general store in our little community.

Like other kids of that period, the Great Depression affected me throughout junior high, high school, and college. Nearly every facet of our lives was touched by this financial catastrophe. The people in our ranch area were probably not as seriously affected as those in big cities. I remember seeing pictures in the newspaper of men, women, and children standing in long lines in New York, Chicago, Philadelphia, and other cities, hoping to get a bowl of soup.

Many people were taking their own lives because they were hungry, out of work, despondent, and unable to go on any longer. A world-renowned bridge in Pasadena, California, the Arroyo Seco, earned the name of "Suicide Bridge" as people in despair hurled themselves to their death in the deep ravine below.

Almost everyone in our community was a farmer, with the exception of the pastor, the public school teachers, and the owner of the small grocery store, so farmers with milk cows, chickens, and hogs could produce some of their own food.

Their challenge was to cut expenses to nearly zero, pay taxes, meet mortgage payments, and ride the Depression out, if possible, for the next eight to ten years. Times were tough, but most families in our community were Christians looking to the Lord for guidance. That gave us hope.

Families passed clothing on from an older child to the next in age. Younger kids grew into their older siblings' shoes. Everybody was doing it.

Was everyone emotionally depressed? No, life went on.

Young people fell in love, got married (although usually waiting until they were a little older), and raised their families. Young fellows often began farming with their dads. Along with this, we had our share of happy community activities. We met occasionally at the schoolhouse, put on plays, sang songs, and had box socials. Single young ladies would bring a dinner box, usually a decorated shoe box, and then the attractive boxes were auctioned off to the highest bidder. Every unmarried fellow tried to figure out which box had been prepared by the girl he liked, and then he would bid on it. Sometimes he was right, but other times he found himself eating with someone he really didn't especially care for! But we had lots of fun.

The community owned a ten-gallon ice cream freezer. This was important inasmuch as no ice cream was available at the grocery store in our community, and summers in Arizona were more than hot. This huge freezer was located at our home, so I got to see everything that happened.

Ladies would come in the afternoon with milk, cream, eggs, sugar, and vanilla. They would mix the ingredients together, pour the mixture into the big freezer can, pack the freezer with ice and salt, attach the belt to a motor, and away it went, turning and freezing. I remember people saying, "It's real homemade—not the store-bought kind!" Before long, the ice cream was just the right texture and frozen almost solid. The best part came when the ladies removed the dash (nearly three feet long) from the middle of the freezer can, and I got to help eat the ice cream that stuck to it.

That evening the freezer was loaded onto a pickup truck and taken to the schoolhouse, the center of community activities. After the festivities of playing games, singing songs, and talking with friends, it was time to enjoy homemade ice cream and cake. On the ranch, I was growing in many ways, and my little place here on earth seemed good to me.

RUNNING AND JUMPING

Teenagers like to run and jump. And I did my share on the ranch. When I wasn't on a horse, I was running around the ranch taking care of cattle and horses, mending fences, and the like.

But at the high school campus it was different. We lived seven miles away, and the only way to get there and back was to take the school bus. Each morning and evening it took about two hours to milk the cows and do all the other chores.

Our school bus arrived at the high school just as the first class was beginning, and it left right after the last class. So athletics at school was pretty well limited to the physical education period.

I saw the kids playing tennis, and it looked very interesting to me. But I had never held a racquet in my hands, and I guess I had never even seen a tennis court before.

But in time I began to play, and in my senior year, at seventeen, I won the school tournament.

"Now" the school principal said, "You'll go to the state finals in Phoenix. Some of those boys will be very good. It is a large high school and the boys play tennis nearly all the time. They don't have to milk cows." He went on to say that some of them might have professional coaches and their dads might be professionals.

Then the day of the state finals came. The first day I played a fellow from Peoria. He wasn't very good so I beat him. But guess who I drew the second day; the champion of Phoenix High School. It only took me a few minutes to learn that he was way out of my class. So he beat me soundly. We were from two different worlds – he from the tennis courts and I from the milking corral!

A few years later as I was finishing college, I read in the newspaper that he had gone to Stanford and had become the U.S. National champion. So

I could console myself by saying I had played the national champion! In basketball things were different. In my senior year I had made the first team. We had one of the best teams in the state, and we won the central Arizona championship.

EXPLODING ON MY CONSONANTS

I was walking down the hallway in high school one day when I saw a notice on the bulletin board---SPEECH CONTEST. It told about a state-wide speech contest that any student could enter. I wasn't especially excited about it, but I knew there was a cute girl who was entering the contest and I thought if I entered, maybe we could practice our speeches together.

So I decided to go for it. I earned my speech, competed, and a couple of weeks later I won. That didn't really mean much because it was a small high school and only a few had entered the contest!

On the following Monday I was walking down the hallway when I met Mr. Smith, my speech coach who was also our track coach. "Narramore," he said, "I want to see you in the auditorium during your study hall". Great, I thought to myself, maybe he's going to compliment me and give me some sort of gift.

But that wasn't what he had in mind. Instead, he said he'd like to hear me give my speech again because I would soon be representing our school in a contest among all the high schools in our part of the state.

So I went on the stage and began my speech. After the first few paragraphs, he stopped me and moaned "Oh no! Oh no!

"Is something wrong?" I asked.

"Yes" he said "nearly everything! First of all, you're dead, completely dead."

I thought for a minute, then said, "I don't feel dead."

"Well," he said, "when you're dead, you don't know how dead you are." And he continued to tell me how stiff and dead I sounded.

"What do you want me to do?" I asked.

"Be energetic," he said. "Be dynamic and persuasive. More energy, more energy!"

"How do you do that?" I asked.

"One way," he said "is to explode on your consonants."

"Your consonants," he continued, "are all the letters that aren't you're a's, e's, I's, o's and u's. Instead of just saying 'm' explode and say a big "mmm uh,' and rather than saying 't' make it a big 'Tuh.' Instead of saying 'j', make it a big 'Juh.' This," he said, "will make your speech come to life."

I thought to myself – What a crazy thing to do!

Then he said, "Now try it!" So I did, and he said, "Oh no! You're still dead! I want you to really explode!"

So I tried it again, thinking I was exaggerating. But it still wasn't enough.

Then he told me, "When you go home this evening practice while you do your chores. Practice exploding on those consonants."

I thought to myself, *I'm from a sensible family and I wouldn't dare "explode" in front of my five older brothers.* But that evening I gave in while I was milking a cow. I began to explode on my consonants---"Mm uhs, Cc uh, Ff uh, Tt uh, Kk uh, Pp uh." I remember my brother Lawrence (Dr. Bruce Narramore's father) who was milking a cow near me, saying, "what on earth are you doing?"

"I'm exploding on my consonants," I said.

Why are you doing that?" he asked. Then I told him about the speech contest and that my coach wanted me to explode on my consonants.

"Well," he said, "do you have to do it here in front of all these cows?"

A day or two later I saw Mr. Smith again in the auditorium and he wanted to hear me explode. I did the best I could, and he said, "Your doing a little better, but you're far from good; you're still stiff and half dead." Then he said, "Now I want you to project."

"Project what?" I asked.

"I want you to project your voice." He said.

"I don't think I can," I said. "It's in my throat."

He smiled and said, "Now as you stand there on the stage, look at the back of the auditorium. Look to the left, then the right. There's a big board about a foot wide all across the back of the auditorium.

"I don't see any board," I told him.

"Just imagine you see a board," he said. "Thousands of large nails are driven part way into the board. And when you speak I want you to look right over the heads of all of these people, and pound the nails right into the board."

By that time I was wishing I had never entered the contest. But my coach felt I needed a lot of work before I went to the valley contest to compete with the best orators from about 18 high schools. I had begun to realize how much a person could do with his voice.

"Next," he said, "I want you to use your body." You're standing there like a stiff post, completely lacking in emotion."

He continued this coaching until a day before the big valley contest. He drove me in his car, and wonder of wonders I won the contest! On Monday morning he said he would see me at 10 o'clock in the auditorium. I wondered what kind of gift he was going to give me. But that's not what he was thinking. He asked me to go to the platform and start giving my oration. Suddenly he stopped me and said, "Oh no, you're still dead and stiff!" I reminded him that I had won the valley contest. "That's because the others weren't very good. In a few weeks you'll be going to the state finals in Phoenix and we've really got to get you in shape, " he said.

So we had more sessions. The finals were held in a beautiful auditorium in downtown Phoenix where a number of dignitaries attended. At the end of the contest they announced that I had won third place. One lady walked up to me and said, "I sure liked the way you spoke. You're so dynamic and full of energy." At that second I only wished my coach had been standing with us and I would have said, "Well I guess some people just have it, and some don't!"

Then the lady said, "Some day you will be speaking to millions."

I blinked my eyes and wondered where that could be. I didn't think there were a million people in Arizona. Millions of jackrabbits, yes, but not that many people. Little did I realize that as the years passed her prediction would come true as I spoke on the radio and at meetings around the world.

GET ALL YOU CAN

I've heard of a mother who was so eager for her children to get a good education that the first three words she taught them were Mama, Daddy and college!

Our family never did that, but my mother encouraged me in my school work. "Get all the education you can," she said. "It will help you to get ahead." In our little country school there were only about eight or ten in the eighth grade. When we graduated I was selected as the valedictorian. I gave a little speech and only Heaven knows what I must have said. But my five brothers didn't criticize me, so I guess I did ok. Our special speaker was John Murdock, Dean at Arizona State University. At the close of the exercise he shook my hand and said, "Young man, that was a good speech. Four years from now when you graduate from high school, see me and I will try to get you a work scholarship at college."

I often thought about that. When I graduated from high school I didn't become the valedictorian, but I did receive another recognition. Our high school awarded each student a certain number of points for each activity we participated in. And since I was interested in most everything such as sports, music, speech, journalism and the like, I was named Campus King. An active, talented girl classmate was named Campus Queen.

So I was happy looking forward to what would happen in college. I knew the Lord was with me and would guide me each day. I had raised several steers and was ready to sell them for $350.00 and take my fortune to the halls of higher learning!

CHAPTER THREE

WHAT HAPPENED AT COLLEGE

I was seventeen years old, bright eyed and bushy tailed! My heart seemed to skip a beat as I walked on the campus of Arizona State University (current name) at Tempe, Arizona. I felt almost rich with my $350 calf money in my pocket. My brother Earl had already been there a year, so that made it easier for me to find my way around and get acquainted.

About the second day on campus, I looked up the dean of students—my "friend," Dr. Murdock, who had been the speaker at my eighth grade commencement four years earlier. He had told me he would help me get a job or a scholarship, so I sought him out with high hopes.

Having grown a lot since he last saw me, I explained who I was and he said, "Oh, yes, I remember you from the eighth grade. I promised you a work scholarship." So he arranged for that.

I was fortunate to get a campus job in the library. I not only came to know lots of students and most of the faculty, but I also learned much about books and did some reading for my own classes during quiet intervals. Attending college was a big change from the ranch, but it was the beginning of a wonderful life. I was ready for whatever God had for me.

As a seventeen-year-old country kid, I didn't know very much. Television had not yet been invented, and I had never even seen snow!

Unlike most of my classmates, I had memorized a great deal of Scripture and felt the Lord was always with me and would guide me. So how could I lose? I did have a core of beliefs based upon the eternal Word of God.

+ I believed the Bible to be the inspired Word of God and that I could depend upon it. When I didn't know what else to believe, I relied on the Scriptures. This gave me wisdom not always found in the classroom.

+ I believed that God had created Adam and Eve and placed them in the Garden of Eden, and since God had formed us, we were responsible to Him. That belief made a great difference in how I felt about others and myself.

+ I believed that Christ was not only human but also divine. If He was able to heal the sick and raise the dead, He could help me with my daily concerns and problems.

+ I believed that all people were sinful and needed to be saved. That was easy to observe, and it gave me focus.

+ I believed that Christ, after having died and been buried for three days and nights, was able to rise from the tomb because He was God.

+ I knew that God could forgive people and save them, giving them new spiritual life. He had done it for me.

+ I believed that Christ was coming back to receive us so we could be forever with Him. That would solve all the world's problems.

Now, years later, as I look back, I realize these basic beliefs helped me over rough spots, gave me tremendous hope, and kept me from living a worldly life. They also inspired me to reach out and help others.

Even though I was attending a secular college, I had a commitment to live for Christ. I liked and respected the other students, and I had many friends. But I knew that the great majority of my classmates did not have a personal faith in the Lord and that their lifestyles and activities did not honor Him. I marched to a different drummer. Consequently, I did not take part in activities that clearly did not honor the Lord.

Did this put me at a disadvantage? Not at all. In fact, it helped me tremendously! I was voted to various positions of leadership. I knew that living a committed Christian life could sometimes evoke criticism. God's Word clearly tells us, "All who desire to live godly in Christ Jesus will suffer persecution" (2 Tim. 3:12). Christians and non-Christians are living in two different worlds. A person who is dedicated to Christ is not trying to win a popularity contest. So in my case, I felt encouraged, since I was endeavoring to serve the Lord, and I was learning early in life that I didn't have to join the secular crowd to be successful.

CAREER GUIDANCE

One day I was walking across the college campus when an upperclassman stopped me. "Say, Narramore," he said, "can I give you a test?"

"What kind of test?" I asked.

He told me he was required to give a vocational test to fifteen people in order to pass his course in vocational counseling.

"What will it show?" I asked.

"It'll indicate which profession would be best for you," he said.

"Is it reliable?" I asked.

"Oh, yes, and I'll give you the results," he assured me.

So I took it, and about a week later, I saw my friend again. "I have the results," he said. So we went into a room and began to talk.

"There's something unusual about you," he said.

I wondered what that might be. I knew I was good at milking cows. I had big hands and years of experience. But that surely wouldn't show up on the vocational test!

"You made a high score in psychology," he said.

"What's that?" I asked.

"That's the study of people and why they act the way they do," he answered. "There's also 'rat' psychology. If you wanted to, you could study rats and do research."

"No, I'll take people," I said. "I don't like rats."

He told me he had also given the test to two psychology professors, and they both made lower scores than I. "You should go into the field of psychology," he told me.

I had never heard much about psychology, and I'd never met a psychologist. We talked it over, and I tucked his suggestion away in the back of my mind but thought about it once in a while. I rather liked the idea of counseling.

At that particular time at that college, all students were required to take a major in education. I picked up an additional major in music along with a minor in business, plus several courses in psychology. I wanted to get all the education I could, and I seemed to be interested in most everything.

One summer, I wanted to take additional courses, so I did housesitting near campus for a faculty family who was traveling. Fortunately, ten-cent hamburgers helped me through that summer.

In my last year of college, a faculty member at a nearby elementary school became ill. So they "scraped the barrel" and asked me to take his place and teach a few classes. I liked having this part-time work while I was able to continue my regular college courses.

But after a month or so, an interesting thing developed. The principal approached me and said, "Narramore, we need a faculty member to serve as dean of boys. We'd like to give you those responsibilities." I agreed, realizing it dovetailed with my interest in counseling.

I was enjoying my work as a student and as an "educator." I figured it was a heap better than milking cows!

A Christian Influence

One of the happy experiences in college was getting to know most of the other Christian students. A widow lady, Mrs. Caldwell, lived in a modest home across the street from the campus. She liked to have young people in her home, so a few of us found ourselves over there a great deal. She was a woman of limited means, but she had a splendid knowledge of the Bible. She gave piano lessons for fifty cents to help make ends meet. But she functioned as though with the Lord she had all she needed. That impressed me.

> I believe one reason many born-again believers are not generous, or don't give at all, is because they were never programmed to be joyful givers in their youth!

Mrs. Caldwell knew we liked popcorn, so she'd buy a brand called Jolly Time and she'd pop a big bowl and put it in the middle of the table. While we munched, we laughed, talked, told jokes, sang Christian songs, quoted Scripture, and had Bible studies. Little did I realize that these informal Bible studies would be so important in the years ahead.

Although she had very little financially, at the first of each month, Mrs. Caldwell took great delight in distributing her tithe. I'd never seen anyone get so excited about tithing. It wasn't long before I saw the significance of using a tenth of my own income (if I had any) for the Lord!

I believe one reason many born-again believers are not generous, or don't give at all, is because they were never programmed to be joyful givers in their youth! So later in life, they tend to squeeze their pennies with a tight fist, never realizing the joy and blessing that comes from giving to the Lord's work.

A Music Combo

In my sophomore year, I became well acquainted with several outstanding music students. One day someone suggested that five of us fellows form a little Western band. "We can go over to Phoenix," one guy said, "and see if we can get on the radio. We could pick up a few dollars that way." So we began to rehearse.

Our violinist was the concertmaster of the college orchestra, and the accordionist was one of the best. We had a string bass player and a talented guitarist. Since I also played the guitar and three of us sang, we formed quite a combo. Occasionally we were invited to a parent-teacher meeting or to play and sing on the radio. I usually sang one or two Spanish songs, which added a little spice and color to the program.

Perhaps one of the best things about the combo was that it provided a small, cordial group where we could have some "non-directed group therapy"! At one point, several of us felt we should "go around the world." We could contact a ship line and offer to be their official music combo. In that way, we could meet fascinating people, visit exotic ports of call, and become world travelers.

But like many other teenage dreams, ours faded away as we settled down to studying and working toward our college degrees.

Squelched!

During my junior year, several of us who attended church near the campus felt that on occasional Sunday nights we should go to various churches and present a youth program. When we brought the idea to the attention of the pastor—a tall, handsome, impressive-looking fellow—he said, "Narramore, you'd never want to do that. You're needed right here in your own church on Sunday night." So he squelched that idea!

I believe that one of the major responsibilities of a pastor and his wife is to notice the young people in their church and encourage each one. Many kids are going nowhere because of lack of encouragement at home and at church. Virtually all pastors have some boys and girls in their congregation who, if they were encouraged, could go a long way. *All pastors and their wives and youth directors should be talent scouts and encouragers!*

All pastors and their wives and youth directors should be talent scouts and encouragers!

Even though I must have shown some talent and promise, I don't remember any pastor ever giving me encouragement in my growing-up years! Praise God, my mother and others were different.

For example, during my first semester in college when I went home for Thanksgiving, I also celebrated my eighteenth birthday. My sister-in-law, Esther, asked, "Clyde, how are you getting along in college? Are you making all A's?"

I blinked because I hadn't thought about such a goal. I guess I was just hoping to get through each course.

> *Encouragement costs nothing, but it pays big dividends.*

"Well, you know, Clyde," she added, "you're special, and we know you'll do well. We're all expecting big things from you."

Can you imagine what that encouragement meant to a scrawny country kid? To this day, I don't know how I got back to college, which was about fifty miles away. I must have floated on cloud nine.

Encouragement costs nothing, but it pays big dividends.

A SPECIAL LIST

It was during my junior year in college that an outstanding Bible teacher from Wheaton, Illinois, came to our church and conducted special afternoon sessions for students. So with a dozen or so other young people sitting under a tree in the shade, we listened as he taught a particular book of the Bible.

During the first session, I opened my three-ring notebook and began to make notes. But they were not about his Bible lecture. Instead, I made a list of the qualities I would like to find some day in a wife. Naturally, no one knew what I was writing. The Bible teacher probably thought I was catching all the choice nuggets as they fell from his lips.

I've often laughed about that list, realizing that if I ever met a girl who had all those qualities and talents, she probably wouldn't be interested in me!

But you know how kids are—they dream—and you know how men are—a little egotistical and unrealistic! The next day, I went to the Bible study again, and I began to make a list of things I wanted to accomplish and talents I would like to develop before I got married. As I think back now, it was a pretty solid list. One was that I wanted to finish my master's degree before I got married. Little did I realize how wise that decision would be in my case.

Another goal was to travel around the United States to see what America was really like. A third desire was to study music, take voice lessons, improve myself, and determine if I had enough ability to do any special work in music. I also wanted to take graduate study—maybe in psychology.

And so the list continued—hopes and aspirations for the future. To this day, I can't remember one thing that Bible teacher taught. But I had my lists, and nearly all of my goals have been realized. And my wife has all (and more) of the qualities I was looking for in a mate. And wonder of wonders, she was willing to marry me!

Parents, teachers, pastors, and other Christian leaders would do well to spend time helping young people sift their ideas about the future. This needs to be done many times during a young people's growing-up years and as they enter adulthood. *Perhaps the great majority of kids, Christians included, settle for very little in life because they don't have clear, definite goals!* Too many wither and die on the vine!

> *Perhaps the great majority of kids, Christians included, settle for very little in life because they don't have clear, definite goals!*

ICING ON THE CAKE

Not long ago I heard a college student say, "College would be so much fun if you didn't have to study."

That might be a little extreme, but it does point up an important truth. We sometimes learn almost as much outside school as we do warming a bench inside the classroom.

Extracurricular activities began to involve me during my second year at college. The school had a top-flight male quartet, which represented the school at many functions. When the second tenor in the quartet graduated, the head of the vocal music department asked me to take his place. The tryout went well, and before long, I was appearing with the quartet and singing solos at functions both on- and off-campus.

Our college president often spoke at state and county functions, civic clubs, banquets, and the like. He occasionally asked the college quartet to appear with him, so we learned a great deal. The guys in the quartet were outstanding students with whom I enjoyed traveling. In short, we were getting a lot of off-campus experience.

Each spring, our official college music groups, such as the orchestra, band, women's chorus, and male chorus, traveled for several days throughout the state of Arizona and into California giving concerts. The purpose was to appear at high school assemblies and attract students to our college.

Since my brother and I were both soloists, we were often asked to travel with these music groups, singing for each appearance. This brought us into close contact with other students in an informal setting. We also learned a lot from the people we met along the way.

Attending class? Yes, I liked that, but I also savored the taste of the extracurricular "icing on the cake."

AN UGLY MOMENT

At the time I attended Arizona State University, the enrollment was small. Consequently, students in any department knew each other well. This was especially true in the music department, where my brother and I were in vocal and instrumental groups. There we learned to know and appreciate the talents and abilities of our classmates.

Only a few African American students were in attendance at the college. One was Mildred. She was an accomplished pianist. When any one of us needed an accompanist, we called on her, because she was an excellent sight-reader.

Mildred and I sat next to each other in the back row of our history class. A new semester had begun, and a number of new students had enrolled from other states. The professor had just started his lecture when a new fellow sitting next to us whispered, "I can't find a pencil. Can someone lend me one?"

Mildred smiled, looked in her purse, and handed him a nice, long, almost-new lead pencil. He glared at her for a moment, then took the pencil, broke it over his knee, and threw it on the floor, saying, "I don't take anything from a n—-!"

As an eighteen-year-old, I sat there shocked and embarrassed, hardly knowing what to do. But I turned to Mildred and said quietly, "Mildred, I'm so sorry he did that. He's just ignorant, and I hope you don't take it to heart." Mildred, a Christian, half smiled and said, "I understand. Thank you, Clyde."

That was my first personal experience with bigotry and someone looking down on a person of a different race. It left an indelible impression on me and flew against everything I had been taught and what I believed. But it helped me to better understand how persons of a minority must feel.

In the New Testament, Christ says, "A new command I give you: Love one another. As I have loved you, so you must love one another. By this all men will know that you are my disciples, if you love one another" (John 13:34–35).

There's no color or ethnic distinction in that!

HAPPY LITTLE REINDEER

Times were hard, and very few jobs were open. But the state of Arizona needed schoolteachers. Our college felt it was preparing us vocationally by qualifying us to teach in the public schools. Since one of my majors was music, I took a course in music education. One day, Miss Norton, our straight-laced music teacher, told us, "This is a song for kindergartners and first-graders. I want you to choose a partner, hold hands, and go around the room singing your song." She looked over to my classmate, Cecil Watson, and then to me. Then we heard her say, "Narramore and Watson, your song is on page twelve. The title is 'Happy Little Reindeer.' Let's see you demonstrate how you would present this song to first graders."

Cecil was about six feet tall and weighed nearly 200 pounds. I was six feet tall and weighed 185. We made quite an "attractive" couple toting nearly four hundred pounds as we began to prance around the room singing, "I'm a happy little reindeer, I'm a happy little reindeer: just look at me!"

About our second time around the room, the other students were in stitches, laughing their heads off. Here we were, two big, clumsy farm boys making fools of ourselves. Miss Norton, whom we had seldom seen smile all year, burst out laughing at the whole fiasco. And our faces were red!

Needless to say, that was the last time we sang, "I'm a happy little reindeer; just look at me."

A REAL, LIVE SENATOR

A few weeks later, the head of the business department called me and another senior student into his office. United States Senator Carl Hayden's office had two part-time job openings for two young men to assist him during his time in his Phoenix office.

Our professor looked at us seriously and said, "You are both good typists and fast in shorthand. Would you like to meet Senator Hayden and his assistant and see if you could work a few hours each week while continuing your college courses?"

My first thought was: *This would be a lot better than prancing around the room singing, "I'm a happy little reindeer."*

We were thrilled to have the privilege of being interviewed and chosen for the job. It was a good learning experience, and we also picked up a few dollars. Later when offered similar work in Washington, DC, we declined.

THE ROSE BOWL

It was late fall when something special happened. I was playing in the college band and one day as we met in the rehearsal room, our director, Carl Boyer, put a question to us: "How would you like to play in the Tournament of Roses Parade in Pasadena, California, on New Year's Day, and then play for the football game in the Rose Bowl?"

We were excited, because it sounded like big-time stuff to us. The director then explained what he had been doing. He realized that times were hard all across the United States and most colleges were having difficulty getting money to support their programs. So he contacted the University of Pittsburgh, the eastern champions who were selected to play in the Rose Bowl that year. He asked if they would like to have the Arizona State University band represent them at the Rose Bowl.

"By all means," they said, so arrangements were made for us to go to Pasadena to march in the New Year's parade and play at the Rose Bowl game. Excitement was running high! A few days after Christmas, we boarded the bus on campus and headed for the west coast. We left early in the morning and arrived that evening. We stayed at a motel in nearby Monrovia. During the next couple of days, we went to the Rose Bowl and rehearsed.

Bright and early on New Year's morning shortly after sunrise, our band assembled on Orange Grove Avenue in Pasadena all dressed in white uniforms with white shoes. Lovely two-story homes with red Spanish tile roofs and graceful palm trees lined the stately avenue. The Wrigley Mansion with its acre of grounds gleamed in all its glory! It was like a real-life fairyland!

We marched a few blocks north on Orange Grove and then turned east and walked for over five miles down Colorado Boulevard. People along the parade route were applauding and cheering! Strangely enough, I don't remember getting any blisters. I think most of us wore double socks!

At the end of the parade route, we boarded our bus and hightailed it to the nearby world-renowned Rose Bowl. Our excitement was beyond belief. The bowl, which seated about one hundred thousand, was nestled in a picturesque little valley surrounded on three sides by mountains, lacy eucalyptus trees, and tall, swaying palms. Our band played off and on throughout the game interchangeably with the west coast band of the opposing university. Then at halftime, we strutted our stuff on the field. I don't think we were all that good, but we didn't know it!

The next day, we boarded our bus and headed back to our Arizona campus. It was one of the most exciting experiences of our young lives. I don't remember who won the football game—but of course, that wasn't important to us! The most important thing was being with our fellow band members and having these exhilarating experiences. We had paraded and played for miles down Colorado Boulevard while being cheered on by thousands of spectators every step we took! Our pictures were being taken and shown around the world. And we got to play in the Rose Bowl. We couldn't imagine things getting much better than that!

STUDENT TEACHING

In my senior year, I taught elementary and junior high school part-time at a "practice school." This was required before receiving a teaching credential. Schoolteachers only made about ninety dollars a month, but that was better than the $1.25 a day I'd been earning on the ranch during the summer.

About seven miles from ASU was an Indian reservation where a number of Yaqui Indians lived. A couple of students from the college were assigned to teach part-time at that public school. I had the joy of being a team teacher as we taught combined grades three and four. Many of these boys and girls were not proficient in English, and some had only been in school a short time.

Christina, a sweet little Indian girl about nine years old, sat at her desk facing mine at the front of the classroom. I would often smile at her throughout the day, and she always smiled back, but I don't ever remember her saying one word all semester. We knew she could talk, because the other children said so. Then one day in her shy little manner, she left her desk, took a couple steps up to mine, and asked an important educational question. "Meester," she asked, "how you make your curlies?" Evidently, she had been studying my crop of wavy hair in contrast to her straight hair.

I realized that perhaps one of her greatest interests in life was to have curly hair, so I said, "Christina, why don't you try this before you go to bed at night. Take a stick about the size of your finger, wrap a lock of hair around it, and then put a little water on it and a rubber band so it stays tight. Then in the morning, see if you have some curlies." A big, broad smile filled her face as she quietly sat down. The next morning, I noticed that a few strands of her hair had a little trace of curl.

> *In other words, you should take a person where he is, or you won't take him at all!*

I have wondered if that was my major educational contribution to that sweet little girl. I've learned that whether teaching elementary school, high school, college, or graduate students, if you don't tap your students' interests, you'll probably not get much response from them. *In other words, you should take a person where he is, or you won't take him at all!*

At college, I took voice lessons and sang solos at various occasions. My teacher encouraged me and said I had real possibilities. However, I knew I did not have a great operatic voice. But who knows how it might develop? My oldest brother had a beautiful high tenor voice with unlimited top notes, and I wondered if I might develop the high range that I needed.

In my senior year, I was chosen to represent the university to sing in a vocal contest with student winners from other Arizona colleges. On the day of the contest, I talked with other students who were competing. I immediately recognized one of them as a student from the University of Arizona in Tucson. He was a Christian, and I had heard him sing the year before at a Christian convention. He had an unusually fine baritone voice. I felt sure he would be my toughest competition. We both sang arias from Italian operas. When the contest ended, the judges awarded him first place and me second place. Years later, I met him again in New York City where he was trying to make it at the Metropolitan Opera Company. We became good friends and laughed about our competition days in college.

ESTABLISHING PRIORITIES

When Billy Graham, world-renowned evangelist, was in his early eighties Oprah Winfrey on national TV asked him about his profound impressions. "The brevity of life," Billy quickly answered.

Indeed, life is short, and as people grow older, they often rearrange their priorities. Realizing that life is brief, they are sorting things out and concentrating on that which seems most important.

Throughout high school and college, along with farm work and sports, I was reading my Bible, attending church, fellowshipping with believers, and in many ways growing in the Lord. Like other Christians, I was learning that spiritual matters were the most important of all.

I was conscious of these Scriptures: "For what shall it profit a man if he should gain the whole world and lose his own soul?" (Mark 8:36) and "It is appointed for me to die once, and after this the judgment" (Heb. 9:27).

Soul-winning became an important part of my life and has continued to be throughout the years.

Two years after college graduation, until I joined the navy at the time of World War II, I was in the teaching profession. During that time, the Lord blessed my priority of personal soul-winning. I witnessed to young people and students and usually followed up their conversion experiences with Bible study. I soon learned that like other believers, I too could lead people to the Lord. I knew there was nothing that could compare to it. *Soul-winning became an important part of my life and has continued to be throughout the years.*

Let me share an experience during my last year in college: Joe Olachea was a seventh grader, twelve years of age. As his teacher, I saw him quite often and was able to tell him about Jesus Christ. He was interested, and within a few months, he surrendered his life to the Lord. He grew spiritually, and upon his graduation from high school, I encouraged him to attend a Christian college. After that, he attended seminary. In time, he became a pastor who has led many to Christ. He came from a large family, to which he was a faithful witness. In time, he led all of his brothers and sisters to the Lord. When I saw him years later, he said, "All of my family are saved, including my grandchildren!"

It's so important to put first things first, to cut through the entanglements of life and to lead people to a saving knowledge of Jesus Christ. *If a person is not saved, he's not anything for eternity!*

If a person is not saved, he's not anything for eternity!

We can help people in many ways to achieve a better adjustment in life. *But the most basic adjustment of all is getting right with God and living each day for*

But the most basic adjustment of all is getting right with God and living each day for Him.

Him. A person can be fairly well-adjusted but still be a sinner heading for a terrible eternity without Christ!

> *Probably nothing causes a person to be as fresh, alert, bright, interesting, and exciting as being a soul winner.*

As I look back over the years, I realize my soul-winning efforts not only helped the people I led to the Lord, but they also helped *me*. *Probably nothing causes a person to be as fresh, alert, bright, interesting, and exciting as being a soul winner.* Why? Because God is working in his life and he is seeing miracles take place week after week and year after year! Indeed, God's Word is true when it says, "He that winneth souls is wise" (Prov. 11:30). And I might add, not only wise, but interesting as well!

COMMENCEMENT

Spring had arrived, and graduation was coming up! My four years of college had passed so quickly.

I was glad that my mother and several other family members were able to attend the commencement exercises. To me it was an important step in life—the culmination of many unusual experiences, nearly all of them good!

But war clouds were gathering in Europe, and they were spreading. What's more, the United States was becoming involved. So as our classmates were saying good-bye to one another, we wondered in what parts of the world we would be scattered next year.

I'm sure a host of feelings filled parents' hearts as they saw the graduates receive their diplomas. I thought about my mother. She was in her early forties when our father died, leaving her with seven children—the oldest were in their teens, and I, the youngest, was only two.

Life was hard for our family, especially my mother, during those Arizona pioneer days. All my siblings except the one just older than I were born on the desert in the Arizona Territory. Then came the Great Depression. In college, as I received letters from my mother, I often found a dollar bill tucked inside. That meant so much to me.

But now the youngest in the family was grown and graduating from college! She was so proud, and I was equally proud of her!

I couldn't help but reflect on the day when I arrived on campus with only $350 to my name. Yet somehow, the Lord had seen me through.

Perhaps you are wondering how a committed Christian student is accepted at a secular university. My answer might be by relating an experience

I had. Near the end of my junior year in college, I received a notice that I had been selected to become a member of the university's "Thirteen" Club. Since my brother Earl had received this honor the year before, I knew it was a special group of thirteen men voted the most outstanding students. They performed various projects at the college. Each year as members graduated, the group chose others to replace them. I was grateful for this honor, especially since I was a committed Christian.

My years of undergraduate and graduate study at five universities have shown me this: *If a student lives a godly life and is friendly, the unsaved faculty and student body may not understand him, but they will usually respect and admire him.*

It's also important to realize that the Christian student who attends a secular college misses out on a world of academic truth, spiritual growth, and personal blessings. On the other hand, a Christian institution of higher learning can offer the following:

> *If a student lives a godly life and is friendly, the unsaved faculty and student body may not understand him, but they will respect and admire him.*

1. Many teachers who are excellent Christian role models.
2. A large number of Christian friends within the student body.
3. Course content that does not omit relevant spiritual facts.
4. Chapel speakers representing various Christian ministries about which students will learn and may become seriously interested.
5. Excellent Bible courses.
6. Learning how a person may magnify Christ in his chosen profession.
7. Teachers who frequently refer students to books, films, and other resources that honor Christ rather than materials that do not.
8. Faculty and students who may offer encouragement, sympathy, and prayer in times of need.
9. A student body of Christians from which a person may choose his or her life's mate.
10. Teachers who identify and expose false and non-biblical points of view.
11. Course offerings that prepare students for Christian ministries.

12. Encouragement and training regarding methods of soul winning.
13. Short-term trips to mission fields.
14. Student social activities that are wholesome and Christ honoring.
15. Christian counseling individually or in groups to resolve problems or life considerations.
16. Special campus concerts, drama, and lectures that are Christ-centered rather than secular.
17. Small group devotion times throughout each dormitory.
18. Opportunities to develop deep Christian friendships that can last many years after college.

Unfortunately, those of us who have attended only secular colleges have missed out on virtually all of the above.

POST COLLEGE

About a week after graduation, my brother Earl, who had graduated a year earlier, said, "Let's go over to the University of Southern California and take some summer courses."

USC, I thought. *Wow, one of the great universities with a big athletic program!* My brother had been teaching school for a year and had saved a little money, so he was all set. But since I had just graduated, I hardly had a nickel. Nevertheless, I began to pray about it and decided to step out in faith. I knew that God would provide the finances, so we left for California, taking our mother with us. She would stay with my brother. At that time, the USC campus had beautiful, spacious grounds with palm trees and colorful flowers. It was more than I expected.

About four blocks from the campus, I noticed a large church on Washington Boulevard. Suddenly an idea popped into my mind: *Maybe they could use a night watchman or someone to keep an eye on things.* I knocked at a few doors and found the pastor. I told him I was a Christian, that I was working on my master's degree at USC, and that I needed a place to stay at night.

"We've a place here that might suit you," he said. "Besides, we need somebody around here during the night." He took me into the education building and showed me a room with a single bed as well as a little kitchen and bath. "We'll pay you a little," he said, "if you would like to stay here. Your only responsibility will be to see that the place is locked up at night and that one or two lights are left on."

What an answer to prayer! I must have run all the way back to the USC campus where I enrolled, bought my books, and prepared for classes the next day.

That turned out to be a wonderful summer. My mother, brother, and I went many places in the evenings and on weekends, including the Hollywood Bowl. We also went one evening to hear Aimee Semple McPherson, the dramatic and charismatic pastor of the Angelus Temple. You might say we were pushing back our "farm boy horizons."

A curious thing happened at the end of the summer. I had taken both the first and second sessions at USC, and the day before we returned to Arizona, I went to the registrar's office to get a transcript of my credits. The registrar was a kindly woman in her late fifties or so. She handed me my card with a smile and said, "Mr. Narramore, you did well. You made good grades."

I smiled as I thanked her. But my eyes got big as I looked at the card a second time. I noticed that it showed I had made an "A" in flute! This, of course, was a mistake, because I had never even held a flute in my hands, much less taken a course in it.

"But," I said to the lady, "I didn't take a course in flute."

She smiled and said, "Oh, yes you did; you're just being modest."

I laughed and said, "No, really! I took these other courses, but I didn't take a course in flute." She thought I was kidding, and I saw she wasn't easily persuaded. She gave me a big smile as she bid me good-bye. I walked out of the building with an A in flute. I could see that it would probably take an act of Congress to get them to change it, so I just left it there. I suppose it's still on their records today.

COUNSELING COURSES

My brother, mother, and I then drove back to ASU in Tempe, Arizona, where I continued work on my master's degree in counseling. I felt very comfortable. So many of the basic things we were learning I seemed to have known instinctively. My master's thesis, "The Rehabilitation of Maladjusted Students," completed the requirements for me. It was doubly helpful, since one of the best ways to assist adults is to understand their childhood. I finished my degree at ASU, realizing that World War II was just around the corner.

CHICAGO AND SEMINARY

Before long, I left Arizona for Northern Baptist Theological Seminary in Chicago, where I had an opportunity during the summer to learn more about the Bible. I took mostly New Testament courses, which I felt would be especially helpful.

I also attended several outdoor summer concerts near Lake Michigan featuring fine singers and orchestras. I also had an opportunity to visit the Moody Bible Institute. One of the personal highlights for me during the summer was being invited by George Beverly Shea, the renowned bass, to sing a solo on his daily WMBI radio broadcast. The song? "I'd Rather Have Jesus." What a wonderful, humble, encouraging man!

My summer in Chicago sped by quickly, and now it was time to head back home to Arizona. Since I didn't have much money, I needed to find an economical way to travel. The idea came to me that I could put an ad in a local newspaper for someone who might be driving to California. So I did, and the following day a man with a big, white Cadillac phoned me saying I could go with him for free if I would do part of the driving. That sounded great to me!

My traveling companion turned out to be an eccentric but wealthy gentleman. Every place we stopped for a meal or any hotel for the night he would ask to speak to the owner because, as he claimed, he was interested in "buying the place." Of course, this was just a ploy, but the owners he spoke to didn't know that. Thinking he must be someone very influential, the hotel and restaurant people gave us the VIP treatment. When ordering in restaurants, he often had the biggest and best steaks, and since he was paying my way, I followed suit. The trip home was turning out to be an unusual experience!

After a few days of travel, I was home on the ranch, and it was good to be with the family again. Little did we realize that the next time we got together, some of us would be in military uniforms.

CHAPTER FOUR

A WORLD AT WAR

As my first year of teaching began to wind down, after I had earned my B.A. and M.A. degrees from Arizona State University, I received invitations from two Christian colleges to come for an interview with the possibility of joining their faculty.

I chose Bob Jones University, located then in Tennessee. What a fine experience to be with committed Christians from around the nation. As I taught in the business department and associated with students and faculty, I felt I was surrounded by some of the best and brightest.

But this experience was short lived, because only a few weeks later on Sunday afternoon, December 7, 1941 a startling radio announcement pierced the airwaves telling the American people we were at war!

I'll never forget President Franklin D. Roosevelt's words on radio about the sneak attack on Pearl Harbor, "A day that will live on in infamy."

The whole nation was shaken. Young men and women rushed to local post offices to see where they could go to join the armed forces. There was unusual unanimity among the American people. We had been attacked, and our citizens were both willing and eager to do their part in defending our land.

Along with millions of others, I received "greetings" from the president saying, "You have been selected to serve in the United States Armed Forces."

> "'For I know the thoughts that I think toward you,' says the Lord, 'thoughts of peace and not of evil, to give you a future and a hope.'" Jer. 29:11

I decided I would prefer serving in the navy, so I applied for a commission as a naval officer. During the interview, they gave me forms to fill out and told me it would be several weeks before I would hear back. In the meantime, I was to report for duty at Bainbridge, Maryland. My brother, Earl, had already enlisted in the navy and was heading for the Pacific.

I had no idea what was ahead; however, I felt confident that Christ who had saved me would never leave me nor forsake me, and the following verse flooded my mind: "'For I know the thoughts that I think toward you,' says the Lord, 'thoughts of peace and not of evil, to give you a future and a hope'" (Jer. 29:11).

BOOT CAMP

The week I arrived at boot camp the navy had just bulldozed, leveled, and built a facility at Bainbridge, Maryland. It was raining, and most of our marching was in mud up to our ankles. A real assortment of young men filled our barracks. One fellow said, "I'm from the South—South Philly!"

The first day we all lined up and got our uniforms, and each of us was interviewed momentarily by a psychiatrist. He asked me about my background, and I told him I had a master's degree and was a college teacher.

"You should be an officer," he said. I explained that I had applied for a commission, but it hadn't come through yet.

"I'll push that along," he said, "and we'll try to get this settled in a few weeks." So I made the best of my situation there at boot camp.

After a couple of days, I met a sailor from West Virginia who was a Christian. He and I decided to conduct a Bible study. We posted signs around the barracks and found a room where we could sing, give testimonies, and study the word. About twenty men showed up. I led the singing and did the teaching. I forget what I spoke on that night, but I brought a gospel message, and when I gave the invitation to be saved, eleven men gave their hearts to Jesus Christ. I knew then why I was to spend a few weeks in boot camp.

When we finished our six weeks of training, we were all assigned to an outgoing unit. We'd been given tests, and the navy was deciding where around the world they would send each of us, and whether we'd be bakers, truck drivers, gunners, or what-have-you. One morning while in this holding area, I was shaving when a sailor walked into the barracks and called out in a rather official voice, "Ensign Narramore, may I speak to you?" That had a different ring to me, but it sounded great. I stepped over to him, and he said, "You have just received your commission as an officer in the United States Navy. Report to the captain's quarters tomorrow morning at 0900."

There was quite a stir in the barracks as the sailors gathered around and asked, "How did you do it?"

One of them asked, "Are you a 90-day wonder?"

"Well," I said, "not to my knowledge. I've spent four years in college and a couple years on my master's degree, so if I'm anything, I'm a six-year-wonder."

On to Princeton

At nine o'clock the next morning, I appeared before the captain to be sworn in as an officer. I was given three days leave to go to Philadelphia, get outfitted for my uniforms, and then report for duty and training at Princeton University in New Jersey.

At Princeton, I joined other men who had recently received their commissions. There were two men to a room and 120 in our company. I enjoyed my six weeks at Princeton—one of the great Ivy League universities. Regular classes had been cancelled, and only military men were on campus. We were given intensive training regarding the U. S. Navy, and there were more tests. Little did I know that I would eventually serve at seven locations.

Great Lakes

Then one day I was called into the headquarters office to be told I had been assigned further training at the Great Lakes Training Center just north of Chicago and that I was to become a gunnery officer. I had made adequate scores in mechanics and high scores in administration, but I was surprised because I didn't know much about mechanics except what my older brothers had tried to teach me back on the ranch. But I guess the other men didn't have any more mechanical aptitude than I did.

A few days later, I reported at Great Lakes with five other officers who had been selected to take similar training there. We were to become executive officers at various anti-aircraft training centers around the world. The training was intensive and thorough. It also gave me an opportunity to go to downtown Chicago, look around, and enjoy fellowship at the Moody Memorial Church.

About forty enlisted men and six officers made up our particular group at Great Lakes. The work was fast and serious. The war was raging, people were being killed, and we were needed to get out and help. But of course, there were some light and humorous moments too. I'll always remember the petty officer in charge of our detail. He was a rather short, crusty, stiff guy who had been in the navy for years. His job was to teach us gunnery, get us in shape, and move us along—fast!

Each morning he'd call our group to attention in formation and then bark out the orders for the day. He was about as metallic and unemotional as they came.

The men had spread the word that Tuesday was his birthday, so on Tuesday morning after he had lined us up and barked out our orders, he asked if anyone had any questions. Bill, an enlisted man, spoke up and said he wanted to say a word.

"Well, speak up!" our crusty little leader demanded. Bill then announced that today was the birthday of a great man whom we were proud to have as our leader. He then handed him a gold watch.

The petty officer, completely surprised and not knowing what to say, choked up as he began to thank us. Meaning to say *cherish*, he said, "Gentlemen, I will *tarnish* this watch as long as I live!" Six of us officers near the back tried to smother our snickers as we ducked inside a nearby room!

LITTLE CHURCH, BIG MESSAGE

While I was in the Chicago area, God gave me a special blessing. I looked in the phone directory to locate a church to attend on Sunday evening. I found one, went there, and worshipped with them. I was in my twenties, and I knew no one, and I was sure no one knew me. The song leader asked us to sing the old hymn, "God Will Take Care of You." I had sung it dozens of times while growing up, but this evening it had special meaning

for me. Naturally, times were difficult and terrible. The world was on fire
with war. Large numbers of our troops were deployed in Europe and other
distant places, and more were scattered throughout the Pacific Rim. Tens
of thousands were fighting—and dying. No one knew where he would be
next week, if still alive.

As we sang the song, my eyes seemed glued to every word.

> Be not dismayed what-e'er betide,
> God will take care of you;
> Beneath His wings of love abide,
> God will take care of you.

Then we sang the last verse.

> No matter what may be the test,
> God will take care of you;
> Lean, weary one, upon His breast,
> God will take care of you.

When we came to the chorus the words seemed to be written especially
for me: "God will take care of you, Thro' every day, o'er all the way; He will take
care of you, God will take care of you."

By the time we finished singing the song, I had great peace in my heart
about the future. I had been saved and living for Christ for a number of
years, but now being away from friends and family, it was just the Lord and
I. I had a wonderful feeling in my heart that God would be with me every
day of the war and that I was completely safe in His care.

Our specialized training at Great Lakes would soon be coming to an
end, and I didn't have the slightest idea where I would be sent next. But God
seemed to speak to me through that song, and I had peace and assurance.
This deep, abiding feeling never left me. It seemed to buoy me up and give
me great expectancy and hope every day.

God says in Nahum 1:7, "The Lord is good, a stronghold in the day of
trouble; and He knows those who trust in Him."

How wonderful that He knows us personally and that He is our
stronghold. God also gives the assurance of His care in Psalm 32:7, "You
are my hiding place; You shall preserve me from trouble; You shall surround
me with songs of deliverance."

He loves His own, and He is our safe hiding place. He preserves you
and me and encompasses us with wonderful songs of deliverance. In Psalm
18:2, we read, "The Lord is my rock and my fortress and my deliverer; My

God, my strength, in whom I will trust; My shield and the horn of my salvation, my stronghold."

> God wants to lead and guide you and me. But it is important that we want his leading and that we are in the place where He can bless us!

That's about as good as it gets! Our rock, fortress, deliverer, God, strength, shield, salvation, and stronghold!

I have often thought about that big message God gave me at the little church on that Sunday night outside of Chicago. I had gone to the right place. I was also with the right people. My heart was open for God's leading and comfort. I also realized the great power that music and words have if they magnify Jesus Christ. *God wants to lead and guide you and me. But it is important that we want His leading and that we are in the place where He can bless us!*

Naval Officer, World War II

10/20/12

Long Island

After completing my training at Great Lakes, another officer and I were assigned to the U. S. Naval Anti-aircraft Training Center at Lido Beach, Long Island, New York. We would be gunnery officers at that facility. Our responsibility was to train large numbers of navy personnel in the use of twenty-millimeter anti-aircraft guns. These fourteen or so guns were mounted on a long cement foundation right at the ocean's edge.

As naval ships came into New York Harbor, the navy would send us as many as a hundred men at a time for four days of intensive training. These young men would then return to their ships and sail across the Atlantic. Chefs and all were trained.

The five training officers at our center had essentially the same duties each day. Every few days, a hundred new sailors would arrive and we would train them; then they would ship out. So we trained men by the thousands— mostly Americans, but also some British, French, and Russians.

A pilot would fly a small plane from the ocean toward the shore. Behind him, a long line towed a big, white nylon sock about twelve feet long and three feet in diameter. An officer commanded the firing from an elevated platform. He would wait to give the command, "Commence firing," until the plane was directly overhead so that the men firing these guns wouldn't hit the plane. The trainees would shoot at the sock. The pilot made run after run.

I soon became good friends with another officer, Lieutenant Lowell Loeffler. One evening, I led him to a saving knowledge of Jesus Christ. After the war, he became a Christian leader and businessman in Nebraska and the head of child evangelism in his area. His wife, four sons, and their children have all trusted Christ as their Savior.

During the nearly two years when I was stationed on Long Island, I began to meet with a group of eight or so civilian Christian men and their wives in a nearby home. They asked me to be their Bible teacher. By exchanging a night duty with fellow officers, I was able to meet regularly with this group. Our studies were simple. We took portions of Scripture, discussed them, and applied them to our lives. These were precious times, as well as a contrast to my daily military life. And as usually is the case, I'm sure that by preparing for each Bible study, I learned more than all the others.

One Saturday while off duty, I took the Long Island train into New York City. I was walking down Forty-Second Street in Times Square when

I noticed a sign on the second floor of a building. It read, "VICTORY CENTER—Servicemen Welcome." So I walked upstairs and was greeted by a Christian lady who invited me to join other servicemen and play ping-pong, have some coffee, play the piano, read, or just rest.

A few minutes later, I found myself seated at a table for four, chatting with three other servicemen. Before long, we got around to talking about serving in the navy, death, and God. It was soon apparent to me that these three guys did not have a personal relationship with Christ, so I asked them if they would like to know about being certain of going to heaven if they should die. They were all ears, so I went through the simple plan of salvation and answered their questions. One of the men who was shipping out in a couple of days asked if he could settle the question right then. We talked a moment longer, and I had the privilege of leading all three to a personal, saving knowledge of Christ.

I went back to Times Square every time I could and continued to lead men to the Lord, week after week and month after month. I had a little card printed that would fit into a sailor's vest pocket. On one side, the card presented a simple, straightforward direction on how to be saved. It had a line at the bottom for a signature. On the other side, I listed six or seven Scripture verses that would help a new convert grow spiritually.

When I went to a printer in New York City to have the card printed, I noticed that he had misspelled the word "neither." When I showed him his error he said, "So vat? Some people say *neether* and some people say *nyther*."

I agreed with him on that but pointed out that regardless of how they pronounced it, the spelling was always the same. So I handed him the box of one thousand cards and asked him to print them again and do it right. In time, the card was printed by the thousands and went to servicemen around the world. During that time, I wrote two tracts for navy personnel that were published by Moody Press and distributed widely.

During my time at Lido Beach, I moved ahead in several areas: (1) studying and learning more about the word, (2) serving Uncle Sam, (3) leading men to Christ, and (4) romancing a lovely girl, Ruth Elliott, who lived only a few miles away and would later become my wife.

THE FIRST FAMILY

One evening while flying from Los Angeles to the East Coast, I boarded a plane in Atlanta to fly to Washington, DC. I had just settled in my seat when the stewardess ushered a lady down the aisle to sit beside me. To my surprise, it was Eleanor Roosevelt, the wife of the United States' president.

The year was about 1944, if I remember correctly. The first lady looked at me, nodded her head, and half smiled. As a young naval officer in uniform, I returned her greeting and introduced myself. She then said, "I am Eleanor Roosevelt."

She was a tall, rather plain-looking lady with a serious expression on her face. She didn't seem very comfortable talking with people. I wondered if she had been on a speaking tour and was tired. She was quiet and evidently seriously preoccupied. Later I wondered if she had been visiting her husband at Warm Springs, Georgia.

I might add that during President Franklin D. Roosevelt's time in office, the public was not aware of his physical handicap due to the effects of infantile paralysis—now called poliomyelitis or polio. Television hadn't yet been developed, so we were dependent upon radio and newspapers to gain most of our information. Unlike today, the media kept many goings-on silent. I remember seeing newspaper photographs of the president seated, with his head tilted upward smiling broadly and giving the impression that he was very confident and that good times were just ahead!

During his presidency, I had heard that at one time he had suffered from infantile paralysis, so occasionally he went to Warm Springs, Georgia, to enjoy the facilities there. Little did we know that the ravages of that disease had been severe and that he was unable to walk without help.

On the positive side of President Roosevelt's terms in office, we were impressed with his ability to organize, to take action, to persuade people to follow his leadership, and to relate easily to other world leaders. But now, many years later, we know more about how he suffered physically and worked tirelessly even though his legs were weighted down with heavy steel braces and he couldn't take a step alone. His great optimism, courage, and triumph over unusual odds were undoubtedly among his greatest attributes, despite some of his policies.

About ten years later, and well after World War II, I had the opportunity to meet another member of the Roosevelt family. It happened one Sunday night at the Eagle Rock Baptist Church in the Los Angeles area. At that time, I was married to my sweetheart, Ruth, who was organist and music director for the church while I served as the choir director. The church was well filled, with about three hundred or more people in attendance that evening. Shortly after the service began, while I was leading the song service, two couples entered the church, walked down the center aisle, and sat about five rows from the front. I knew immediately that one of the men was Elliott Roosevelt, son of FDR. He was a tall, well-muscled man with a fine bearing and appearance. He looked a little like his father. He sat attentively during the service. I was told later that the lady with him was a personal friend and that the other two were acquaintances of Elliott's companion.

I had personally selected the congregational hymns before the service. But since we had no printed programs, I immediately made a few changes, making sure that at least one of the hymns would probably be familiar to Elliott. I wanted him to feel comfortable singing a song I thought he might know. I also selected two hymns whose words gave the plan of salvation plainly.

At the end of the message, the congregation stood to sing the closing hymn. The pastor, Dr. Roy L. Laurin, gave an opportunity for people to accept Christ. Elliott and his three friends remained standing until the benediction. People in the church respected their privacy. However, there were a few who greeted them cordially.

> We, as believers, should be alert to present the blessed gospel of Christ. We never know who might respond and be affected—for eternity.

Later at home, Ruth and I talked about the experience. We were glad Elliott Roosevelt and his friends had attended the service and that they had been able to hear a salvation message, along with gospel music!

We, as believers, should be alert to present the blessed gospel of Christ. We never know who might respond and be affected—for eternity.

So the war continued, finally shifting from Europe to Asia. Families were torn apart, and thousands of service personnel and civilians were tragically being killed. What a terrible time! Like others in the service, I lived each day not knowing what the future held. But, praise God, as a believer, I knew Who held the future.

By the way, in 1951, I met and talked with Captain Fuchida who had led the attack on Pearl Harbor. By this time, he had trusted Christ as his personal savior, and he was speaking at public meetings in America, earnestly encouraging people to give their hearts to the Lord to be saved!

Off to Honeymoon

CHAPTER FIVE

LOVE AT FIRST SIGHT

Not long after reporting for duty at Lido Beach, Long Island, New York, I met another Christian Naval Officer, Lt. Ed Daverman, who had been stationed in Brooklyn for about a year. Consequently he had attended various churches and had become acquainted with many of the Christian people in the area.

On Saturday evening, we decided to go into Times Square and attend a youth rally held by Jack Wyrtzen. Ed and I sat next to the aisle so that we could "see everything." We had hardly gotten settled in our seats when two beautiful girls walked down our isle near us. I nudged Ed and whispered, "Who is she?"

"Which one?" He asked.

"The tall blonde," I said.

Then Ed told me that her name was Ruth Elliott who was attending a Christian college and who was a fine musician. I don't remember what the message was about that evening, but I sure remembered the girl. As soon as the service was over, I went over to where she was standing with friends and introduced myself. I also met her mother, who had been singing in the choir, and her brother, Gordon, who was the student body president of one of the high schools in Queens.

My mind flashed back to my college days when I had made a list of the qualities I would like to have someday in a wife. I could tell immediately that Ruth had a lot of these qualities.

Was it love at first sight? It was at least definite attraction at first sight! Since Ruth lived with her family not many miles from the naval station, we began to see each other regularly. I learned that she had been raised her early years in China, where her parents had been missionaries. Everyone in the family was a good Bible student and musical. In time, she transferred to Columbia University. I began to see how intelligent she was and how gifted in speaking, writing, music, and art.

When the bomb fell on Hiroshima and the war ended, we decided to announce our engagement on Thanksgiving Day. That was also my birthday. We invited a number of friends to the Elliott home for a Thanksgiving evening celebration. Little did they know that we would announce our engagement and I would give her a ring.

We were married a few months later at the Calvary Baptist Church in New York City across the street from Carnegie Hall. The platform of the auditorium was decorated with large arrangements of apple blossoms. The bridesmaids wore rainbow colors, and the groomsmen were dressed in naval uniforms or tuxedos. And the bride? In white satin and veil, she was as radiant and beautiful as could be!

It was a near-perfect wedding followed by a dinner in the recreation hall. There we had the cutting of the cake and a time of beautiful music. It could hardly have been more wonderful.

A few months earlier, I had become well acquainted with a staff member of the Waldorf Astoria Hotel who was in charge of reservations. He had arranged for us to have a honeymoon suite. We stayed there until Monday morning. Then we flew to Bermuda. A month or so before the wedding, we tried to make arrangements to stay at a hotel in Bermuda, but every place was filled with U. S. military personnel. I contacted Jack Wyrtzen, a prominent Christian leader on the East Coast, whose radio broadcast was heard regularly in Bermuda. Jack graciously gave us the names of several of his contacts there. We wrote five of them asking if they knew of any hotel available in Bermuda. All five wrote back saying there was nothing available but that we could stay at their home! One letter was from a lady, Mrs. Newman, who said she lived in Hamilton. Her husband had died a year or so before, and she would be delighted to have us stay in her big home overlooking Hamilton Harbor. So we graciously accepted her invitation.

On Monday morning, we flew to Bermuda. The military gave us a ride into the city of Hamilton. We then phoned Mrs. Newman, saying we had just arrived and would be taking a buggy taxi to her home. Cars were not allowed, and the only way to go short distances was by taking horse drawn buggies. When we drove up to Mrs. Newman's lovely home, she was standing at the front gate. We introduced ourselves, and then she looked at Ruth and me carefully and then turned to me and said, "You are a lucky boy."

Bermuda was unbelievably beautiful, with whitish-pink beaches and turquoise water. We attended church on Easter with Mrs. Newman. When she introduced us to her pastor, she told him we were both musicians, so he invited us to sing and play for the evening service and to speak the following night to the young people of their church. We brought a Bible message and reasoned with that group of high school and college students. At the close of the meeting, about twelve of them gave their hearts to the Lord, including the pastor's daughter.

At the end of our honeymoon, we flew back to New York, where Ruth resumed her work at Columbia and I continued my work with the navy in downtown Manhattan close to what became the famous World Trade Center.

The next few weeks become very special to us because my mother flew from Arizona to New York and stayed with us a few weeks. We had the unusual joy of touring Washington, DC, sights around New York City, Boston, and Cape Cod.

Little did we realize that a few weeks later I would receive orders from the navy to report to duty in Iceland.

And poor us, dependents were not allowed!

CHAPTER SIX

UNITED STATES, HERE WE COME

World War II was over; June of 1947 was approaching, and I was out of the Navy. Ruth and I, along with millions of others, were settling into civilian life.

We planned to begin work on our graduate degrees at Columbia University in September. But first we wanted to take a trip across the United States to visit friends and relatives, to see the sights, and especially to spend time with my family in California and Arizona. After all, there were many Narramore family members out west, but only my mother had met Ruth.

But how do you travel across the United States when you don't have much money and you want to save what little you have for graduate school? Ruth and I talked this over with her nineteen-year-old brother, Gordon Elliott, who had just finished his first year of college. We decided to form a gospel trio and preach, sing, and play our musical instruments on our way across the United States. Ruth was an excellent pianist, organist, vibraharpist, trumpet soloist, singer, and chalk artist. Gordon was a good trombonist and baritone soloist. I was a speaker, singer, and somewhat of a pianist. Together, we could have numerous vocal and instrumental solos and combos and present quite a varied program. Since my college days, I had held onto a dynamic Scripture verse, "For I will give you a mouth and wisdom which all your adversaries will not be able to contradict or resist" (Luke 21:15). That gave us encouragement.

But our problem was that no one had ever heard of us. So how would we get engagements?

We studied a U. S. map and located towns about every three hundred miles apart from New York to San Francisco. We thought there must be a church in each of these cities where we could hold a meeting. I suppose it was presumptuous, but we printed a card with our photos and biographical information. We enclosed the card with a letter to selected churches across the country where we wanted to hold an evening service and have overnight accommodations. We called ourselves "America's Newest Gospel Team." We didn't have much time, so we just sent the mailing to the "pastor" of the First Baptist Church, thinking there would probably be one in each of these cities! We bathed it all in prayer.

Within a couple of weeks, we began to receive answers. In nearly every town where we wanted to hold a meeting, we were invited to come to a church. I suppose few speakers and musicians were passing through these towns. So Monday night, Tuesday night, Wednesday night, and right on through Saturday night, and of course, Sunday morning and evening, our schedule began to fill up.

OFF WE GO

We loaded our car with a trombone, folding vibraharp, trumpet, collapsible chalkboard with special colored lights, plus clothes. Then we headed west. We were really packed in tight. At most meetings, Ruth drew a chalk board picture while I furnished a piano background. The attractive drawing with the multi-colored lights coordinated with my message.

By ministering along the way, it helped us financially, because in most places we were given a nice play to stay, including dinner and breakfast, and sometimes, a love offering. We praised God for the dedicated pastors who invited us, unknown and sight unseen. Their congregations were appreciative and enthusiastic. Most importantly, we saw people trust Christ as their Savior at nearly every service. It was a real blessing and encouragement. (Ruth said my speaking was also improving. I'm sure it needed it!)

BIG, BAD BUFFALO

One morning while traveling across Nebraska, we stopped momentarily to take motion pictures of a small herd of buffalo grazing in a field next to the road. Two of them were nearby with only a flimsy wire fence between us.

I put the sixteen-millimeter camera lens in an opening of the wire so there was nothing between the lens and the buffalo. A mother buffalo with her baby calf at her side looked at us suspiciously. I wanted some action, so I picked up a clod and tossed it toward them to get them to move. And move they did! The angry mother buffalo charged full force at me and the fence. Ruth screamed at me from the car, "Forget the picture and get in the car!" I guess she didn't want to lose her husband to a buffalo, especially since we were newlyweds!

But, foolishly, I was determined to get a motion picture. So I kept the film rolling until that angry buffalo got within a few yards of me. Clicking the camera off, I jumped back and dashed into the car, scared to death. That angry beast could have ripped me to pieces! But I knew I had taken some rare motion pictures!

When we sent our film to be developed, the buffalo film was completely missing! Evidently someone at the photo lab saw what an outstanding shot it was—a buffalo charging and getting up to within a few feet of the lens—and decided to keep the film. We wrote the Eastman Kodak Company and complained, but all they did was send us some new blank film. Oh well, that's life! At least we have this incident engraved on our memories.

SPECTACULAR ENTRANCE

We kept traveling west until we arrived at Salt Lake City, Utah. There arrangements were for us to speak at a radio station. A pastor who had a regular Sunday morning radio feature asked me to be his guest speaker.

We met the pastor at the station about twenty minutes before nine. That would give us a few minutes to get settled in the studio, then make the broadcast.

The pastor was a fine gentleman with a rather quiet, reserved, yet self-assured personality. The building was beautiful, quite new, with a big glass front door. As we approached the door, my minister friend said, "It looks like the door is locked." Then we could see that it surely was—locked tight.

"I wonder what the problem is," the pastor said. "They're supposed to be here long before this to open the door, turn on the lights, and get everything ready for us to make the broadcast."

We looked around for a moment, but no one was arriving at the station, so about five minutes before we were to go on the air, he said, "We'll just have to take action."

He stepped out to his car and got an old-fashioned tire iron. It was big and heavy. This mild-mannered Christian gentleman said, "Stand back." Ruth and I saw what was coming, so we quickly stepped back to avoid catching any flying glass.

At that point, the pastor drew the tire iron over his shoulder like he was going to knock a home run. He swung and crashed the glass door into a hundred pieces. "Okay," he said quietly, "now we can go in and get started."

He rushed into the radio studio, picked up a microphone, and calmly said, "Dear friends, this is Pastor So-and-so." He went on to say, "What a joy it is to be with you on this beautiful Sunday morning." He introduced me, and I brought a half-hour message. As I remember, the topic that morning was "Peace."

During the message, I looked at Ruth, who had a peculiar expression on her face. We had never had such an experience before, and I believe she was having a hard time reconciling the shattering of a big glass door, then sharing with people the "peace which passes all understanding!"

MINISTERING AND SIGHTSEEING

Although Ruth, as a child, had traveled to China and back, there were many parts of the United States she had never seen. It was delightful to watch Ruth and Gordon become so enchanted with the beauties of our American West. During a spectacular sunset, Ruth said, "Oh look at the green in the sky. Now it's turning turquoise!" Sure enough it was, but I had never noticed it before. My wife was opening my eyes!

After Ruth and Gordon had taken a dip in the slimy, salt-heavy Great Salt Lake, we continued west to Yellowstone and the Grand Tetons. We finally arrived in San Francisco early Saturday evening, where we were to appear at the Area Youth For Christ rally. As a dramatic prelude to the rally, hundreds of people marched through a city street behind a brass band, like a Pied Piper, bringing the followers right into the auditorium where we would hold our meeting. That night a large number of teenagers gave their hearts to Christ. We also held other meetings in the Bay area.

Next, we drove along the spectacular California coastline to San Luis Obispo to see my sister, Lela, and her family. From there we continued on to the Los Angeles area where we stayed with my brother Earl and his wife. They showed us many sights.

I remember one special evening at the Hollywood Bowl. The tenor soloist was a man I had never heard of—around thirty years of age. It was a spectacular night at the bowl, with its beautiful natural setting. However, the bowl was only about one-third full. I presume the crowd was not large because the singer was not well known, so we were able to move down front into choice seats.

The tenor soloist was sharp looking, and when he sang his first aria, we were totally thrilled. What a voice! We knew we were listening to one of the nation's finest tenors. The crowd stood and applauded enthusiastically after his first group of songs.

My brother said, "Let's look at the program again and see what this fellow's name is—he's tremendous!" It was Mario Lanza! He sounded much like I supposed Enrico Caruso would have. He was young, vigorous, and in excellent voice. Having studied voice ourselves, we were thrilled. His rendition of *"Una Furtiva Lagrima"* by Donizetti still rings in my ears! He was gracious with his encores, and the report in the Los Angeles papers the next day read something like: "Mario Lanza takes the bowl by storm!" And he did! Soon he was known everywhere.

HEADING HOME

After two exciting weeks in California, we headed east to Arizona to see the Grand Canyon, then south to Palo Verde in the farming community where I had grown up. There we met the rest of my family—five brothers, sisters-in-law, nieces, and nephews, as well as many friends. Ranch life, cattle, horseback riding, steak fries—these and many other western things filled our days. How different from the navy and Iceland! And how different for Ruth and Gordon, who had never been out West.

Now the calendar was telling us it was time to return home to New York City. So we drove across the southern part of our country to Washington, DC, then on to the Big Apple. We arrived just in time to complete enrollment at Columbia for our graduate study. Now we were ready to hit the books!

A few days later, we thought about what had happened during the past two months. We knew we wanted to go across the nation and back, but we had no plan and very little money. But we had a gracious God. He arranged for transportation and lodging, wonderful meetings, and all the rest. We were reminded of Psalm 32:8—"I will instruct thee and teach thee in the way that thou shalt go: I will guide thee with mine eye." We knew that nearly every day of our trip there was great rejoicing in heaven because people were being saved. What a Savior!

CHAPTER SEVEN

COLUMBIA UNIVERSITY

HARVARD, YALE, PRINCETON, OR COLUMBIA?

World War II had just ended. I wanted to work toward a doctorate, so I visited all four. But Columbia seemed to be the best for me. Furthermore, Ruth was already enrolled there. So with the Lord's help (and the financial aid of the GI Bill) I also enrolled at Columbia in New York City. I already had my bachelor's and master's degrees, so I started on a doctorate. Ruth resumed work on her master's degree. By the end of the year, she had finished, and I had picked up a second master's. We were both in the commencement exercises, and since our last names were the same, we walked down the aisle together. In fact, we did a little hand holding as we marched to the orchestra's playing of Elgar's magnificent "Pomp and Circumstance"!

In time, we came to know some of the students and faculty quite well. Although there was nothing spiritual or biblical about the program, neither was it anti-Christian, and we were treated fairly. Ruth and I made a special effort to get to class on time, speak up in class, write good reports, and attend faculty teas and meetings. We wanted to cooperate.

Except for their lack of spiritual insight, I believe our professors were among the best in the nation. Columbia was not only excellent academically, but the faculty and administration also had reasonable and considerate attitudes about many things. While there, I had the opportunity to be the student assistant to one of the prominent psychology professors. That was a real plus because we had many conversations, and I learned a lot.

DISSERTATION DAYS

During the time that I was working on my dissertation, Ruth accepted a position teaching in a nearby private elementary school. There were perhaps fifteen of us in the same stage of the doctoral program, each with his own cubicle where we did research and writing. You could find these graduate students at their workspaces almost any hour of the day or night. If I got too tired at nine PM, I would set my alarm for an hour of sleep then put my head on the desk. An hour later, I'd wake up and start working again. This daily routine was broken with other activities Ruth and I had, including a job as music directors at a Long Island church. My intensive study continued week after week and month after month.

> Interestingly, during the years I was at the university, I never saw a tract discarded, thrown away, or lying on the floor.

Each time I went downstairs to the cafeteria, I took several gospel tracts to put in a line of vacant telephone booths located on the first floor. When I returned, I noticed they had all been taken, so I left more. One of my favorites was, "The Best Thing In Life." *Interestingly, during the years I was at the university, I never saw a tract discarded, thrown away, or lying on the floor.* Evidently, students and faculty were picking them up, taking them home and reading them. Tracts are excellent soul-winning tools that minister to people right where they are. I have known of people dying, clutching a gospel tract in their hands!

WHAT IS THE DISTINCTIVE?

I'll never forget an experience I had at Columbia. About one hundred students were enrolled in a certain class. I had come a few minutes early that Tuesday evening, and as I waited for the lecture to begin, another doctoral student came and sat beside me. He was, I believe, the assistant minister of education in India.

Just before the class began, this stranger turned to me and asked, "What is the distinctive of the Christian religion?" Naturally, I was surprised to hear him ask this question, and to ask it of me, a complete stranger. But I was glad he did.

"There are a number of distinctives," I explained. "But one stands out above all the others. Every religious leader who has ever lived has died and remained dead." His head was nodding in agreement. Then I added, "Except one—Jesus Christ. He lived and died and rose again on the third day. We have the names of people who talked, walked, and ate with Him and who recorded where He was going and what He was saying. In fact, over five hundred people at one time and place saw Him and heard Him speak."

"I never realized that," he said.

"Well," I continued, "while you're here in the United States, you'll learn many interesting things, but without doubt, you'll never learn anything more important than this fact: Christ died, arose from the dead, and publicly ascended to heaven."

"But how could He rise from the dead?" he asked.

"Because Jesus was not only man; He was also God," I replied. "Since He was God, He had power to give up His life, as well as take it back. That is why we trust Christ as our personal Savior; not because He was a good teacher and a good man, but because He, being the Son of God, was able to die and rise again."

About that time class began, and I praised God that He had given me such a fine opportunity. Later I thought, *Some of the most important things you learn in college may not come from the faculty.*

THE CLASS CLOWN

About a week later, I had another interesting experience in a different class. It was held in an auditorium where five professors on the platform spoke to a topic and answered questions. During the second hour of the class, students broke into small discussion groups of about fifteen.

On the first day as we broke into small groups, I noticed a young man about twenty-nine years of age by the name of Joe. He was quite a clown, talking a great deal, laughing, and being the life of the class. After a few days, I told Ruth about this guy and suggested that we pray for him. "His name is Joe Raffa, and he's always laughing and joking."

"Well, what's wrong with laughing?" she asked.

"Nothing," I said, "but life really isn't that funny. I think he's trying to cover something, and down deep he's really hurting. I haven't met him personally, but let's just start praying for him."

About a week later, Joe and I entered the college cafeteria at the same time. "Hi Joe!" I said.

He looked surprised and asked, "Have I met you?"

"We're in the same foundations of education class," I said. "Let's have lunch together."

"Great," he said.

We sat down and talked about our experiences. He had been an officer in the army and I in the navy. As we sat at our table, I said, "Joe, I don't know how to say this, but I'm quite concerned about you."

"What do you mean?" he asked.

"Well," I said, "in our class you're always laughing and clowning. I wonder if you might be trying to cover your real, deep-down feelings."

He looked at me quizzically and aside, "Are you a psychology major?"

"Yes," I said.

"Well," he said, "they should give you your doctor's degree this afternoon." He went on to say, "I suppose I'm the most unhappy student here at Columbia. I've tried all kinds of things, but nothing satisfies. Just this morning as I was coming over to the university, I stopped at the big Riverside church nearby and tried the front door. It was unlocked, so I walked in, but there didn't seem to be anybody around. So I walked about halfway down the aisle of the sanctuary and threw myself on the floor and began to cry out to God, 'If there is a God, reveal yourself to me. I don't want to live as I am. So if you're there, reveal yourself to me.' I pounded the floor and cried."

"Joe," I said, "God has answered your prayer, because He has sent me to reveal Him to you."

I explained that God put Adam and Eve in the garden of Eden with free choice. But they disobeyed Him and sinned, so He had to drive them out. Since that time, every person has sinned. But God in His great love and mercy sent His Son Jesus Christ to die for us. And if we trust in Him, God's Holy Spirit will indwell us, make us new, and also take us to Heaven when we die.

"That sounds sort of like a fairy tale," Joe said.

10/21/12

"Maybe it does," I said, "*but spiritual conversion has been put in the scientific test-tube more often than anything else—under every condition with all ages of people, in every culture and in every generation, and the results are always the same: a new life in Christ!* Millions have experienced it and have found that it's real, and I'm one of them."

As Joe sat there, tears began to come to his eyes.

Then I added, "Joe, don't let anyone poke anything down your throat. But when God does move in your heart, accept Him." Then taking a paper, I wrote out four Scripture verses and suggested that he carry it with him, reading it as he rode back and forth on the subway.

He took the paper and began to read the verses as he left the cafeteria. Every day or so after that, I would see Joe momentarily as we passed each other in the halls. About a week later, I came into the library, and just as I stepped in, Joe saw me and called out, "Narramore, Narramore!"

Oh my, I thought, *they're going to kick us out of the library for yelling like that. This is supposed to be a quiet place.* But I walked over to where he was standing.

> *"But spiritual conversion has been put in the scientific test-tube more often than anything else—under every condition with all ages of people, in every culture and in every generation, and the results are always the same: a new life in Christ!"*

"Clyde," he said, "I want to ask you a question. One verse on that paper says, 'That if we confess our sins, He is faithful and just to forgive us our sins and to cleanse us from all unrighteousness' (1 John 1:9). Will God forgive me of *every* sin I have ever committed, no matter what and when?"

"Yes!" I said. Then I gave him another Scripture verse: "'Come now, and let us reason together,' says the Lord, 'Though your sins are like scarlet, they shall be as white as snow; though they are red like crimson, they shall be as wool'" (Isa. 1:18).

After a moment Joe said, "I think I'm ready now to be saved. How do we do it?"

I thought fast and said, "Let's go down the hallway of this building and find a room that's vacant. Then we'll go in and pray and ask God to save you." So we walked down the hallway as Joe looked in each room on the right side and I glanced in the rooms on the left, but every one was in use. So I suggested we go up to the second floor. We did, but as we met each other at the end of the hallway, we found again that every room was filled with classes. Then we went to the third and found the same situations. So I said, "Joe, maybe the gymnasium is vacant."

"I doubt it," he answered, "it's used by so many students."

But we went to the gym anyway, and to our amazement, we didn't find one soul there. So we knelt down on a wrestling mat in the corner of the gym, and I said, "Let's pray."

"Well, I really don't know what to say," Joe said.

"Just tell God you're a sinner," I suggested, "and ask Him to come into your heart and save you."

Then Joe said, "Just before we do it, Clyde, I want to tell you something that I'm very happy about. You see, I've come from a family that's very emotional—my dad's very emotional, and so is my mother and so are all my uncles and aunts. I have a degree from Cornell University, and I've tried to get over a lot of this silly emotionalism. And I want to thank you for the fine, intelligent, clear way you have presented the gospel without a lot of emotion."

"Joe," I said, "I know what you mean. But I would not avoid emotion, because when you see yourself heading for hell where there's never a baby's cry, where there's never a rose, or a sweet song—only misery. It's enough to make you cry. And when you think of spending eternity in heaven with God where all is perfect, it's enough to make you cry for joy—at least on the inside."

Then Joe began to pray, "Oh God, I'm not only a sinner—I'm a bad one!"

"Tell Him you're sorry for your sins," I said.

So he went on to tell God how sorry he was about his sins ... and then he began to cry relentlessly. He sobbed and sobbed.

Finally, Joe regained his composure, and said, "Lord, come into my heart and save me. I'll serve you the best I know how every day that I live."

I prayed also, and we both shed a few tears. Then we got up from the wrestling mat, and still no one had come into the gymnasium. *God had saved it just for us to transact eternal business!*

As we came out of the building, Joe said, "It feels like a thousand pounds have been lifted from my back. I know that if I should die this very minute, I would be in the presence of God!" Then he asked, "What do I do now?"

"Joe," I said, "it's good to get a Bible and read the book of John, and also the book of James plus the book of Psalms." Then I gave him a paper with

John 10:28 written on it: "And I give them eternal life, and they shall never perish; neither shall anyone snatch them out of My hand."

"Anytime Satan tempts you," I said, "or tries to make you doubt your salvation, just say that verse wherever you are."

From that point on, Joe and I had regular Bible studies together. He began to visit Ruth and me at our home and come to church with us. He grew so fast spiritually. About a year and a half later, after he had completed his work at Columbia, he moved to California and attended seminary for awhile. In time, he met and married a fine Christian young lady. A little later, Joe joined my staff in California as a counselor.

In time, Joe Raffa and his family moved to Atlanta, Georgia, where he has lived for many years. What a tremendous blessing he has been as he has held seminars and counseled with hundreds of people! As I look back, I realize that leading people to Christ was one of the most important things that took place during my time at Columbia. I enjoyed all my courses and learned much on my Ivy League mission field! But God says, "He that wins souls is wise" (Prov. 11:30). How true!

Note: Today, as I was writing this story about Joe, I received a wonderful letter from Joe's youngest daughter, Cynthia, who lives in New York City. Yes, you guessed it: she was thanking me for leading her dad to Christ some fifty years earlier!

IT'S A PIZZA

When I think of my days at Columbia, a special culinary experience comes to mind. Near the campus was a tasty little restaurant about big enough for ten or so people. One evening I went there, and as I sat on a stool at the counter, I saw something unusual. The cook took a ball of dough and flattened it with a rolling pin until it was about the size of a large plate. Tossing it into the air several times, he caught it with his fists. He then put this flat piece of dough on a board and covered it with what looked like tomato sauce. After that he sprinkled a generous layer of cheese all over the top. Then came some thin slices of pepperoni and olives, along with a few chips of green pepper. I wondered what it was and what he was going to do with it.

Next he took a long, shovel-like paddle and shoved his creation into a big, open oven. It began to smell wonderful! Some minutes later, he reached in with his long-handled paddle, slipped it under the crust, brought it out, and placed it on his little table not more than four feet from my inquisitive nose.

"What's that?" I asked.

"It's a pizza," he answered with an Italian accent.

"Can I try about half of it?" I asked.

"Sure," he replied as he took a knife, cut it down the middle and put it on my plate. *That was the beginning of a new addiction!*

The rest is history! It was the first time I'd ever seen or heard of a pizza, even though I'd traveled extensively and eaten many kinds of food. About ten years later I began to see them appearing in specialty restaurants around the country. I'm glad that I got in on the early days of the popular American Italian pizza!

A SECONDARY CONSIDERATION

As I was learning more about the field of psychology, I was beginning to realize the great potential Christian psychology could have in the lives of people, including born-again believers. So my interest and enthusiasm was growing day by day.

Music was also important to me, but I felt it was secondary in my career. Yet I kept thinking about it. I had grown up in a musical family, and even in elementary school I had sung solos for various events. In high school, I took leading roles in the school operettas, and I was the soloist at graduation. In college, among other things, I had received a major in music and was a soloist for a number of college functions. In my senior year, I was asked to represent the college in a state-wide contest of male vocalists from the major colleges in Arizona. There I won second place singing an aria from an Italian opera. A year or so later, I placed third in a contest for soloists at the American Conservatory of Music in Chicago. And while at Columbia, I gave a recital in one of the smaller auditoriums at Carnegie Hall.

In short, I had experienced at least a little success in music ever since I was a child. And now, having married Ruth, a talented musician, my interest in music was still very much alive. Interestingly, voice students are always hoping to find a teacher who can "unlock" their voices so they can add several notes to their upper or lower ranges. *Who knows,* they wonder. *Maybe I have the potential to be the best.*

While studying at Columbia I was introduced to a fine voice coach at the Metropolitan Opera Company. I rather enjoyed opera, and I had learned a number of arias. So I made arrangements to have two evaluation sessions with him. I was aware that my oldest brother, Leslie, had an unusually high tenor voice. I'm sure he could have done opera work if he could have had training instead of, at eighteen, running the ranch and helping to raise all of us children after our father died. So, when I met with the voice coach, I asked him if he thought it would be possible for me to develop those high tones also. I was a second tenor, and I knew I could never go to the top as a singer unless I could develop a higher range.

At the end of our second session, he advised, "You have a good voice, and you'll always be able to make a living singing. But your voice by nature is not sufficiently high to do unusual singing. You have the quality, volume, and musicality. But no amount of training will develop the needed top tones. They're not there."

I left his studio feeling happy to have had his professional evaluation. He confirmed what I had believed for a long time, so I was not disappointed. I realized that many singers do spend a lifetime studying voice but never singing professionally because they are lacking what it takes to reach the top.

> God knows what he is doing when he gives us our potential as well as our limitations.

As I look back, I think God used this experience with the voice coach to point up the importance of encouraging people, but at the same time helping them to be realistic about their possibilities. *God knows what He is doing when He gives us our potential as well as our limitations.*

SIFTING AND REASONING

My years at Columbia were very important. I knew I was attending one of the world's outstanding secular institutions of learning. The faculty members were among the brightest and the best. And I wanted to learn all I could. It was also a relatively quiescent time of life. World War II was over, I was newly and happily married, and we were employed on weekends as the directors of music at a fine church near our home. The music job proved to be a delightful ministry as well as a source of income to meet our expenses. There were few distractions, and I was able to concentrate on my studies.

This was a time of careful sifting and reasoning. When I attended lectures, did research, and read books, I was intent on sifting what was true and what was false. If it was in conflict with the plain teaching of the eternal word of God, I knew it was not true. If what I was learning was not discussed in the Bible, I would ask myself, *Is this in opposition to, or agreement with, the general inference and spirit of God's word?* Having a fair knowledge of the Scriptures helped me in this sifting and reasoning process.

Another thing—as I learned, I kept asking myself:

+ *How could this apply to my life or the life of another person?*
+ *Is there spiritual significance in what I am studying?*
+ *Can I explain this clearly to someone else?*

These mental processes went on day after day and month after month. To make it even better, I talked things over with Ruth, who was well-educated and a good student of God's word. I also discussed many things with my godly father-in-law, Edwin Elliott, who was an astute student of the Scriptures.

In short, I was aware that millions of people were studying, but many were doing as the Bible describes, "Ever learning and never able to come to the knowledge of the truth" (2 Tim. 3:7). And I kept praying I would not be among that crowd!

WHAT'S YOUR ADVICE?

In time, as I was moving through the doctoral program, I went to my major advisor and said, "I'm having some thoughts about several things. I like the field of psychology and counseling, I have two masters' degrees, and, as you know, I'm working on my doctorate. But I also have a real interest in college administration, possibly becoming the president of a university someday. I don't have anything particular in mind, but I am wondering what you think."

My advisor, a mature man who had been a professor at Columbia for many years, said, "Narramore, you don't have to put yourself into a corner. Here at Columbia we want our graduates to be as broad as possible in their academic backgrounds. By taking an extra semester or so here you can get a major in both psychology and college administration. I think one field will help the other."

I was encouraged and followed that path, never realizing that someday I would not only be a licensed psychologist but I would become the founding president of the Rosemead Graduate School of Psychology, offering a doctorate in Christian counseling!

Near the end of my study at Columbia, I received a very sad letter from my mother. She told me that she had not been feeling well and that the doctors had found she had cancer. I felt so badly and arranged to fly home to see her. Those were precious days together.

"How long will it take you to finish your doctor's degree?" she asked.

"Mom," I said, "it's hard to tell because I'm dependent on committees and my major advisor. But I think I can finish in three months."

"That's okay," she said. "I can last that long. So go back and finish it and come see me."

As always, I was impressed with my precious pioneer mother's practicality and determination. So I returned to Columbia, finished the degree, and Ruth and I moved to California. Yes, Mom was still with us, praise God!

ARE YOU A REAL ONE?

As we go through life, there are always people around who help us keep our feet on the ground. I suppose that's good. It happened to me on commencement day. The time finally arrived when I had completed all the requirements for my doctorate and I was handed my diploma. Ruth and I were so thrilled, considering all the study, discipline, and hard work it had represented. *The final day had come, and we rejoiced as we left the campus with sheepskin in hand.* We seemed to be floating on air as we drove to our home on Long Island.

When we arrived, we got out of our car and started walking up the sidewalk to the front door. A little boy about seven years of age who lived next door was standing there looking at us. Evidently his parents had told him that Mr. Narramore was now receiving his doctor's degree and that he should address me as "Doctor."

"Hi, Dr. Narramore!" he said as we approached our apartment. "Do you have your doctor's degree now?"

"Yes, I do," I answered. And I thought to myself, *Isn't this nice that someone has recognized my doctorate even before I get into my house!*

Then he asked, "Dr. Narramore, are you a *real* doctor, or are you just one of those other kind?"

Ruth looked at me and smiled, and we've often laughed about that moment of deflation.

A few weeks later, Ruth and I headed west. My childhood summer visits to Southern California probably influenced my wanting to go to the "Golden State." Ruth hated to leave her family and friends, but she wanted what I wanted. Short on money, but full of faith and lots of education, we said good-bye and headed west. We owned our car, a piano, and a bookcase. We had only about a few hundred dollars and no job prospects, but we felt we were in God's will, and we were both certain He would open opportunities. What followed was amazing!

CHAPTER EIGHT

GO WEST, YOUNG MAN

School had already begun by the middle of September in 1949, and we had just arrived in California. We had no home and no job, but we had lots of hope. I said to Ruth, "When we were back at Columbia a few weeks ago, I saw a book published by the California Test Bureau in Santa Monica. It's a good book on counseling. Let's go over there and look around."

Unexpected Meeting

As we entered the building and turned a corner, I bumped into a man, who said, "Oh, I'm sorry. Can I help you?"

I laughed and said, "The kind of help my wife and I need, I doubt if you can give us."

"Well, what is it?" he asked.

"We've just arrived from New York," I said, "and we're going to be living in California, and I'm looking for a job."

"What's your field?" he asked.

"I have a doctorate in psychology," I answered.

"Where did you get your degree?" he asked.

"Columbia University," I said.

"Well, that's as good as gold!" he commented. Then, to our surprise, he took us into his office and said, "One of the best jobs in America in the field of educational psychology is open right now! It's with the Los Angeles County Superintendent of Schools—a large office—and the schools in California are among the best in the nation. There's a strong possibility that if you go over and apply for the job, you can get it!"

By that time, he really had our attention.

"There are," he continued, "about a hundred people who work for the county superintendent of schools—professionals representing different specialties. Their job is to fan out over Los Angeles County, which is growing tremendously, and serve as consultants to the local school districts. It's a top-flight job and a great place to learn and work."

Then he added, "Take your wife with you; she's an asset!"

INTERVIEWS

So we jumped in our car and headed for the office of the Los Angeles County Superintendent of Schools in downtown Los Angeles. When we went into the research and guidance department, the secretary said, "Our department head is out of the office today, but he'll be in tomorrow. Can I help you in some way?"

"We just arrived from New York City," I said. "I have my doctor's degree from Columbia University in the field of psychology, and I'm looking for a position."

So we talked for a few minutes. Then she asked, "Do you have a license to practice in California?"

"No," I replied, "we just arrived, and I didn't know a license was required."

"Yes," she said, "but it sounds like you will qualify. I'm sure our director, Dr. Harry Smallenberg, would be interested in meeting you tomorrow. Can you come back?"

We returned the next day and met Dr. Smallenberg, and found him to be a prince of a gentleman. "We do have an opening," he said. After a good talk, he handed me the phone number of the state department of education in Sacramento. By contacting them, they could determine if I had taken the necessary courses to get a California license.

I got busy and filled out forms and sent telegrams to the University of Southern California, Arizona State University, and Columbia requesting them to send transcripts of credits directly to Sacramento. Then I phoned Sacramento, telling them to expect the transcripts. A few days later, I received a letter saying they had received the transcripts and that I had taken every course required to receive the psychologist license for the state of California. Ruth and I praised the Lord! You know how it is, you're in college taking a required course you may not like, but years later you find it's actually needed to gain a state license. How wonderfully God works!

GET ON BOARD

We went immediately to the county superintendent of schools' office and showed them the letter. "You're employed," they said.

Little did I know what a fine position it would be. There were about thirteen psychologists in our department. Some were specialists in clinical psychology, others in research, counseling, and some in educational psychology. But they all qualified for a license in California. I didn't realize how much I would grow and develop, and how much it would prepare me for the work God had for me in the years to come! It all happened so fast and so well. As I settled into my new position, I took some postdoctoral work at USC. (But I made sure it was in psychological testing, not flute!)

In the meantime, I had taken the position of choir director, and Ruth as director of Christian education as well as organist for the Eagle Rock Baptist Church in Los Angeles where Dr. Harry MacArthur (grandfather of John) was pastor. Before long, we were privileged to know all three generations of these remarkable preachers: Harry, Jack, and John.

Now Ruth and I were both employed. But where would we live? We had only a car, a piano, a bookcase, and a flat billfold! But God provided a place to live not far from Dr. Keith L. Brooks, who wrote and distributed Bible studies throughout the world. Our times with this brilliant and humble man were precious. His simple lifestyle while having a worldwide ministry impressed us deeply. In fact, it became our lifetime example.

BILLY GRAHAM ARRIVES

A few weeks after Ruth and I had settled in California and the Lord had opened a professional career for me, a benchmark event took place. A young evangelist, Billy Graham, came to the Los Angeles area and conducted his first major crusade at Washington and Hill Streets.

Ruth and I had heard Billy a few years earlier at Percy Crawford's Pinebrook Bible Conference in the Pocono Mountains of Pennsylvania. We were impressed with his unusual ability to speak and lead people to Christ, so we were eager to attend his tent meetings in Los Angeles.

Under the power of the Holy Spirit, Billy impacted the city, and many prominent people along with thousands of others surrendered their hearts to Christ. It was evident that this would be the beginning of a great public ministry.

And indeed, God has used him to lead perhaps more people to Christ than any man in history. Billy Graham holds nearly everyone he meets in high regard, and people respond to his love, humility, integrity, and clear presentation of the saving grace of God through Christ.

Billy and I were born near the same time and commenced our ministries at the same time in the same area. In addition, because of the choice of our wives, neither of us was "Ruthless!" Like millions of others, I will always be grateful that God has put me on earth during this remarkable period so I could see firsthand the marvelous working of God through Billy Graham's ministry.

SERVING AND LEARNING

My professional work for the next thirteen years was more than exciting. Can you imagine working closely with thirteen licensed psychologists day after day and year after year? (Perhaps you wouldn't think that exciting.)

We had two clinical staff meetings each week. We shared cases of children and teachers with whom we were working—mostly boys and girls with severe problems. Each psychologist added his insights and experience. We discussed almost everything having to do with psychological testing, counseling, child development, parent education, rehabilitation, and the like. I don't suppose there was a better place in America to learn from professional associates.

This was coupled with going into local school districts and doing hands-on work with children, parents, teachers, nurses, and administrators. I soon learned how much I didn't know!

Dr. Smallenburg, our department head, set a sterling example as a top-flight, well-adjusted administrator. I'm sure we "caught" more than he "taught." He also brought in medical, psychiatric, and other specialists to give our staff special training. What an opportunity!

In time, I had the privilege of co-authoring two books for our office, *Guiding Today's Children* and *Guiding Today's Youth*. The two volumes have been used in schools and colleges around the nation.

Mixed with these days of joy and blessing came a very sad time—the homegoing of my precious mother. All seven of us children loved her so much. And since our father had died thirty-one years earlier, she meant even more to us. But she was a strong believer in Christ, and we knew we would see her again in heaven. We were comforted with God's word, "Precious in the sight of the Lord is the death of His saints" (Ps. 116:15).

No Room in the Inn

As we settled down in California, we took several weekend trips around the state, plus a couple of summer trips to the East Coast.

Most young people entering the twenty-first century are not aware of the tremendous changes that have swept into our lives during recent years. They take conditions for granted.

Just think of the hotel and motel industry. Millions more lodgings for travelers have sprung up offering a smorgasbord of options. Some, for example, are "vacation destinations." You go there not only to stay for a night or two but also to swim, sweat it out in the sauna, soak in the hot tub, pump iron in the exercise room, hold conferences, play tennis, and surf the Internet. You can choose to eat in your room, in a choice of several restaurants, or order box lunches to take out.

What a contrast to the conditions only a few years back!

I remember an incident early in our marriage when my wife, Ruth, and I were traveling to the Sequoia National Park in California. In those days, if we found any place at all to stay, it would be in a little row of cabins near the road. Each one was about big enough to get in, go to bed, get up, and then be on our way.

But on this occasion, we weren't that lucky. Night was settling in, and we didn't have any place to stay. After searching up and down the roads, we finally came to a little campground with a lonely gas pump out in front. We asked the man there if he knew where we could sleep that night. "There's no place around here," he said, "nothin' at all."

"But don't you know of just any place where we could sleep?" I asked.

The man thought for a moment, scratched his head, and answered, "Well, out in back there's a tiny place. I think there's an old straw mattress up there. It's in an old windmill about ten feet high, and you'll have to climb a ladder to get up there … and there ain't no bathroom."

I looked at Ruth, who sort of frowned, then smiled and said, "Let's look at it." We climbed the ladder, and at the top, we found a platform room about eight feet square. An old straw mattress took up most of the space.

We knew it was this or nothing at all, so we told him we'd take it. I think he charged us a dollar. Actually, he should have paid us for staying there!

Ruth was frightened of spiders from experiences in China as a young girl. I tried to assure her there weren't any spiders in this part of the country! I don't think I was all that convincing, but Ruth was a good sport, so we stayed overnight. What an experience, especially when your wife happens to be pregnant!

On another occasion, we stayed at an interesting "motel" when driving through New Mexico on our way from California to New York. We kept our eyes open for anything that resembled a motel or cabin. We saw a few places, but each had a "No Vacancy" sign hanging outside the front door where a weak, little forty-watt bulb lit it up. Everything else was dark. We kept traveling east for miles, when finally we saw a police car alongside the road. We stopped and asked the officer where we could possibly find a place to stay that night.

"Well," he said, "I don't think you'll find anything for the next hundred miles or so and maybe not even there. However, up ahead about a mile there's a hospital. Maybe they'd have an extra bed." I looked at Ruth who smiled and said, "Let's go for it."

So we traveled on until we saw a sign pointing to a hospital. We went in and told them we were really in a bind. "We need a place to stay and can't find any. Do you have an extra bed we can use tonight?" I asked.

The dear, compassionate nurse at the desk thought for a moment, then told us they did have one small area that was vacant. "It doesn't have a regular door," she said, "and it isn't really what you'd call a room. But a curtain hangs between it and the hallway."

We assured her that it would be okay. So we went in and found the "room," a space with two narrow, vacant hospital beds. And it was hospital clean. As we drew the curtain, we began to laugh.

"Well, Honey," Ruth said, "this is quite an experience, isn't it? I'm just glad that neither one of us is sick!"

Today we use the computer, Internet, and what have you to learn what hotels and motels in which cities are available. When I see all of the first-class amenities available now, I think about the times we climbed the ladder to a windmill, and again, when we stayed in the hospital. Believe me, those were times when there was no room in the inn!

Cobo Hall, Detroit

CHAPTER NINE

MINISTERING AND PARENTING

When Ruth and I completed our graduate degrees at Columbia, we moved to California. There I joined the staff of the Los Angeles County superintendent of schools. This would be a thirteen-year professional experience of unusual blessing.

I was assigned to eight elementary and junior high school districts in Los Angeles County. Each had several schools, and all were "bursting at the semesters." In Los Angeles County, which is more than one hundred miles wide, six new complete school plants were springing up, ready for use every Monday morning.

More than a thousand people were rushing into Los Angeles County every day. They flooded in from everywhere, but especially from the Midwest. It was one of the greatest migrations of human beings that had taken place in America, and I found myself in the middle of it. Developers were bulldozing thousands of orange trees and erecting homes for families. Towns were springing up, and new freeways were threading their way north and south as well as east and west.

Ruth and I found a residential lot on a hill with a lovely view in the Pasadena area where we built our home. In time we moved in, furniture or not. We slept at a friend's home for a few weeks until we had enough money to buy a bed and were able to sew some draperies for our living room. But we were just as happy as though we owned a bank. The house met our needs, so we have continued to live in it for more than sixty years!

Financially, those were difficult, struggling days, but I thank God for a wife who stuck with me. She'd been raised on the mission field, and although she had quality tastes, as I suppose I did, we were willing to get by on very little in order to serve the Lord. My salary was four thousand dollars a year—not a month. Furthermore, I had no employment during the summer—which meant no income during that time. I taught courses one summer at Long Beach State College in California, and another at Montclair State College in New Jersey. After that, we spent many summers crisscrossing the nation, speaking at Bible conferences. We financed these conference trips by borrowing money. But we were reaching thousands of people in person who were learning about Christian psychology.

FROM NINE TO FIVE

Friends often asked me what I did as a consulting psychologist for the public schools.

I tested children for gifted classes, as well as those with difficulties who needed to attend special classes. I studied youngsters who had severe problems and worked regularly with groups of teachers and parents. I was challenged by the things I learned each day. *I soon found that when a person finishes his doctor's degree, he needs a job where he can learn.* And I surely had that. On a typical day, I would arrive at school at 8:30 or 9:00 AM. There the superintendent would hand me a stack of manila folders, each containing information about a child who had rather serious problems.

I selected four or five to see, administered tests, interviewed their teachers, and visited their parents. Then I met with the principal and teacher to make recommendations for helping the child. It was not unusual to follow a child for several months, or even an entire school year. As I worked through on a case, I made sure that the teachers and administrators understood what we were doing. This was especially important inasmuch as their understanding of the problem, as well as the solutions, would help them the next time they identified a child with a similar problem.

We sometimes found that the basic causes for the child's difficulties were rooted in the family, perhaps a broken relationship or dysfunctional parent and siblings. *But in serious, longstanding problems, the causes frequently stemmed from physical factors.*

During the years I served as a psychologist on the staff of the Los Angeles County superintendent of schools, I worked rather closely with Dr. Harold Burk, another psychologist on the staff who had a strong clinical background. Dr. Burk found, as I did, that many of the boys and girls who were referred to us with severe problems seemed to have neurological impairments. Over a period of time, he teamed up with a neurologist in the Southern California area. Together, they studied several hundred students they suspected as being neurologically impaired. These boys and girls (more often boys) were carefully interviewed, observed, and given psychological tests. Their teachers and parents were also interviewed.

The neurologist then gave them electroencephalograms (EEGs). Finally, for those whom the neurologist and psychologist identified as neurologically impaired, Dr. Burk then made a study of their most frequent classroom behaviors that were *not* characteristic of the average child.

As he worked with the teachers of these children in their classes, he found there was a common set of behaviors that were characteristic. The following were listed in three behavioral categories. It has proven helpful in identifying boys and girls who might have a neurological problem.

If at least six or eight of these persistent behaviors are identified by the parents and teacher, the counselor might suggest to parents that they take the child to a neurologist. This list included the following:

BEHAVIORAL-MUSCULAR

1. Hyperactive and restless
2. Erratic, flighty, or scattered behavior
3. Easily distracted, lacks continuity of effort
4. Behavior goes in cycles
5. Quality of work may vary from day to day
6. Excessive daydreaming, alternating with hyperactivity
7. Explosive and unpredictable behavior
8. Can't seem to control self (speaks or jumps out of seat)
9. Poor coordination in large muscle activities

PERCEPTUAL-DISCRIMINATIVE

10. Confused in spelling and writing
11. Inclined to be confused in number processes
12. Has difficulty reading

13. Lacks variety of responses, repeats himself in situations
14. Upset by change in routine
15. Confused in following directions (three or more simultaneous commands)
16. Confused and apprehensive about rightness of response
17. Classroom comments are often "off the track" or extraneous
18. Difficulty reasoning things out logically with others

SOCIAL-EMOTIONAL

19. Demands much attention
20. Tends to be destructive, especially of the work of others
21. May evidence stubborn, uncooperative behavior
22. Often withdraws quickly from group activities
23. Has constant difficulty with others purposelessly
24. Has shallow feelings for others
25. Cries often and easily (younger child)
26. Is often more confused by punishment
27. Seems generally unhappy
28. Often tells bizarre stories

Rehabilitation involves (1) counseling with the parents, (2) a different educational classroom approach, (3) medication, (4) a more understanding approach to the child in his home, (5) a Christ-centered atmosphere for the child, (6) nutritional considerations.

As the principal or superintendent understood what I was doing, he would often say, "We need to get this information and understanding to every one of our teachers. Can we set up a series of meetings where you will speak to all of our teachers?" This, of course, led to meeting with groups of educators and administrators during the year.

THE GREATEST THOUGHT

There were many sharp psychologists on our county schools' staff, all of whom I liked, and from whom I learned.

One day, a psychologist who occupied the office next to mine came to my desk and asked, "Narramore, what do you think about this spiritual conversion bit?"

Being a psychologist, I didn't answer, but instead asked him, "What do you think about this spiritual conversion bit?"

"That's what I came in to ask about," he said.

I had other ideas up my sleeves, so I asked, "How did you come to think about this anyway?"

"Well, I try to keep my ears and eyes open," he replied. "As you know, I'm not a religious person, but there's a man on TV by the name of Billy Graham. Have you ever heard of him?"

"Billy Graham," I replied, "yes, I have."

"Well, he's very high on this spiritual conversion bit!" he commented.

"Oh, is he?" I asked. "What does he do?"

"I'm not sure," he said, "I've only seen him on television, but I see that he goes to a major city and has a meeting in a stadium or somewhere, and thousands come to hear him speak."

"That sounds like a lot of trouble and expense just to promote your ideas," I said.

"It seems that way to me, too," he said. "But if I understand it correctly, he gives his philosophy about the Bible, then at the end of his speech he asks people to come down front by his podium, and he speaks to them there."

"Pray tell, what does he do with them when they come down front?" I asked.

"I'm not sure because I've never been there," he replied, "but I understand that when he gets through with them—" and bringing the forefingers of each hand together, the psychologist continued, "they're supposed to have a personal relationship with God."

"Oh my," I said. "Do you think that could actually happen?"

"I don't know," he continued, "that's why I came to ask you. But I would say this, that *if it is possible for a human being to have a personal relationship with the One who created everything, then that just has to be the greatest thought that could ever occupy the human mind!*"

At that moment I thought, *What a brilliant statement from a sinful man!*

I assured him that, indeed, it could happen, because it had happened to me! Then I explained God's plan of salvation.

> "If it is possible for a human being to have a personal relationship with the One who created everything, then that just has to be the greatest thought that could ever occupy the human mind!"

As I drove home that evening, the concept kept going through my mind—*if a human being can have a personal relationship with the God of the universe who made all things, then that must be the greatest thought that could occupy the human mind!*

His statement impressed me so much that eventually I prepared a message along that line and gave it to the president's staff at the White House and other places around the world. Each time I have given it, God has blessed with the salvation of souls!

PARENT-TEACHER MEETINGS

As I traveled from district to district day by day, administrators began to invite me to speak at school functions, such as evening PTA meetings. I usually brought a challenge about raising boys and girls and how to help them become well adjusted. In my last point, I stressed that children are spiritual beings and we should help them grow spiritually because their souls live on for eternity.

After the meeting during coffee and doughnuts, it was common for young couples to approach me and say, "We enjoyed your speech tonight, but what caught our attention was when you said we should be doing something spiritually for our children. We don't think we're doing that. We've never felt the need to attend church ourselves, and we wouldn't know what to teach our children, or where to start."

"Let's sit over here by ourselves with our coffee and doughnuts," I would reply, "and discuss this." On scores of occasions, I explained the plan of salvation to couples, and right there as we talked, they would trust Christ as their personal Savior and surrender their lives to Him!

Within a year or two, the word got around that I was a speaker. Other staff psychologists would say, "Look, I'm having to give a speech in my district, but I'm the world's worst speaker. Would you come over and speak for me? Then I'll come to your district and help you with some of your work." So I took them up on it, and before long, I was speaking throughout the county, dedicating new schools and the like. I sometimes felt like an official "school dedicator" for Los Angeles County! I was reaching parents in many professions, as well as educators. For most, I was the first psychologist they had ever met or heard.

A few days before I spoke, I would make an outline of my message. After speaking, I filed these outlines away. Before long, I had a large three-ring notebook filled with outlines of speeches, along with audience reactions. (Some I never used the second time!) Little did I realize that a few years later, Christian publishers would ask me to write books. So many of these message outlines eventually found their way into books and into the lives of people around the world.

In short, I was deeply grateful for the privilege of working in such an outstanding organization. We also had many professional growth opportunities. Every few months, the head of our department brought in specialists, one at a time, who would speak to our staff for several days to upgrade our own

> *"If you want to understand adults, study them when they are children."*

education and professional understanding. These included endocrinologists, neurologists, educators, psychiatrists, and many others. So we were gaining a broad education ourselves. We would ask each one to go with us for half a day, or an evening, to our own districts. As we rode along together, I picked his brains. What an opportunity to grow professionally. And what a foundation for the years ahead! I was also learning the wisdom of the saying, *"If you want to understand adults, study them when they are children."*

I also had opportunities to direct Christian teachers to our area. A number of public school districts in Los Angeles County were headed by Christians. I was able to alert Christian teachers across America and tell them where to apply for jobs in the public schools. Before long, Christian teachers were flooding many schools in the Los Angeles County area. What an opportunity to be a blessing to the students!

I'd been at my job for about six or eight months when I received a phone call from a Christian businessman in Southern California. He asked me to speak at the annual banquet of the Christian Businessmen's Committee (CBMC), which was to be held in Los Angeles. "We have never had a psychologist," he said, adding, "in fact, few of us have ever met one. I think you'll draw a large crowd."

The evening came, and the banquet hall was packed. I did my best to bring a solid message from the Bible while integrating psychological concepts. I recalled what one of my professors in college had said: "Illustrations are like windows, and if you try to erect a building without them, it'll be very dull." I also remembered a professional writer telling me that it's almost "immoral" to bring out a point when speaking or writing without using an illustration! So that night I used plenty. They were easy to come by since I was living each day in the middle of them.

As I got up to speak, I noticed that the waitresses were standing around the edge of the room and listening. At the end of the message when I challenged people to be saved, five of them gave their hearts to the Lord, along with thirty-five or forty of the men and women at the banquet.

That was the beginning of a larger outreach. Many of the businessmen who attended that regional meeting came from other parts of the West. Within a few weeks, I was receiving invitations to travel to other California towns and nearby states to speak at CBMC meetings. The Lord had launched me into a speaking ministry along with my regular work with the county superintendent of school's office! Thousands were learning basic psychological principles. I was working during the day in school districts and speaking in the evenings and weekends to various groups.

These were some of my initial experiences in the growth of the Christian psychology movement in America.

EXPERT WITNESS

One day, I received an unusual phone call from the office of the Los Angeles City Attorney. The deputy attorney who called said that an important case was coming up and he wanted to know if I would be willing to serve as an expert witness. After talking a few minutes, we decided on a time and place where we could meet and consider the details of the case.

A few days later, I met with the attorney for lunch at the downtown Hilton Hotel. He was intelligent, well-trained, and a born-again believer.

"We've a case coming up in a couple of weeks," he said. "It concerns a man who is selling pornographic books and other lewd materials at a small downtown store. We'd like to bring him to justice and get rid of such stuff."

They had contacted me because I was a licensed psychologist, had college teaching experience, and was the author of a best-selling book, *Life and Love*, a wholesome Christian book on sex for teenagers and their parents.

"This porn vendor," he said, "has a very sharp attorney, and we've run into him before. He's bright, cunning, and aggressive. He'll twist and turn everything he can. He often handles cases for publishers of dirty books."

I agreed to help if I could. So we met again in a few days. Then he told me their plan. "We'll give you about a half dozen of the books we have confiscated. You can take them and read them so you'll know what you're talking about when you're called to the stand to testify. We want it made plain that these books are vicious and harmful to young people and adults alike."

After a few more instructions, he handed me a sack containing the six books. They were each about forty-eight to ninety-six pages in length. I took the books home and reviewed them in preparation for the lawsuit. They were poorly written, most of them by the same person, and designed to stimulate the reader sexually. *They were sordid, vile, filthy, perverse, degrading, vulgar, unnatural, abusive, evil, lascivious, and prurient.*

I wondered just how the "filth" attorney would approach the case and what my best course of action should be. As I prayed about the matter, I realized I had an opportunity, in a sense, to represent multitudes of Christians and other decent citizens to whom these books would be altogether offensive.

I felt that the attorney for the other side would not be able to refute my credentials inasmuch as I had an earned doctorate from Columbia University, was employed by one of the largest school organizations in the nation, and was a successful author. However, I felt I would probably be asked specific questions about the contents of the books, hoping that I had not read them, therefore disqualifying me as a reliable, creditable witness. Although I disliked reading this garbage, I went through each of the paper-bound books and selected specific pages I could refer to if he asked such question. I tabbed each one so I could refer to it quickly.

The day arrived when we met in court. I found that the attorney for the pornography vendors was bright and as cunning as a snake. He looked like something the cats had dragged in. When I was called to the stand, I was asked about my credentials. He couldn't refute them, so he went on. Surely enough, he said, "Mr. Narramore, could you give me an example from these books of anything you feel is offensive and improper?"

I prayed silently. "Thank you, Lord, for making me prepared." I then turned to the first book and a certain page I had marked. I began to read the foul stuff. I thought back to the time when I prepared for an oratorical contest as a senior in high school, and the many things my speech coach had taught me. So I stood up and read the portion as dramatically as I could, emphasizing the passionate portions. The porn attorney, who was a little shriveled-up guy and looked like an underworld character, jumped to his feet and cried out, "Stop, stop. We've heard enough!"

The judge smiled, and I grinned on the inside. I suppose the attorney had gotten a lot more than he had bargained for. After he gained his composure, he said, "Is there any other portion of other books that you feel is offensive?" So I picked up book number two and turned to the passionate page I had marked. Again I used all the techniques I knew in speaking as I read it, and I'm sure it sounded twice as turgid and pungent as the author had intended. Their attorney twisted and turned and said, "Stop. That's enough! That's enough!" The judge smiled again.

Finally, their attorney in his last attempt, asked me to read any portion of another book that was offensive. And I innocently asked him, "Which book do you want me to read from?" He said I could choose any I wished. So I picked up book number three and read from it as pungently as I could. At that point the porno attorney shouted nervously, "That's all! That's all!" He had evidently had enough of me.

So the judge said I could leave the witness stand. The city attorney won the case. Later his deputy thanked me and said, "You were more than adequate!"

I laughed, got in my car, and went on my way praising God. As I returned to my office, the Scripture that came to mind was Philippians 4:8, "Finally, brethren, whatever things are true, whatever things are noble, whatever things are just, whatever things are pure, whatever things are lovely, whatever things are go good report, if there is any virtue and if there is anything praiseworthy—meditate on these things."

WHAT KIDS WILL SAY!

Anyone who works with kids knows how totally frank they are. You never know just what they're thinking or what they might say. Since several years of my life were spent ministering to boys and girls in the public schools, you can imagine the various things they told me. Just look!

While serving one day in the West Covina School District, I was asked to spend some time with Benny, a six-year-old in the first grade. I had never seen the boy before and found him very interesting. I met with him that morning to give him an IQ test. We were alone in a room at a small table—he on one side and I on the other. I had spread several things out that I would be using in the test.

We were looking down at the table where he was fingering some of the objects. Suddenly he looked up and said, "You know, something, Mister?"

"No, what?" I asked.

"Today's my mother's birthday." Benny looked up again and said, "Do you know how old she is?"

"No," I replied. "I don't know."

Then Benny looked me squarely in the eye and volunteered, "She's twenty-nine."

Knowing that kids go home and tell everything to their parents, I was careful what I said. "Well, that's interesting," I replied.

Benny kept looking at me as if he wanted me to respond. So I asked, "Is twenty-nine young or is twenty-nine old?"

He sighed and said, "Well, mister, she's getting around a lot better than I thought she would at twenty-nine!"

I didn't pursue the conversation any further, nor did Benny bring it up again. But on the way home that evening, I was thinking about the perceptions we all have regarding age. *We tend to think of anyone ten years older than we are as being quite old. But when we reach that age, it seems quite young.* I guess age is in the eye of the beholder and whether we're on one side of that age or the other.

I remember Ethel Barrett, the famous Christian storyteller, saying publicly, "I'm pushing thirty-nine, but I'm not telling you which way I'm pushing it!" I understand where she was coming from.

> We tend to think of anyone ten years older than we are as being quite old. But when we reach that age, it seems quite young.

Once I was holding an all-day seminar for ladies in the Toledo, Ohio, area. The auditorium was packed with Christian women who had come from many miles. Most of them had heard our daily radio broadcast, "Psychology for Living."

During the seminar, I was stressing the point that children pick up information early and often learn a great deal, even when we're not formally instructing them. At that point a lady laughed and raised her hand saying, "I'd like to tell you what happened this past week." She went on to say, "We have a little boy who's five years old, not quite ready for school. I listen to your broadcast every day, and my son is usually around playing or doing something. The other morning he did something that he shouldn't, so I grabbed him and told him I'd have to give him a little paddling. Suddenly he turned his face toward me and said, 'Mommy, don't spank me! Call Dr. Narramore first, 'cause you might injure me for life!' "

10|22|12

The ladies laughed, and I have thought about that ever since. *Even when we think kids aren't listening, they're learning.* This particular mother had heard our broadcast each day not realizing that her son was picking up on it and putting it all together.

> *Even when we think kids aren't listening, they're learning.*

Early in my career, I had an assignment in the Downey school district southeast of Los Angeles. The principal had asked me to give an IQ test to a little boy named Jimmy.

We were sitting quietly by ourselves in a room where I had some test items on a table which we were looking at. Quite suddenly Jimmy looked at me earnestly and asked, "Mister, ya want to know something?"

"Yes," I said, "what's on your mind?"

He looked at me again and said, "My daddy loves me."

"Jimmy," I asked, "How can you be *sure* your daddy loves you?"

"Because," he answered, "he likes to play with me."

That incident taught me a great lesson. Kids feel that if someone wants to be with them, he must really like them. In other words, *spending happy times with a child is interpreted by him as being loved.* Parents often buy gadgets for their kids to show their love, hoping to make them happy. Actually, what a child wants more than anything is to spend time with Mom and Dad.

> *Spending happy times with a child is interpreted by him as being loved.*

One day I went to the Charter Oak School District located a few miles east of Los Angeles. There again I had been asked to work individually with an eight-year-old boy named Brad who was having problems in school. I was to see him just after the lunch period at one PM.

During those years, most men were wearing their hair short in crew cuts, often called "flattops." I didn't wear mine that short, but I realized I did need a haircut. So during the lunch hour, I jumped in my car and dashed down to Covina, grabbed a sandwich, got a haircut, and rushed back to the school feeling proud of myself for getting everything done within the hour.

10/22/12

A few minutes later, Brad came into the room where I was to talk with him and give him a psychological test. In the midst of it, he looked up at my head and said, "Mister, you sure need a haircut!"

That was rather deflating, since I'd been in the barber's chair only twenty minutes earlier. But I suppose his dad had a flattop, and he felt that was how all men should look!

Shortly after coming to California, I had photos taken at a shop near the Eagle Rock Baptist Church in Los Angeles. The photographer was a young man, new in the profession, who was highly creative and eager to establish himself as an avant-garde photographer. So when he took my photo, he had me turn to the left, the right, looking up, looking down, with bright lights here and there. After he had the photos printed, he felt he had done a good job with one of them, so he put it in the front window of his shop, along with other examples of photography.

On Sunday mornings, week after week, a family from our church, Mr. and Mrs. Johnson, and their eight-year-old son, Steve, walked by and noticed the photos in the window of the shop. I knew the Johnsons well inasmuch as Ruth and I were so involved in the music of the church. Every Sunday when walking by the photo shop, Steve would point to my photo and say, "There's Dr. Narramore." Weeks later, Mr. Johnson told me, "Last Sunday morning on the way to church when we went by the photo shop, Steve looked at your photograph again, then turned to me and said, 'Gee Dad, they're sure having a hard time selling Dr. Narramore's picture, aren't they!'"

One Sunday evening, after the regular church service, an interesting thing happened. Dr. Roy Laurin, the pastor and noted author, asked Ruth and me and our little daughter, Melodie, to come to the platform for special recognition, and to wish us Godspeed on our summer's ministry at Bible conferences across America. Ruth and I were the church music directors—I conducted the choir, and Ruth played the organ, directed the orchestra, and wrote musical arrangements. Melodie was nearly four years of age.

He stood Melodie on a chair so she could reach the microphone and then asked her, "Melodie, are you proud of your father?"

"Yes, I am," she answered.

Then Dr. Laurin asked, "And why are you proud of him?"

"Because he is a psychologist and he helps people with their problems," was her answer.

That's an intelligent answer, I thought, swelling with pride.

"And are you proud of your mother?" Dr. Laurin continued.

"Yes, I am," she responded.

Probing a bit further, Pastor Laurin continued, "And why are you proud of your mother?"

In a loud, clear voice Melodie proclaimed, "I'm proud of my mother because she writes all of Daddy's books!"

The entire congregation roared with laughter.

I guess that was Melodie's way of showing her frustration at that particular time. Ruth was helping me edit as I was writing two books, and Melodie evidently felt she needed more time with her mom! Kids do have their own ways of getting even!

CALLED TO ENCOURAGE

> Most people have much more ability than they realize, but they lack encouragement and training.

One of the greatest joys in life is to inspire and encourage others. *Most people have much more ability than they realize, but they lack encouragement and training.* However, if they are inspired and trained, they can make unusual contributions in life.

During my first year as a licensed psychologist, I began to realize the dire need for Christian psychologists in America, and in fact, around the world.

Wherever we went, people asked if I knew of a Christian psychologist in their area. And I usually had to tell them I didn't know of any. In fact, everywhere I went I asked local leaders if they knew of such, but they rarely did.

> In reality, I was on a crusade to encourage Christian young people to enter the profession.

So I began to encourage dedicated Christian young people to go into the field of psychology and receive their doctorates. I also spoke to parents about encouraging their own sons and daughters. I announced the need from the platform and then took a few minutes to answer questions. *In reality, I was on a crusade to encourage Christian young people to enter the profession.*

I often saw Christians, perhaps through no fault of their own, who were having serious problems. But to whom could they turn except an unsaved (and sometimes humiliating) psychologist or psychiatrist? I realized that if a therapist did not know the Lord, he would be limited in how much he could help a person. In fact, he could possibly do damage, because a person's entire spiritual nature would be disregarded. *Trying to help a person without recognizing his spiritual nature would be like trying to help a sick person without recognizing that he had a body!*

I saw the need for licensed Christian psychologists in the *public schools*. And there was a need as well, for men and women to establish *private practices* where they could counsel people individually. There was also a definite need in *industry* and many other places.

Large evangelical churches, of which we have hundreds today, were just beginning to develop in the 1950s and 1960s. I could see that, in time, thousands of people would be attending mega churches every Sunday, and surely counselors would be needed on their staffs.

> *Trying to help a person without recognizing his spiritual nature would be like trying to help a sick person without recognizing that he had a body!*

Christian psychologists were also needed on *the mission field*. Thousands of men and women were going to foreign countries to serve the Lord. They and their children would benefit greatly from the services of a godly person professionally trained in counseling.

I felt almost alone in the field, and I longed to see others get their training and begin serving people who were hurting. Now as I look back, I believe this has been a major contribution of my life.

> *I felt almost alone in the field, and I longed to see others get their training and begin serving people who were hurting.*

You can imagine my joy when one Saturday afternoon a young man came to my home to talk about the possibility of becoming a Christian psychologist.

The doorbell rang around three o'clock, and when I opened the door, a tall young man about nineteen or twenty years of age introduced himself. "Dr. Narramore," he said, "my name is James Dobson. I'm a college student, and I wondered if you would have a few minutes to talk to me about the field of Christian psychology."

I was delighted, so we talked for perhaps an hour or two. He asked a question that today seems strange, but which was actually appropriate at that time.

"Is there room," he asked, "in the field of Christian psychology for anyone beside yourself?"

I knew where he was coming from. There was hardly any other Christian in the field, and no other Christian psychologist on national radio, traveling around America. We both realized, too, that psychology was not very well accepted in Christian circles. In fact, several pastors told me later that some of their best sermons were about the dangers and detriments of psychology. Naturally, James didn't want to major in a field and spend years earning graduate degrees if there would be no real place for him to serve.

I remember telling him, "There's a great need. In fact, if I knew a hundred Christian psychologists with their doctorates, I could place them all, and their schedules would be filled in a matter of weeks!"

As we talked, I wondered about his motives. As you may know, many students who are laden with problems go to college and major in psychology. And whether they realize it or not, some are searching for solutions to their own problems. I was not interested in encouraging a person to enter the field who had major unresolved conflicts in his own life. We already had too many of those!

But as I talked with James, I felt his motives were good and that he was eager to help people. I could see that he was a well-adjusted guy. I knew, also, some young men were wanting to enter the field because they felt it was a way to make big and quick bucks. But as we visited, I was impressed that he was not driven by a strong desire to make money.

Another area that concerned me was his spirituality, his commitment to Christ. I think the feeling at that time, and perhaps still is, to some extent, that if you are not spiritual enough to become an evangelical minister or a missionary, you can make it okay as a psychologist. In other words, these spiritually fuzzy, half-hearted Christians felt that a psychologist need not be very committed. (Of course, this is far from the truth.)

As we visited, it was evident that James loved the Lord and that his life was on the line for Christ.

Two hours later, when we had finished our visit, I was convinced that this young man had good motives, much ability, and could become an outstanding person in the field. So I definitely encouraged him and kept in touch with him down the line. In fact, I had the opportunity a few years later to recommend him for his first counseling position in the public schools. I'm sure, too, that the ministries of the Narramore Christian Foundation (radio, literature, phone referrals, and public speaking) provided examples of some ways a Christian psychologist might minister.

Today the work of Dr. James Dobson and Focus on the Family is almost unfathomable. To go to Colorado Springs, Colorado, and see their great headquarters and understand the many facets of that extensive ministry is, indeed, impressive. But more significant is their impact on people around the world.

Some years after Dr. James Dobson established the ministry to which God called him, it became evident that he was more than a licensed Christian psychologist. He became a national leader with a definite influence on many people in high places in our nation.

In the Bible, we read that God told Moses to encourage Joshua. We all need to encourage others, and God commands it. I'm so glad I had the opportunity to encourage James Dobson. And I might say that I'm still looking for men and women who might do great exploits for Christ!

I will always be grateful to a Christian leader who took time to encourage me personally. He was Dr. Walter Wilson, medical doctor, educator, and author. Dr. Wilson, from Kansas City, was in demand as a speaker throughout the nation. In fact, he was one of the best-known Christian leaders in his day. From time to time, he wrote to encourage me. My, what a lift! I think it all started when I held an all-day seminar in Kansas City. Dr. Wilson sat in the front row and took copious notes and seemed to be intently interested. I presume he recognized, perhaps for the first time, the importance of Christian psychology in the believer's life. At any rate, from that time on he wrote or phoned me quite regularly. His letters were all the more significant since he was an extremely busy person himself.

Encouragement is so important that God tells us, "Therefore, as we have opportunity, let us do good to all, especially to those who are of the household of faith" (Gal. 6:10).

Family Vacation

A HERITAGE OF THE LORD

The Bible says, "Children are an heritage of the Lord" (Ps. 127:3). In other words, God gives us sons and daughters to love, train, guide, teach, comfort, and in every way help them develop to be their best for Him. In a sense, this relationship continues all through life. But in another sense, God gives them to us for just a few years, and then they are out on their own. But we are never to lose sight of the fact that they are a heritage—a gift from God.

Ruth and I were eager to have children, so when our first baby was on the way, we were ecstatic. Ruth continued with her work at the church, playing the organ and writing and directing music. One Sunday night after she had played the organ, she also played a trumpet solo. The next morning, she woke up to give me some exciting news. "Honey," she said, "I think our little one will arrive shortly." So we hurried to the Huntington Hospital in Pasadena, were Ruth was soon taken to the delivery room. We didn't know whether we were to have a son or a daughter, but we didn't care; either would be perfect.

Two hours later, the nurse came out to the waiting room and said to me, "Sir, you have a baby daughter! Both mother and baby are doing fine."

"How much does she weigh?" I asked.

The nurse smiled and said, "Five pounds and twelve ounces."

"That's a little small, isn't it?" I asked.

"Well, a little," the nurse replied. "But she's all there and she's healthy, and she'll grow."

We named our little one Melodie Lee. We liked the name Melodie and thought that since both of us were musical, she would probably be musical, too. The name Lee was given because that was the Chinese family name Ruth and her parents were given when they lived in China.

A few years later, God gave us a son, whom we named Kevin. "What a perfect combination," I told Ruth, "one girl and one boy. Some people fill up a whole yard before they get this combination!"

As soon as the children came, Ruth stopped her professional work as an educator and Christian education director so she could dedicate full-time to the children. And what a wonderful, sensitive mother she has been! Early in their lives, both Melodie and Kevin accepted Christ as their personal Savior. This helped them to side-step a multitude of problems.

About two years after we had moved to California, Ruth's father, Reverend Edwin Elliott, accepted a position with Moody Bible Institute as its west coast field representative. Moody suggested that he make his headquarters in Southern California, so it wasn't long before Mom and Dad Elliott sold their New York home and moved to Pasadena. We were delighted. Now we had family nearby. That was a real comfort to Ruth when I had to be away so many weekends. It was also a tremendous blessing to our children to have loving, caring grandparents next door. This added a rich dimension to their lives and gave them a strong, godly example.

During our children's growing-up years, we helped them with their school work, attended parent-teacher meetings, took them to school and church functions, and had lots of fun times together. The four of us felt very close.

The children were aware that God had given Ruth and me a unique international ministry, and they cooperated. We wanted them to know as much as possible about our ministry, so we shared a great deal. Nearly every day we talked about something that was happening—helping someone, a new building, a new aspect of the ministry, a special gift, or whatever. This made them feel personally involved and gave them cause for rejoicing and praising the Lord.

At the same time, we tried not to burden our children with needless details or financial hardships. We did not share much about negative situations with people or circumstances. They knew that developing a ministry involved disappointment and setbacks. But we tried not to dump issues onto them they could do nothing about. As a result, they grew up with a positive view of life and Christian ministry. They were never turned off on the Lord's work.

Through it all they learned much about Christian psychology. We often discussed the causes and solutions to problems and why people acted as they did. In short, they had the equivalent of several "courses" in human behavior before they entered high school! When problems came up in school or with playmates, we tried to help them understand why they and other people acted and felt the way they did. In other words, Christian psychological principles were being applied to their own lives.

"What happens to your children when you are away speaking?" people have asked. Ruth and I have been alert to this problem. So I have tried, when ministering alone, not to be away for more than a day or two. Also, whenever possible, we traveled together as a family. So this has kept us close through the years.

> *When compared unfavorably, you dislike the one with whom you are compared as well as the one who did the comparing. You also dislike yourself, and you dislike the place where it usually happened. So everybody loses.*

We made it a point not to compare one child with the other. Comparisons are usually odious. *When compared unfavorably, you dislike the one with whom you are compared as well as the one who did the comparing. You also dislike yourself, and you dislike the place where it usually happened. So everybody loses.* But good sibling relationships pave the way for good brother and sister feelings all through adulthood. It's amazing how many people dislike their brothers and sisters. A man once said to me, "When we have family reunions, I'm the only one everyone will speak to." And the causes can usually be traced to childhood.

Ministering in the United States during the regular school year usually called for my leaving California on Friday evening and returning on Sunday afternoon. So I would only be away one full day—Saturday. And while away, I always phoned the family. At the same time, I was usually able to hold one full-day seminar and speak three other times.

Music was always an integral part of our lives. And since our children were also musical, we had wonderful times together singing and playing.

Later, as Melodie and Kevin grew older, they were a special blessing as they participated in concerts and made recordings.

Ruth and I were both devoted to the Lord, to each other, and to our children. You can't beat that arrangement. *We tried never to let them go to sleep at night without encouraging them and telling them how much we loved them.*

I deeply appreciated the fact that Ruth was a fine student of the Bible, so the two of us shared in the spiritual development of our kids. At home, church, Sunday school, and Christian schools, they learned about Jesus. And as we traveled to Bible conferences, they had the privilege of hearing many of the nation's great Bible teachers. We were also careful to mix their spiritual training with fun, sports, fellowship with other young people, and happy times at home. *With some children, spiritual things do not make much sense and are not easily internalized unless they are mixed with a good measure of fun and fellowship, along with lots of love.* In short, we tried to always remember that they were "a heritage of the Lord!"

> *We tried never to let them go to sleep at night without encouraging them and telling them how much we loved them.*

> *With some children, spiritual things do not make much sense and are not easily internalized unless they are mixed with a good measure of fun and fellowship, along with lots of love.*

IN THE NICK OF TIME

Most speakers give real thought to how they will begin their speeches. But sometimes circumstances take care of that. I know from experience.

One Saturday, I was scheduled to speak at 11:00 AM at a Youth For Christ convention at Pismo Beach, about two hundred miles north of Los Angeles. I flew from Los Angeles to Santa Barbara, where we were to change planes for the flight to Pismo Beach. My schedule was tight, and I didn't have time to spare.

While waiting to depart from Santa Barbara, I was told there were problems with the plane, so they couldn't take me on to Pismo Beach until later in the afternoon. But I knew that wouldn't work for me.

So I looked around and saw a sign—"Private Planes." I walked over to a gentleman and asked, "Do you fly a private plane?"

"I sure do," he said.

"My flight to Pismo Beach has been cancelled," I said, "and I need to get there by eleven o'clock. I have to speak at that time."

"Well," he replied, "it's getting pretty near that time now, so we'd better hurry!" I hopped into his little plane, and we took off heading for Pismo Beach.

As we neared our destination, the pilot said, "The airport is several miles from the auditorium where you're to speak, and your time is short. What I can do is land you right on the beach below the auditorium, and then you can climb up the sandy bank and a long stairway up to the auditorium."

I didn't have much choice, so we went for it. We made a rather spectacular landing on the beach near the long, wooden stairway. I jumped out of the plane with my case in hand and scrambled up the sandy bank to the stairway, then on up to the top. I arrived breathless at the front of the auditorium at five minutes before eleven!

My friend, Ben Wise, a leader in the Youth for Christ ministry, greeted me at the front door and said, "Narramore, we've been wondering what to do. We're sure glad you're here! You're on now, so go right up to the platform."

As I began my message, I told the teenagers who filled the auditorium what had happened. They blinked their eyes, sat up straight, and followed everything else I had to say.

It was probably the most interesting intro I'd ever given, but I wouldn't want to risk it again. Our beach landing *could* have been reported in a *deadly* manner in the local newspaper the next day! But God took care of that.

THE MAN ON THE BULLDOZER

One day, I was working as a consultant at a school district, just east of Los Angeles.

During the lunch period, I went out to sit in my car and have a sandwich. Nearby, the kindergarteners and first graders were outdoors eating their lunches by a chain-link fence next to a grove of orange trees. Just beyond the fence, a man on a bulldozer was pulling up the trees and leveling the ground in preparation for building new homes.

Several kids were standing by the fence, pressing their fingers and noses through it. All eyes were focused on the man running the bulldozer, who kept driving by the fence and waving at the kids.

I noticed that the next time he came around, he got off his bulldozer, walked over and began talking with the children, especially to one boy.

When the bell rang for the kids to go inside, I got out and went over by the fence. The worker got off his bulldozer again and asked me, "Do you work here?" When I told him I did he said, "Well, a very strange thing has happened, and I'm really shook up."

Then he told me that about six years previously, he and his wife had been married in the Midwest. She became pregnant but was unhappy in their marriage. "I had my own problems," he said, "so we got a divorce. She moved away without telling me where, and I never got to see my child. But," he said, "The moment I saw that little boy, I realized he looked like me and my twin brother, and I felt sure that I was his father and he was my own son. So I asked him his name and he told me. His first name is the one my wife had chosen for him. I asked him about his mother—what she was doing."

After a moment, the man got back on his bulldozer and continued his work. That afternoon when parents came to pick up their children, I noticed the mother who came for this particular child. Then the boy evidently told her he had met a man who was driving a bulldozer.

How much he told her I don't know, but she sought me out and asked, "Are you the psychologist who comes here?"

"Yes," I said.

"Did you see a man on a bulldozer talking with my son?" she asked.

When I told her I did, she asked, "Did you speak with him?"

"Just briefly after the kids had gone back into their classroom," I said. She asked what he had told me. "He told me," I said, "that when he saw the boy, he realized it was his own son, and that he looked like his twin brother and himself."

The mother became furious, saying, "I never ever wanted my ex-husband to know where I was. Never, never!"

I talked with her for a moment and tried to calm her; then she took her son home.

I don't know how the story ended, but I was impressed with several things, including the fact that nearly everyone—like this man, this mother, and this child—has some concerns that need God's help and people's understanding. And you and I should be alert to their needs. It's true: *Every Person Is Worth Understanding!*

A Few Minutes from Eternity

As I read the Scriptures, I'm impressed with the many instances in which God has used someone to help another person in need. And whom did He use? It was usually someone who was handy and someone who was willing to be used.

> *As we reach out to help people in Christ's name, the Lord enables us to function far above and beyond our limited natural ability.*

I believe this helping principle is still working today. God will use almost any Christian who is available. We may look around, hoping that someone will come along and do a more professional or spectacular job. We may feel we're not qualified, not experienced enough, or without the proper training. But God actually wants to use *all* of us who are His children. Furthermore, our expertise or effectiveness is not within ourselves, it is in God. We are merely the conduit or the local vessel. *As we reach out to help people in Christ's name, the Lord enables us to function far above and beyond our limited natural ability.*

This fact was impressed upon me one evening when I was riding on a plane. I was flying home from a weekend meeting in the Midwest. I was tired, so I managed to get a little sleep. But I woke up about ten minutes before we landed in Los Angeles. I asked the man sitting next to me if he was heading for the Los Angeles area.

"Yes," he said.

"You live here?" I asked.

"No, I'm coming to see my brother. He's sick and not expected to live," he said.

As we talked, I learned that his brother was in a hospital just a couple of miles from my home.

"Do you have a way to get there?" I asked.

"No, I'll have to take a taxi."

"I left my car at the airport," I explained, "and I'll be glad to take you to the hospital to see your brother."

Obviously, he was grateful, not only for the ride, but also for the company. He was an unsaved man who was grieving and who felt ill at ease about seeing his brother, who might be dead by the time he got to the hospital.

As we arrived at the hospital, I thought to myself, *I guess I'm the one who must serve the Lord in this tragic hour. No one else is here, no pastor. This dear man isn't saved, and his brother probably doesn't know the Lord either.* So I prayed silently, asking the Lord to guide me.

When we entered his brother's room, the nurse told us that the patient was not expected to live. After a minute or so, he seemed to arouse, and he spoke his brother's name. I stood close to his bed, held his hand, and told him I was his brother's friend. When I asked him if he knew Christ personally, he said he didn't. So I asked him if he would like to know Christ and be sure of heaven; he said he would.

So I witnessed briefly to him, and he asked God to forgive him of his sins and to save him. A few minutes later, he slipped into eternity. Both he and his brother heard the gospel. For several days, I kept thinking about that crucial hour. I had nothing to offer myself, but I knew someone, the Lord, who offered him heaven! Jesus said, "Likewise, I say to you, there is joy in the presence of the angels of God over one sinner who repents" (Luke 15:10). I'm sure there was great rejoicing in Heaven that night.

THE NEW KING JAMES BIBLE

While serving as a psychologist on the staff of the Los Angeles County superintendent of schools, I became good friends with a colleague who had a doctor's degree from a major university. This guy was unusually bright and perceptive.

As time went on, I shared the good news of salvation with him. Before long, he surrendered his heart to the Lord. This friend really meant business with God. As he began to read the Bible and pray, a beautiful change came over his life.

One morning he said to me, "Everything is so different since I've found the Lord."

I asked him what he had in mind. "Well, among other things," he said, "I've begun to notice things I had not been aware of. For example, this morning as I drove to work I noticed a street lined with beautiful trees. I've been driving that same way for two years, but I had never really noticed the trees before. I suppose God is opening my eyes to all kinds of things."

Then we began to have Bible studies together in a park during our lunch hour. After a couple of weeks, he tossed me a little bombshell.

"Why don't they bring this book up to date?" he asked as he thumbed through the Bible.

"What do you mean?" I asked.

"Well, there's so much gobbledy gook," he said. "Look at some of these words— 'whither thou goest.' And hundreds more that are roadblocks to understanding." Then he asked, "Why doesn't someone do something about this problem—and bring the language of the Bible into modern English."

At first I felt a little offended. I thought the language of the Bible was classical. In fact, I thought it sounded rather *holy*. I had heard the Bible from the time I was a young child. In my Sunday school classes, I had memorized many portions. So I felt comfortable with the King James Bible and hadn't even noticed such expression as "Wilt thou then that we go and gather them up? But he said, 'Nay, lest while ye gather up the tares,' etc."

From that time, I began to think more seriously about the archaic words found in most Bibles. So when I heard that several of the major Bible publishers were beginning to print Bibles with more understandable words, I was happy.

One day I received a letter from Thomas Nelson Publishers in Nashville saying they were planning to update the King James Version to a New King James Version. They wanted to leave it essentially the same, yet change the outmoded, archaic words. They invited me to become a member of their general committee to make the changes. Since I was not an outstanding Bible scholar, I realized they probably invited me because I was a psychologist who was interested in speaking and writing.

Thomas Nelson Publishers formed a top-flight committee of Bible scholars to make the major decisions. But a larger committee, of which I would be a member, would give them feedback and help in various other ways.

At our first meeting in Chicago, about forty of us met with the primary committee. We spent the first few hours talking about the need for updating archaic words in the King James Version. Some of the committee members, especially the younger ones, thought it was an excellent idea. Some were not sure how they felt. And a number of the well-respected Bible teachers felt that the project was unnecessary. They thought we should leave "the best" alone.

As we shared our feelings openly, I sensed that those who were against updating the words were probably feeling the way I did when I was confronted by my newly saved PhD friend.

As we concluded our Chicago meeting, the majority agreed that the time had come to update "difficult to understand" words. Each of us who served on the committee was invited to review certain Bible portions and make suggestions. I selected two books of the New Testament as my responsibility. We were to review every word and leave the old as it was unless we definitely felt that another word would be as accurate and certainly more understandable.

Fortunately, Mr. Robert Weber was on the staff of the Narramore Christian Foundation at that time. He was a licensed psychologist and also a fine Bible student. He and I worked together, and he did much of the work. We prayerfully suggested substitute words that were in common use in the English language. I then sent our review back to headquarters in Nashville.

A few months later, our larger committee was invited to come to another meeting, this time in Nashville, Tennessee. We then spent the next few days together in the Opryland Hotel. That was a delightful experience in itself.

Those were precious days when we got together to consider each other's suggestions, praying that the Lord would guide us as we contributed our small part. I felt that God blessed and that we would now be able to enjoy the best of the old King James but with the updating of many outmoded words.

It was a joyous day when Sam Moore, president of Thomas Nelson Publishers, sent me one of the first copies off the press. I thank the Lord for the privilege of being involved in this important project. And I've often thought back to the time when my newly saved friend asked why someone hadn't done something to make the Bible more understandable.

> *So when we offer leadership and guidance to people, we must remember that they need time to change because feelings adjust slowly.*

Actually, life's road is strewn with conditions and situations that need change and improvement. But most of us don't see them, or we resist change. We like what we are accustomed to; we feel secure and comfortable. Revision and change may bring feelings of threat, insecurity, rejection, suspicion, anger, and pain. *So when we offer leadership and guidance to people, we must remember that they need time to change because feelings adjust slowly.* But if people are led thoughtfully, in time they may believe the idea for change was their own!

THE MENNINGERS

During the years when Ruth and I were raising our children and ministering, I was also on the lookout for opportunities to grow professionally. Interacting continually with the large psychology staff at the Los Angeles County superintendent of schools offered a stimulating environment. Specialists from around the nation who consulted with our staff also helped to extend our horizons.

But I was wishing there was a Christian organization from whom I could gain more insights and information. As I traveled around America, I found very little. Most Christian colleges were beginning to offer majors in psychology, but none offered a doctorate at that time. The Menninger Foundation in Topeka, Kansas, interested me because its leader, Dr. Karl Menninger, upheld Christian principles in his writings.

So I took a week off and went there to learn more about their approaches. I stayed at a nearby motel and each day drove to the headquarters in Topeka. They were expanding and utilizing various approaches to help people with emotional and mental problems. The professional staff of psychiatrists and psychologists was cordial and helpful.

One day I had an opportunity to sit in on a clinical staff meeting where about twenty health care professionals were considering specific cases. When they came to a child's case, they invited me to share my thoughts about the youngster. I was impressed with their multi-disciplinary approach. Each person who had any contact with the one being studied was asked to share his or her insights. However, in all the discussion relating to the six or eight cases before us that day, very little of a spiritual nature was mentioned. I felt that a spiritual approach would have been acceptable, but almost none was introduced. I made several suggestions while several nodded their heads.

The highlight of my week's visit at the Menninger Foundation with its various outreaches was a personal visit with Dr. Karl Menninger. We spent much of an afternoon together talking about many aspects of psychology. He was practical and open minded in his approach to therapy, including the spiritual.

With a humble beginning, Karl's father, Charles S. Menninger, started a medical clinic in Topeka in 1890. He was eventually joined by Karl, who helped him form the Menninger Foundation in 1925. They felt they could provide a more humane treatment for those suffering from mental illness. Up until that time, about the only options offered to the mentally ill were asylums and custodial care.

The Menningers believed that doctors and mental health specialists should collaborate and treat each patient as a whole person, so the father and son purchased a twenty-acre farm on the outskirts of Topeka and converted a farmhouse into a thirteen-bed clinic. Karl's brother, William, joined the group in 1926. Eventually, the Menninger Foundation not only treated people but also provided research, training, literature, and public awareness on mental illness.

Charles died in 1954, William in 1966, and Karl in 1990. A third generation, Roy and Walter, became medical doctors and joined the foundation as psychiatrists. Walter Menninger has served as president since 1993.

At the close of my week's visit, I came away with the feeling that headed by Karl, the Menninger Foundation was viewing people as total persons who could change, improve, and frequently become productive citizens. I felt their philosophy fitted into the slogan of the Narramore Christian Foundation: *Every Person Is Worth Understanding*.

PROFESSIONAL ATHLETES

One day I received a phone call from Charles Morgan, a prominent attorney friend in Miami, Florida. Charles has had an interest in professional athletes for some years and was personally acquainted with several members of the Miami Dolphins football team.

"Clyde," he said, "the Dolphins are playing this weekend, and I know you'll be ministering in south Florida. Would you have time to come over a few hours before the game to speak to the Dolphins? We invite certain speakers to challenge them spiritually, but we've never had a psychologist."

"What do you want me to speak on?" I asked.

"Whatever you think," Charles answered, "something that would help them spiritually. Some of these men already know the Lord."

We worked out the details, and Charles and I went together to their morning meeting place in Miami. The game would begin several hours later.

I was impressed with their friendliness and tremendous size—not only where they tall but also broad. But I noticed one smaller guy, and when I asked Charles who he was, he said, "Oh, that's Garo Yepremian. He's their place kicker and one of the best in the nation." Then I remembered hearing his name on TV.

I began my talk by briefly explaining my background so they could understand where I was coming from. Then I opened a time for questions and it was interesting to hear the matters that concerned them.

Next I brought a brief message on the importance of being born again. As I was speaking, I noticed several nodding in agreement. At the end of the presentation, I asked if there were those who wanted to make a commitment of their lives to Christ. About seven hands went up. Then we prayed and asked the Lord to come into their hearts. At the close of the meeting, eight or ten of the men asked further questions about being saved and other personal matters.

Joining them for breakfast afterward was something else! I've rarely seen so much food! Most of the men took one or two big steaks with four to six eggs. All and all, it was a tremendous time.

On another occasion, I received a phone call from a chaplain for the Houston Oilers.

"The Oilers are going to be in Anaheim, California, next weekend," he said, "but I can't be with them. It is possible for you to come and speak to them? They'll meet for a couple of hours before the game."

I told him I'd be happy to.

It was on a Saturday, and my son Kevin went with me. He is nearly six-feet-six himself, so he blended in fine as far as height was concerned.

Like my meeting with the Dolphins, we began with a period of questions and answers. Interestingly, they raised many of the same questions: marriage, children, personal hang-ups, and quite a few questions about career plans for the future.

Then I brought a brief message challenging them to surrender their lives to Christ. Several made commitments to the Lord. Kevin and I came away with the feeling that these were *real* men with *real* lives and *real* problems, and like the rest of us, in need of a *real* Savior. What a joy sharing with them!

CHAPTER TEN

BIBLE CONFERENCES, SEMINARS, AND RADIO

About three years after joining the staff of the Los Angeles County superintendent of schools in 1949, I received an invitation to speak at the well-known Word of Life Bible conference at Schroon Lake, upstate New York. The director was Jack Wyrtzen, our long-time friend. *This was a significant development for the Christian psychology movement in America.* To my knowledge, it was the first time a licensed psychologist had been invited to speak at a Bible conference.

Hundreds of such conferences sprinkled throughout America are attended by thousands. They attract entire families representing many denominations. Since most people stay for a week or more, it gives the speakers an opportunity to know the people, while being a blessing to them. In addition, these Bible conferences give a speaker credence. *In short, Christian psychology began to receive the stamp of approval of Bible conferences nationally.*

LIFE AT CONFERENCES

Since I had only a ten-month contract with the Los Angeles County schools, I was free to travel nearly all summer. Over a period of twelve years, I attended Bible conferences in many parts of America, including Winona

Lake, Indiana, Mt. Hermon, and Forest Home in California. Ruth and I and our little daughter, Melodie (and later our son, Kevin), flew to many places and spent one or two weeks at each conference. Large crowds (sometimes several thousand) came from many miles, and I counseled individuals free of charge when I wasn't on the platform.

We were having opportunities to bring new insights to people we had not met before—showing the causes and solutions to problems, not only from a *spiritual* point of view but also from *physiological* and *psychological* perspectives. The response was unusually positive. As I spoke, people nodded in agreement. Then after each message, many rushed to the platform to share their personal concerns.

We would leave California each summer having borrowed money because Bible conferences paid very little and there were many expenses connected with our traveling. But when we returned home in September, we were happy that large audiences had heard our message and Christian psychology had been introduced in person to many across America.

You might ask what topics I spoke on at Bible conferences where people had never heard a psychologist before. I gave this a great deal of thought and prayer. I realized that the other conference speakers were remarkable Bible teachers who knew much more about the Scriptures than me, so I should concentrate on my own field. Yet if I spoke only about psychological matters, at least part of the audience would surely be turned off.

So for my first message I often used "Why a Psychologist Believes the Bible." Several points in the message would be similar to those most pastors and Bible teachers would present. But for my last point, I stressed the *psychological accuracy of the Bible.* I wanted my listeners to know exactly where I stood on the word of God, but I was also eager to introduce some psychological content. In another message I mentioned that if you should bring one hundred psychiatrists and psychologists together and ask them to list the basic emotional needs of people, they would fairly well agree what those needs were.

Then I took several of those needs and explained how they are met on a human level but on the other hand, how they are met at the deepest level through understanding teachings of the Bible and applying them directly to one's life.

During the week, I brought other messages regarding the family, children, marriage, and emotional disturbances. I started each session by answering questions that had been written and handed to me. In this way I could understand what the most common problems of the people were, and at the same time, bring practical help and insight.

I did not want to be placed in the same category as a young psychologist I heard about. Acquaintances said they heard him speak twice—both times to a group of evangelical Christians. And both times his topic was: "Why Christians Go Nuts."

One of the interesting conferences we attended each summer was a two-week Youth for Christ conference at Winona Lake, Indiana, southeast of Chicago. Bus loads of young people and their leaders arrived from around the nation. I spoke every morning as well as at special sessions for YFC leaders only. I felt privileged to conduct sessions for these talented young leaders.

At the close of evening meetings, an invitation was given for people to come to the front of the tabernacle and talk with a counselor about their soul's salvation. Then the counselors took them out of the large Billy Sunday Tabernacle into an adjacent tent that had been set up with about a hundred chairs. In this prayer tent, Youth for Christ spiritual counselors sat and talked one on one to these young people about their relationship to the Lord.

Each evening I stood in the back of the room, alert to any counselor who felt the person he was talking to had rather deep problems with which I could help. Two or three times during the evening, one of the spiritual counselors would come back and ask me if I would talk with a young man or girl he had been counseling. Often a person would come forward in a meeting ostensibly to trust the Lord, yet he had other serious problems that needed attention. So I was able to help him and possibly refer him to a professional in his home community he could see for a period of time.

Later, I would meet with the counselor who had referred the young person to me and explain what I had done and why. I felt this would help the youth leader as he returned to his home state to lead Youth for Christ groups. I realized these youth leaders might direct large, national ministries of their own some day.

I often thought how helpful that approach would be for all churches across the nation. People with various problems trust Christ, but they may have physiological or psychological problems no one has detected. Or perhaps they have a problem that needs special longer-term attention.

We had remarkable speakers all week at Winona Lake, such as Billy Graham, Bob Cook, Ted Engstrom, and many others, plus great musicians. It was also a good time for the Narramore family to sit under the ministry of some of the nation's finest Bible teachers and to learn and grow.

One of the delightful Bible conferences where I spoke each summer was at Forest Home, located in the mountains about ninety miles east of Los Angeles. Every year we looked forward to spending two weeks there with Dr. Henrietta Mears, director of Christian education at the Hollywood Presbyterian Church. She was also a prolific writer, teacher, and one of the nation's fine speakers. We learned so much from her. What a great lady!

Our experiences at Bible conferences were unusual, to say the least. For example, one woman who attended the Mount Hermon conference near San Jose, California, came year after year. When I first met her, I learned how negative she was, not finding anything good to say about anyone. The second year proved to be the same ... she always complained about something. The third year, I noticed her right after I had spoken at the morning service. As I was walking alone to the dining hall, she said, "I liked your message this morning."

I was surprised to hear her say something positive, and I thanked her. As she turned to walk away, she said, "You sure have improved!"

Radio Broadcasts

RADIO

We had been in the conference ministry for just a few summers when I spoke at a large church in Grand Rapids, Michigan, where Dr. Martin DeHaan had been pastor. After the evening service, a man came up to me and said, "You're a good speaker, but you're even better at answering questions about problems like you did tonight. You should be on the radio."

"Pray tell," I asked, "what would I do on the radio?"

"You could talk about problems," he said. "There isn't any other Christian talking about problems on the radio." Then he told me, "I have one of the best radio stations here in central Michigan. You could make tapes in California and send them to me. Then we could play them over the air without charge."

After recovering from the shock of a Dutchman offering something valuable free of charge, I looked at my wife and said, "Honey, when would we find time?"

"We have twenty-four hours in a day," she said, "just like everyone else! Besides, I think you could reach more people in one week by radio than you could in ten years by traveling around the nation speaking like you're doing now!"

"She's right!" the radio station owner added.

Ruth had been on the radio as a musician for several years with Percy Crawford and Jack Wyrtzen, Christian leaders on the East Coast, so she knew the value of radio.

When we returned to Los Angeles, I called Dr. Charles E. Fuller of the Old Fashioned Revival Hour, and asked him about it. "Narramore," he said, "I think it would be a good idea. You could approach people on the basis of their problems and concerns, and then you could show them how the word of God applies to such problems. It would be an excellent combination!"

"But Dr. Fuller," I replied, "I have a problem! I'm a licensed psychologist and I've tried to abide by the rules and regulations of the American Psychological Association. One of those rules is that members can never mention money on radio or TV."

"Well, if you don't ask," he said, "you won't get!"

I thought to myself, *This is from the lips of a man who has been on radio for years, so he knows.* "Well, what do I do?" I asked.

"I guess you'll just have to starve for the first few years," he replied. I soon learned that he knew what he was talking about.

I talked the situation over with Ruth at home. We didn't want to run up bills we couldn't pay. Yet I knew if I observed the American Psychological Association regulations, I could never ask for money on the radio. I also thought about something else! *Some day I may be the one to found a Christian graduate school of psychology. If so, I'll need the cooperation of the APA.*

TAKING THE BIG PLUNGE

We decided to buy some Ampex recording equipment. We set it up on the dining room table in our home and made our first broadcast. We were advised by the station in Michigan not to have all speaking. Since my wife was a musician, she would take one verse of a hymn, stylize it on the organ, and include it on each of our broadcasts. We decided to call our broadcast "Psychology for Living."

The format was simple. Without identifying anyone, Ruth would read a paragraph or so from a letter, and I would discuss it. We tried to cover three problems on every broadcast—one about children, one about older people, and one about marriage or some adult problem.

As I discussed each problem, I considered the possible spiritual factors, the psychological causes, and possible physiological factors. I knew that all problems fell into one or more or a combination of these three areas. Such consideration was new in American radio, and listeners began to see the wisdom of such an approach.

We sent program tapes to the station in Michigan and soon received an avalanche of letters in response. One would think that everyone in Michigan had a problem! Thousands of people wrote us asking for help. We saw that we were becoming involved in a very important ministry. Christian radio was new in America, so as Christians began to build radio stations, they asked us to air our program on their stations. They knew they could build their listening audience if they featured a broadcast that dealt with problems. As listeners wrote us, "You're the only radio personality who doesn't scream and 'holler.'"

This was the first time a Christian psychologist had discussed everyday problems regularly on the radio. Some counselors felt it wasn't the right thing to do, that anything we knew should be kept to ourselves and be shared only in our private offices. However, I felt the opposite. If there was anything I knew about human behavior that would help others, I should share it at every opportunity! I also felt that we could explain psychological concepts clearly and simply so everyone could understand and benefit.

The following statement by a psychologist shows the need to say things simply:

> ... Mediating his or her developing relational capacities and abilities to regulate effectively both self states and affect. These emergent systems, identical to the psychic structural regulatory systems described by Freud, play out in the regulated and unregulated states of patient and therapist. His seminal findings about biopsychosocial development are especially relevant in all psychodynamic endeavors to the psychotherapy of "primitive emotional" or "severe personality" disorders, and to nonverbal object relations.

Uh!

Now I'm sure you understand!

A couple of psychiatrists told me that a psychologist should only do psychological testing and then let the psychiatrist do the counseling. In other words, they were saying that a psychologist was not competent to counsel. But I knew differently. I knew that a born-again psychologist who understood God's Word, who had spent four years on his bachelor's degree, two years on his master's degree, four more years to complete his doctorate, then took an internship and qualified for a license, was qualified to do more than give a person a test! So I pressed on in spite of that negative "encouragement"—and the Lord blessed. In fact, today psychologists probably do the majority of the professional psychological counseling throughout the world!

Letters kept pouring in from radio listeners, and we hardly knew where to turn. I was employed every day from nine to five by the Los Angeles County superintendent of schools, so any radio work had to be done in the evenings.

Since we could not afford chairs, Ruth and I bought some barrels for fifty cents at a Salvation Army store in Pasadena. We set them up on the lower level of our home and put cushions on them for the secretaries to sit on. We also put boards across sawhorses, commonly used by carpenters, and made tables.

We had only one typewriter, so I asked people around the community if we could borrow their typewriters for awhile, and three of them agreed. We needed someone to do the typing, so I asked several ladies if they would like to donate half a day, a week, or whatever time they had. Praise the Lord, several of them said they'd be glad to work for free of charge. As they read the letters asking for help, they realized this was a ministry that was long overdue.

Each day the ladies opened the mail while I was at my regular work in downtown Los Angeles with the county office. I devised a form so a long letter could be summarized onto one sheet: name, address, the nature of the problems, what treatment they'd already received, whether they knew the Lord, and several other things. After our evening meal, I'd study the sheets, pray, dictate the letter into a machine, and give whatever help I could. I worked late into the night.

The more we did this, the more people wrote in, and soon several secretaries came to our home every day to help carry on this ministry. People sometimes wrote long letters of a hundred pages or more. One day a lady from Washington, DC wrote me a 365-page letter—a page for each day of the year! I don't know why she had such a serious problem. (Perhaps it was because she worked with politicians!)

As people wrote and phoned about their problems, we realized we had a serious problem ourselves. We didn't have the money to pay the bills for stationary, envelopes, postage, printing, and so forth!

Finally I said to Ruth, "I don't know what to do. Dr. Fuller was right. Since we can't ask for money on the radio, nothing is coming in. I guess people think we're wealthy. I'm wondering if we should stop before we go any further in debt." However, I certainly didn't want to end this one-of-a-kind ministry to which people were responding so vigorously. But neither did I think we should let the bills pile up.

Ruth looked at me in surprise and said, "Oh, I don't think we should give up now. Why don't we pray earnestly and see if the Lord might touch someone's heart to send in a gift—say by Monday." (This was Saturday).

So we did. On Monday, we opened the mail and there was a check for one hundred dollars!

"See," Ruth said, "the Lord wants us to continue!" And we did.

In short, we were heard on many stations, and Christian psychology was exploding all over America through radio!

During the years, we have had many difficult times financially buying office supplies and equipment, eventually operating a ten-acre campus with nine major buildings, and meeting the salaries and expenses involved with an emerging worldwide ministry. Many times we didn't know until the eleventh hour where help was coming from. But God has always proved faithful! And although Ruth and I have had to sacrifice and have gone without salaries for several years, our organization has ministered to people throughout the world, including many well-known Christian leaders who now have international ministries themselves.

LITERATURE, TOO

The days were difficult because the work load was heavy, people's problems were severe, and finances were short. But one day while driving on the freeway, the Lord gave me an idea. Perhaps we could offer a "Fellowship Plan." It would work something like this: to anyone who wrote us wanting help, we would enclose with our response letter a folder telling about our Fellowship Plan. If anyone wanted to send a gift, we would mail him a tax-deductible receipt, plus a magazine and a booklet on some problem, each month—all for ten dollars a year!

When I talked to Ruth about it she said, "Sure, when do we start the magazine?" Since both of us were writers, we knocked out the magazine in a few evenings and gave it to a local printer. Although it was small at the beginning, it was filled with articles about the solutions to everyday problems. In time, it grew to be a full-fledged, award winning-magazine with international distribution. After our children were grown (and with their encouragement), Ruth worked full-time in our offices as Director of Publications and Editor of *Living* magazine. She continued in this position for the next twenty years.

A problem that was asked us many times in those days had to do with adoption. It was a common concern. So I wrote our first booklet and called it, *The Psychology of Adoption*. I numbered the booklet "Number Three." I was embarrassed to call it Number One because it seemed so small. Furthermore, I might want to number another booklet Number One.

One of the first women to whom we sent booklet Number Three wrote back and said it was excellent, and to please send her booklets One and Two! So we decided to get busy and write more booklets. After all, there were plenty of problems to write about. As time went on, we did produce booklets on various topics based on the most common problems about which people wrote us.

Now many years later, we have printed booklets on about two hundred human problems. We have sought to be a blessing to people through Bible-based, psychologically sound literature. As time went on, we improved our periodicals and bought our own printing presses. Before long, we were writing, producing, and sending out thousands of pieces of literature every month.

We could write volumes about the unusual and humorous things people told us after they read our literature. For example, a woman wrote us from Africa. She had a medical problem and had been to numerous doctors for help, but no cure was found. However, one day she went to the fish market and brought home a fish to cook for supper. When she arrived home, she found that the fish had been wrapped by the store clerk with our magazine, *Psychology for Living.* As she opened the magazine, she found an article about a certain medical problem. "Oh my!" she shouted. "Those are the same symptoms I have!"

She learned from the article that certain types of specialists could offer help to a person with that particular ailment. "I went to a nearby city," she said, "and found such a specialist who began to treat me, and in time I became well!"

Eventually our radio ministry and speaking engagements became so extensive that I left my position with the Los Angeles County superintendent of schools and went full time into Christian work. We called our non-profit organization the Narramore Christian Foundation. Actually, it's not a foundation as you ordinarily think of one, since most foundations distribute funds. We are the opposite in that we are a nonprofit, faith organization with a tax-exempt status, dependent on gifts.

By now we were reaching many thousands daily through radio, literature, in-person conferences, and by phone. Christian psychology was well launched in America!

WHERE'S THAT HOLE TO CHINA?

I suppose most of us who are public speakers have at times been guilty of creating embarrassing times for ourselves. We say things that may have been well-intentioned, but they turn out to be red-faced moments!

I'm not going to tell you all of my embarrassing moments, because that would take too long. But one that took place some years ago has always stood out in my mind. Ruth and I and our little daughter, Melodie, and later our son, Kevin, traveled across America each summer when I was speaking at Bible conferences.

This embarrassing moment occurred during my first year at beautiful Camp-of-the-Woods located in upstate New York. I think I was the first psychologist to speak there.

It was the eleven o'clock hour, and the auditorium was packed. Some probably came out of curiosity, since a Christian psychologist was sort of like a prize mule at a county fair! Some came to see me personally about their problems. But all seemed to appreciate the message. When I opened the meeting for a period of questions and answers, a man from the metropolitan New York City area raised his hand and asked, "Do you know of a Christian psychologist in private practice in New York City?"

I told him I received many letters from listeners in New York and that people there had often asked the same question. Ruth and I had lived in New York, and we were fairly well acquainted with Christian referrals there.

I told him (with everyone listening) that I did not know of a born-again Christian psychologist in all of that area. In fact, many pastors had written, asking if I knew one.

Suddenly I remembered a lady psychologist who had written me from New York City a few weeks earlier. So I relayed that to the audience. I said that in her letter she mentioned nothing about the Lord, and I doubted if she was a believer. I felt justified in telling them this because I thought it was true. Furthermore, I sensed a responsibility to Christians to not mislead them and not refer them to a counselor who was unsaved. I wanted people to know that when they asked straight questions, they would get straight answers and that Christians could depend on the Narramore Christian Foundation to represent a definite biblical point of view. I added that since I didn't believe she was a Christian, people would probably be disappointed if they sought spiritual help.

With that explanation, the audience seemed to be satisfied. Then suddenly, from the back of the auditorium a lady held up her hand and said, "Dr. Narramore, I am the psychologist who wrote that letter."

Oh no! I thought to myself. *What have I said? I've judged this dear lady before even knowing her.* I was completely embarrassed. *If only there were a hole, I would like to fall through all the way to China!*

What was I to do? Well, as I stood there with my face hanging out, I apologized to the lady publicly for judging her spirituality.

The audience grew silent, wondering how she would feel and how I was going to get out of the predicament. So I apologized further and asked her to forgive me.

After the meeting the lady walked up to me and said, "Dr. Narramore, I want to thank you for being so frank. I have gone to church most of my life but I don't believe I'm saved or even know how to be saved." She was, in fact, twice as gracious as I was. I apologized again in private, and she was kind and understanding.

During the week, we talked several times, and I had the privilege of leading her to a personal knowledge of Jesus Christ.

How true the Scriptures are that say, "Let your speech always be with grace, seasoned with salt, that you may know how you ought to answer each one" (Col. 4:6).

FLORIDA IN FEBRUARY

In 1969, we decided to offer our own one-week Bible conference at Lake Yale, Florida. This would give us an opportunity each February to minister to many who lived in the Midwest and on the East Coast.

We used the large campus and facilities of the Southern Baptist Convention of Florida. Since it was located about thirty-five miles northwest of Orlando, it was easily accessible. We had a talented staff, including Larry and Bonnie Whiteford, Lee and Gloria Bendell, and others. Ruth was in charge of the music program, which featured a great deal of vocal and instrumental numbers.

The conference attracted large crowds, and we continued to hold it annually for the next twenty-one years. In addition to featuring Bible messages from my brother-in-law, Dr. Gordon Elliott, along with lots of great music, we had sessions on resolving everyday problems. People came from throughout the Midwest, the South, as well as the East Coast from Maine to Florida. Some even came from California. Many attended year after year, enabling us to make a significant impact on their lives. Thousands were learning about Christian psychology.

After a few years, we added a special feature, new in America. *This was the availability of licensed Christian psychologists who could give psychological tests and offer individual and group counseling.*

I had spoken at many Bible conferences and knew their great value. Those who came had a good time, were blessed, and heard Bible messages. But they usually went home much like they had come. I was certain that if people in attendance could take psychological tests, they might identify specific problems in their lives. Then, through professional counseling, they would begin the process of growth and change.

The first year when we offered psychological tests and counseling, I wondered how the people would react. At the very first session, we explained the new added features of the conference. Several of the group had been to our headquarters in California and had taken psychological testing and counseling. So when I announced that these would be available, several people jumped to their feet and asked if they could give testimony as to the benefit of tests and counseling. That did the job! People wanted to try it.

We included five licensed Christian psychologists that week to offer their professional services. When we announced the special opportunities, nearly everyone in the audience stood up and hurried to the appointed place to sign up for the tests and counseling. Every appointment for the week was filled within ten minutes! The benefit the people received was especially satisfying. All of the weeks' Bible teaching was given more impact and significance because people were focusing on their specific needs.

It was an intensive conference, and the counselors were impressed with the progress their clients made during the week. Their usual comment was, "We see more change in a week than we see in a month back home at our offices." Many messages and most activities around the campus focused on understanding, improving, and applying the word of God to individual lives.

At the close of the conference, many told of the unusual growth they had experienced. Even to this day, people still phone and write us about the value of Christian psychological services at a Bible conference!

A few years later, we also began offering vocational tests and career counseling. People of all ages were interested. One elderly man took the tests and later told me, "I just wanted to know if I had been in the right vocation all my life." I might add that, indeed, he had!

Later our same team introduced a similar Bible conference week at Bibletown, Boca Raton, Florida; and at Sandy Cove, Maryland. During the twenty-one years we held this "Florida in February" conference, thousands of people, including many pastors and their wives from many states, saw and experienced the value of Christian psychology.

COUNTING MONEY

One time, while ministering in Pennsylvania, this happened. I held a seminar for ladies near Reading, Pennsylvania. My traveling companion was T. J. Reese, a prominent and highly respected business man from Elkhart, Indiana. Our driver was Dr. Ken Markley, who had made the travel arrangements.

The seminar was attended by a large number who had paid a one-dollar admission. When the meeting was over, we headed for Lancaster, where I was to speak that night. Just before we reached Lancaster, Ken said, "That bag of one-dollar bills is in the back seat. Why don't you fellows count it and put rubber bands around each twenty? That will make it easier tomorrow when we stop at a bank and exchange it for a few large bills."

So Mr. Reese in the back seat and I in the front each took a bunch of dollar bills to count and sort. About that time, we were arriving in Lancaster and Ken said, "We're getting low on gas and stations may be closed after the meeting, so I'm going to pull in here and fill it up."

As we drove up to the station, a couple of service station attendants came out and noticed what we were doing, and one began to put in the gas. What we didn't know was that the day before, two scam artists from California had fleeced the town and had gotten away with a lot of money.

Suddenly two police cars drove up—one immediately in front of us and one in back, locking us in. A policeman got out of his car, approached my window, and said, "Sir, where are you from?"

"California," I answered.

"And what are you doing?"

"I'm counting money," I said.

He looked in the back seat and asked, "Sir, what are *you* doing?"

"I'm counting money, too," Mr. Reese said.

"Well," the officer said, "we want to look into this further." Then he said to Ken, our driver, "The police station is right down the street. I want you to leave the car and come with me. We need to make a report." Then he looked at Mr. Reese and me and said, "You two can keep counting you money. You're covered."

Not knowing what was wrong, Mr. Reese and I continued counting our dollar bills and quietly prayed that everything would be all right. Ken walked with the policeman to the station where he learned why they had stopped us—yesterday's scam artists from California.

"What?" Ken said. "We're not robbers or gangsters. The man with me in the front seat is Dr. Narramore, whom you hear every day on the radio. His program is called 'Psychology for Living.' Don't you hear it?"

"No," the policeman replied. "I work every day."

Then Ken began to wonder what to do. It was almost time for the meeting to begin. He phoned two local pastors so they could tell the police who I was. But neither was home. We learned later that they had both gone to the meeting. Suddenly he thought of the barber shop next door and wondered if they might have a newspaper telling about our big meeting in Lancaster that night.

So he went in, and sure enough, he found one. The newspaper carried the story, as well as my picture. So Ken and the policeman went back to the car and held my photo next to my face and Ken said, "See, he's the same guy!"

Then the policeman relaxed and told us what had happened the day before. "When we found you were from California and counting money, we figured we had really nabbed the right criminals."

They let us go, and we dashed downtown to the auditorium where the meeting was ready to begin. Ken and I walked to the platform, where he introduced me. We acted as cool as cucumbers, even though we had just evaded the slammer.

As I began speaking I thought, *This is a lot better than looking through the bars in the local jail!*

In summary, life can be quite exciting, especially if you're a pioneer psychologist serving the Lord!

Kevin, Melodie, Ruth, Clyde

Narramore Christian Foundation

CHAPTER ELEVEN

A BETTER PLACE, A BETTER WAY

Driving to the airport on a Friday evening, boarding the plane, flying to a distant city, holding an all-day Saturday seminar, speaking at a Youth for Christ rally Saturday night, speaking at two churches on Sunday morning, then flying back to my home in California on Sunday afternoon ready to go to work on Monday morning. This was a typical weekend for me for many years.

Considering this schedule, I was away from my wife, Ruth, and two young children one full day—Saturday. I kept thinking I should make a change. I didn't like being away from my family if I could help it. But as a pioneer in the field, invitations to speak and write were coming from almost everywhere. It was not unusual to receive three or more a day, often from large conventions with opportunities to minister to many at one time.

I had been criss-crossing the nation from Maine to California and from Florida to Washington. There was hardly a larger city I hadn't visited. And I had been to hundreds of smaller towns, governor's breakfasts, Christian publishing companies, Bible conferences, radio stations, missionary conferences, Christian colleges and seminaries, television stations, federal government agencies, plus a host of other places. In fact, a friend accused me of being omnipresent!

A SERIOUS DECISION

One weekend I found myself ministering in Pennsylvania. It was a Saturday seminar of about nine hundred, mostly pastors and their wives. After the meeting, I began to think more about what was happening. The crowds were getting larger, and people were traveling many miles to attend the meetings or to talk privately about a problem. For the first time, most of my listeners were challenged to consider the multiple causes of problems. I emphasized the physiological, emotional, and spiritual roots. This was a rather new concept—but usually accepted (at least mentally) when I explained it. In other words, we were considering the whole person.

But still, I was concerned about being away from my family. I could see what was happening to pastors and evangelists who were away from home in ministry. Many of their families were falling apart, and they were phoning or seeing me in person for help. So I didn't want to be caught in the same predicament.

At our public meetings, people were gaining insights, but there was not enough change! Because of our daily, national broadcast, *Psychology for Living*, plus literature and public meetings, people were beginning to recognize personal and family problems that needed attention. Christian psychology was becoming more respectable and important. A lady wrote me, "I have listened to your broadcast for nearly five years and I've come to the conclusion that you are probably saved!" She had a hard time believing that a psychologist could be born again, even though I was emphasizing salvation on nearly every broadcast!

Except for spiritual conversion, I had to admit that insufficient growth was taking place in the lives of those to whom I was ministering. This was the problem: *there was little or no individual diagnosis or treatment.* So I began to pray earnestly that God would give us an international headquarters in California where we could minister month after month to people, group by group, at an in-depth level. I felt a personal responsibility since at that time there were hardly any other Christian psychologists in America who were offering seminars of any kind. To enrich people's lives and bring about change, we needed to spend more time with them. *But first we needed a place!*

A PLACE AT LAST

It was noontime when a man about fifty years of age walked down the corridor just outside my office door in Pasadena, California. He had passed by two or three times, so I stepped out and asked if I could help him.

"I've come to see one of your counselors," he said. "We're going to have lunch together, but I see his door is closed."

"I think he is with a client just now," I said, "but he should be finished in a few minutes." I invited him into my office, and we visited for a short time.

"You're busy around here, aren't you?" he said.

"Yes," I replied, "we're pretty busy."

"You're terribly crowded, too."

"Yes, in that corner are three secretaries where there should be no more than one."

"Well, what are you doing about your space problem?"

"We're praying about it!"

"What do you need?"

"We have in mind an international headquarters, and we need several acres and a number of buildings."

"I know a man who has some property." He said, "Maybe he'll give it to you."

I immediately asked him, "Where is it, out on the desert?" (*Oh ye of little faith.*)

"No," he said, "it's right here in the San Gabriel Valley in Rosemead. There's an elderly gentleman who has a beautiful piece of property, ten acres, high on a hill." He continued, "He's very religious and also very peculiar."

"Religious and peculiar," I repeated. "What does he do that's so religious?"

"He reads the Bible every day," he said. "You can see him sitting out on his porch. He's a man in his early eighties, and he's always reading the Bible."

"Does he really do that?" I asked.

"Yes, he does!" he continued. "Even though he's a graduate of Princeton University where one of his teachers was Woodrow Wilson."

"Now that's very interesting!" I commented. "What else does this man do that's so peculiar?"

"Well," he replied, "he wants to give his property away. Have you ever heard of anyone in his right mind who had an expensive hilltop property of ten acres that wanted to give it away?"

"That *is* different," I agreed.

"Maybe he'll give it to you."

"Are you pulling my leg?" I asked.

"Oh no," he replied.

"Well, when you're finished seeing your friend, the counselor," I said, "will you take me out to see the man?"

He agreed. So about an hour later, one of our staff members, Wallace Wright, and I got into my car and followed this man. He took us to the hilltop property in Rosemead. A small frame house was perched at the very top. We knocked at the door, and our host introduced us to Mr. Weaver and then left.

Mr. Weaver, who was small in stature, stuck his head out the door and said, "Who are you anyway?" I told him, and he wasn't impressed. Then he said, "Do you believe the Bible?"

"Yes I do! I said.

"How much?"

"I believe all of it."

"Are you a liberal or modernist?"

"No, neither of those."

Continuing his questioning, he asked, "Well, do you believe in people being saved?"

"Yes I do!"

"Are you saved yourself?"

"Yes sir, Mr. Weaver, I am saved," I answered.

"Are you busy getting other people saved?"

"Yes I am," I replied, "I often witness for Christ."

He shook his head and said, "Well, then, I guess you can come into my house."

So he let me in, and oh, what a mess. His wife had died several years before. He told me she had died early in her eighties because she ate bacon. When I told my wife about it later, she said, "If I could be assured of living to my eighties, I think I'd start eating bacon every day!" The house was strewn with old newspapers; they seemed to be four or five inches deep in every room. He also had a little dog of whom he was very fond.

Finally he said, "Let's go out on the porch and talk." It was a beautiful day, and for many miles we could see the valley below with the giant San Gabriel Mountains as a backdrop for this spectacular view. Directly across the road was an extensive golf course. It was a lovely sight. He said, "Do you know if you get up on the roof, you can see the ocean at Santa Monica!" Wally and I were certainly impressed with this beautiful property!

Before long, Mr. Weaver asked me about the ministry of the Narramore Christian Foundation. I explained that we were helping people through radio broadcasts, literature, counseling, seminars, correspondence, speaking engagements around the nation, and overseas trips to help missionaries.

As I returned home that evening, I had a strong feeling that perhaps God was going to do another great thing. We had worked so hard for so many years. Most people did not understand Christian psychology, and didn't know the value of it, and few people had sent us financial help because we could not mention money on the radio. It was a difficult time, but perhaps now God was going to give us an international headquarters.

Before we left, Mr. Weaver asked me to come back the next day. During this second visit, we talked and had a nice time. Then he said that he would like to see our headquarters in Pasadena. So the following day, I took him there. We went into one room where we had several thousand Elliott addressograph address labels, and some were marked with a little red dot.

"What are those with the red dots?" he asked.

"Those all represent pastors," I said.

"Do pastors have problems?" he asked.

"Well, yes. These have written to us for help." I said. He was impressed as he looked over our work at the office, and he asked me to come out to see him again the next day.

When I arrived at Mr. Weaver's the next morning, he said, "There's something that's been going on lately—a big jet plane has been flying over this area several times this week. Have you seen one?"

"Yes," I said, "I saw my first jumbo jet in Seattle just a few days ago. They're enormous!"

Mr. Weaver had received a degree in engineering from Princeton University, so he was interested in things of a mechanical nature. I asked him, "Would you like to see one of those jets close up?"

"Oh yes, I'd like that very much," he said.

So I phoned one of the major airlines and made arrangements to take Mr. Weaver to the airport so he could see a super jet the next day. After the plane had landed and they had cleaned it up and serviced it, we were escorted on the plane—just the two of us. They let him sit in the cockpit, and he was awed by the hundreds of instruments and gadgets. He was having a great time!

As we got off the plane, he looked around and said, "You know, we're not very far from the beach."

"That's right," I said, "it's just a couple of miles from here. Let's go!" So we went to the beach and walked out on the pier.

"My wife and I were here about half a century ago, and we had some cotton candy," he said.

"Well, let's you and I have some right now!" I said. So we walked around eating cotton candy. It was a very special day for both of us!

Then pretty soon he said, "You know my wife and I used to go down here by the water's edge and wade in the ocean."

"Mr. Weaver," I said, "that's exactly where we're headed next!" In those days, you could drive your car out on the beach next to the water and take off your shoes and socks, roll up your pant legs and start wading. So that's what we did!

That week we had several long talks. He was a brilliant man but one who didn't trust people. Many negative experiences in his childhood had taught him he couldn't put confidence in people. I told my wife it was a wonder that he was able to trust the Lord and be saved years earlier because he was so untrusting.

It was just one week from the time I first met Mr. Weaver that he said to me, "Young man, I believe God wants me to give you this property so you can help pastors and people around the world." He continued, "If you'll come back in the morning and take me down to the bank, I'll get the papers and deed this property over to you."

So the next morning, I took him to the bank, and he went in and brought out the papers. "Let's go to the attorney's office," I said, "to sign the deed."

"No, don't see an attorney," he said. "They charge too much, and they tend not to be honest."

"Mr. Weaver," I said, "you're giving us a beautiful piece of property, and the least I can do is to pay to have the deed transferred."

"No," he said, "just take me down to the escrow office, they're just as legal."

So we did, and the deed was recorded that day. About a month later, at our insistence, we deeded the two acres on top of the hill back to Mr. Weaver for the remainder of his life. This was where his home was located. I wanted to be sure that if anything happened to me, he would always have a place to live.

I continued to have many long talks with Mr. Weaver. About two years later, he went home to be with the Lord. It was a pitiful funeral; only the pastor, my wife and I, and two people from our staff attended. But I thought to myself, *God has used this man, whom almost no one knew, and who was a recluse, to give a beautiful piece of property for our international headquarters so that thousands of people throughout the world can receive help.*

I think it is often this way. People who are basically well-adjusted may not see the need for reaching out to others. *But when people are hurting and they've suffered bitterly, they may be more sensitive to the pain of others and more likely to want to be a blessing to them.*

I believe that was the case with Mr. Weaver. We'll always be grateful to God for providing this beautiful land where we could establish our headquarters.

Our ministry had entered a great new phase. I felt the finances would now come in for erecting buildings, but not so. People were still not accustomed to giving to psychology and counseling ministries.

When we first began our seminars for ministers and missionaries and other groups, we had no housing facilities. Yet, the people coming were from all over the United States, as well as from foreign countries. So we contacted friends and neighbors who were fairly close by and placed the seminar attendees in various homes around the community. Meanwhile, we kept on praying, and before long, we had completed our first housing facility. Little by little we developed a splendid ten-acre headquarters with a counseling clinic, an auditorium, an administration building, an educational building, a dining center, a shipping building, two motel-type facilities for housing our seminar guests, as well as a repair shop. Now we had a better place where we could serve the Lord in a better way!

INTERNATIONAL COUNSELING CENTER

One of the important services we provided at our new headquarters was individual counseling through our large counseling center. We designed a large counseling center that would meet the needs of those who came for individual help. Four major entrances and exits led to outside patios. In this way, a counselor and his client, especially a child or teenager, could go outside the office for a few minutes and talk.

Our professional staff of Christian therapists grew until it numbered sixteen. In addition, we had one full-time medical doctor and a part-time psychiatrist. It wasn't long before we had one of the largest counseling clinics in America. People came from all over the United States, as well as from many foreign countries. Most stayed in our on-campus housing facilities.

The individual counseling aspect of our work actually began years before we had a counseling center. People would ring the doorbell of our home, asking if they could talk to me about their problems. Since our home phone was listed, and in those days, addresses were included, it was not difficult for people in Pennsylvania, Florida, Texas, or other places to locate our home and ring our doorbell for help. If I was still at work at the county office, they would sit in our living room and wait until I arrived.

Actually, it was the same all over America. People had problems that were not being addressed by churches or others. And now that there was a Christian Counseling Center, they rushed to it to get relief and resolution of their long-standing problems.

We have never had an unlisted phone number. We figured if a person was facing a serious crisis, we wanted to be available. Consequently, our phone would ring day or night. Sometimes a person would be calling from back East and would forget about the time change. We must have sounded very drowsy when answering the phone at three or four in the morning.

As our counseling clinic developed, it soon became evident that it would also become a prototype for Christian clinics around the nation. In fact, we established a clinic in the Harrisburg, Pennsylvania, area and one in Phoenix, Arizona. We maintained these for several years until they were able to develop a staff and practice of their own.

In the early days, I declined most requests from people who wanted to be a part of our professional staff unless they had a doctorate in psychology and a license to practice. I was intent on having licensed personnel who could diagnose as well as treat a person, using the best knowledge available. Each licensed psychologist was required to be a born-again Christian, committed to the word of God and able to apply the Bible to human problems. Being a large staff, we were able to share with each other and upgrade our own understandings and techniques. This was through daily conversations as well as weekly clinical staff meetings.

I have always held these attitudes about Christian psychologists:

1) God usually uses people to help other people. He gives us dentists, engineers, plumbers, physicians, pastors, psychologists, and others. So when we need help, we seek it from one another according to our needs. This honors God.

2) In a counseling session, a Christian psychologist is God's servant here on earth. Therefore, he should be as well-trained professionally as possible, and he should have a substantial knowledge of God's eternal word so he can share and apply it appropriately with his counselee.

3) A Christian psychologist's life should be above reproach, being made conformable to the image of Christ. His clients should see Christ in him, not only in his knowledge of God's Word, but also in his behavior.

4) The basic adjustment in life is spiritual conversion. This affects a person throughout his life and for all eternity. A Christian psychologist is responsible for sharing this fact with his clients and leading them to Christ, if possible. *Spiritual conversion is central to effective therapy.*

> *Spiritual conversion is central to effective therapy.*

Not long after we moved into our new counseling center building at our international headquarters, people came from near and far to get help. Some would arrive with sleeping bags, willing to sleep on the ground or anywhere just as long as they could get counseling! However, in time, we built two motel-type housing facilities on the campus.

We've always tried to be aware of our limitations. We have not encouraged clients to come to our clinic unless we felt we were qualified to help them. Furthermore, we have been alert to refer them to other professionals.

Through the years, the transformation of lives through counseling has been nothing short of amazing. In fact, God's word says, "Where there is no counsel, the people fall; but in the multitude of counselors there is safety" (Prov. 11:14). We were humbled to have among our clients a Miss America, great Bible expositors, and leaders in business.

One day a client handed me a poem. It was written by a lady who had grown up without a caring father. This deprivation, along with other conditions, resulted in extreme personality problems. As an adult, she had extensive professional counseling at our clinic, and it was during her therapy that she wrote this poem and addressed it to her counselor.

To My Counselor

When I was just a little girl, I could not understand
Why father didn't seem to care, or even take my hand
And walk with me, or talk with me, or even seem to know
Whenever I would hurt inside, because I'd need him so.
He didn't know I used to dream, when I felt extra sad,
That someday there would come to me, an extra special dad.

The heart is like a garden, and I have heard folks say
That what you sow is what will grow, and come up tall some day.

The days and years just slipped away and in no time I'd grown.
But nothing grew way down inside, 'cause nothing had been sown.
Well, I'm a grownup now you see, but I'm so small inside,
I never could get bigger, though I had often tried.

Through hurt and pain I'd lost my dream to find that special Dad,
But now I've got the nicest one that any child has had.
It may be slow and painful, and very hard to do;
But maybe now I'll grow inside, as big and strong as you!

We began to offer in-depth one- and two-week seminars throughout the year. We tailored different seminars to meet the needs of each. In the very early days, most of the Christian psychologists in America were on our staff or located in nearby communities. They were the source of our seminar presenters. I soon learned that most licensed psychologists were bright, good listeners, and talented therapists. But few were good speakers. So we screened them carefully and featured for our seminars those who were talented communicators. I'm sure this was of special interest to pastors, because they usually were experienced speakers and teachers with real ability to communicate. They recognized a good or poor speaker almost instantly!

10/24/2
5

SEMINARS FOR MINISTERS AND MISSIONARIES

The first seminar we developed was for ministers and missionaries. It was about three weeks in length. Later we condensed it to two weeks because many people couldn't get away for three. These forty or more servants of God came from many parts of the world and lived on campus. We did not usually accept a man without his wife since we felt she was an integral part of the "team" and certainly vital to the family.

Upon arrival at the campus, *we gave the attendees several diagnostic personality tests.* Then a licensed Christian psychologist sat with each person individually to review and carefully consider the test findings. This helped each one to understand why he or she was feeling and acting the way he or she did. There was almost no embarrassment because everyone was going through the same process and knew we respected him and held him in high esteem. We provided, of course, a strong biblical basis for all that we did. People developed both spiritually and emotionally; after all, they go hand in hand. Basic emotional needs, at their greatest depth, are met through salvation, Bible knowledge, application of God's eternal truths to one's life, and Christian maturity. *But careful, skillful, and sometimes long periods of counseling are needed to help a person reach the point where he is able to apply the eternal word of God to his life and to think and act differently.*

Both spouses went daily into small group therapy sessions (husbands and wives in different groups), and each day they considered issues that were important to them. The group leader, a Christian psychologist, had access to the personality test results of those in his group, so he knew the nature and extent of each person's good or poor adjustment. With test and interview results, and some medical information, we were not working in the dark. We could focus on specific needs.

Of the thousands who came through the years, perhaps 80 percent wanted private counseling while they were on campus.

Our aim was to help each person be as well-adjusted as possible. For example, a pastor's wife or a lady missionary may have found through the test results and interviews that she had made high scores in one particular trait—such as *manipulation.* Although she had not been aware of this, it had been hindering her from being her best for the Lord. So as she had private counseling and small group therapy, she came to understand the reality of this personality problem, its effect upon her life, its origins, and what she could do to resolve it.

Another example might be a pastor who learned that he had a high level of hostility. He had not been cognizant of this, but it had prevented him from being the husband, father, pastor, counselor, and Bible teacher he could have been. People in his congregation may have thought of him as being a "fiery speaker" or a man of God who "called a spade a spade." In fact, he may have taken some pride in his ability to quickly "critique" and "set things straight." But now at our in-depth seminar, he came to realize that he had a problem with long root systems that needed to be resolved. So he focused on this issue and received help that would last a lifetime. Indeed, the opportunity to have private counseling and small group counseling daily with a licensed professional who loved the Lord Jesus Christ was very important. We also helped each person become more aware of the psychological and physiological causes of problems in the lives of *other* people.

The ministers and missionaries came from many mission organizations and scores of different denominations. In some instances, it was the first time a pastor had associated closely day by day with someone who was not a member of his own denomination. As one pastor said to me, "These men are not in my denomination, but some of them are the most spiritual people I've ever met!" It's helpful to realize that many of the most spiritual people may not belong to our denomination!

At the beginning of a two-week or three-week intensive seminar, you'd never think that at the end of the period a pastor, or missionary, or his wife, would grow and change so much. But he or she did!

The time it takes to help a person is shortened if the therapist is well-trained and gifted, if the person's problem has been correctly diagnosed, and if both are looking to the Lord to wonderfully fill in the cracks of childhood emotional deprivations. Of course, the nature of one's problem is important when considering how he or she will respond to counseling.

I knew we could always hold one-day or weekend seminars around the nation and reach people where they were living and to help them some. I had been doing that. *But I also realized there was no substitute for a person or a couple staying on our campus for a period of time, having psychological evaluation, test interpretations, private counseling, group therapy each day, and instruction from 8:30 AM to 8:30 PM.* We were always amazed at improvements that could be brought into people's lives with such in-depth seminars.

In each seminar given for pastors and missionaries and their spouses, we focused on many topics. Here are several brief comments on a few factors that relate to counseling.

1. *Personality adjustment. Few things other than spiritual conversion are more important than good personality adjustments.*

   It affects the way we think, the way we feel, and the way we relate to other people and to God Himself. Our personalities are made up of numerous traits. A man or woman can be rather well adjusted in some areas of personality but not in others. As Christians, we should be acutely aware of how we are functioning personality-wise. Fortunately, as we begin to understand our own personality dynamics, we better understand other people. What is going on inside us may be similar to what is transpiring inside others, except to a different extent. Take the trait, security-insecurity, for example. We all have some feelings of insecurity. But some people are continually devastated by such feelings. Through spiritual and psychological means, personality maladjustments can be resolved.

2. *Serious long-term problems. It is a general rule of thumb that if a person is manifesting personality problems that have existed for a number of years, the basic causes are often physiological.*

   For example, Jim, an adult, has numerous personality maladjustments. Since his problems have been evident for a number of years, it is very likely they are of a physiological, rather than a spiritual or psychological nature. We often see this in the case of neurological impairments. In Jim's case, he may need three kinds of help: medical, spiritual, and psychological. This understanding has significance for anyone who is working or living with a problem-laden person.

3. *Concepts of God.* Everyone, whether he knows it or not, carries with him a picture of God. These images may be quite fuzzy or erroneous, or they may be accurate, in line with the teachings of Scripture. *A person's thoughts and concepts of God are overwhelmingly important.* When helping a person, it is essential to understand what his concepts of God really are. Such understanding unlocks a world of insight about that person. Interestingly, a person's concepts of God are often

influenced by his relationships early in life with his mother and father, especially the father. Merely telling a person to change his perceptions of God usually does little good. A patient and thorough process of scriptural and psychological counseling is needed and is highly effective.

4. *Attitudes toward Christianity and religion.* People have various attitudes toward Christianity and religion. I remember counseling with a man who had very negative attitudes toward the Bible. One day during a counseling session, he stumbled onto some hidden experiences of his youth. His father usually punished him by forcing him to stand in a corner with his arms extended in front of him holding a large black Bible. In that terribly tiring position, the boy was forced to recite Bible verses he had memorized or that the father asked the boy to repeat after him. Occasionally the boy would faint while being punished. He grew up with extremely negative attitudes toward preachers, churches, the Bible, and Bible memorization. It does little good to tell an adult with such attitudes to "snap out of it." He needs to be helped out of it. *A study of thousands of people who have negative attitudes regarding spiritual matters would reveal that many of them have had known or forgotten experiences that took place during their growing-up years.* Such negative attitudes toward Christianity should be understood and if possible, carefully resolved before expecting the person to trust Christ and develop spiritually.

5. *Marriage.* We know that a person's marriage may be quite happy or unhappy. During our seminars, we have often asked each person to seriously consider a dozen or so aspects of his or her marriage. Each was encouraged not only to identify these factors, but also to gain understanding of how they developed and how they can be resolved and improved. Counselors should avoid "using" their counselees to gain understanding for themselves. Counselees sometimes say, "My counselor talks and talks. I think he has more problems than I do." It is important for Christian counselors and Christian leaders to seek help for their own problems as easily as they would for a strep throat or some other ailment. As they do so, they can

more easily help others. *Counselors with unresolved personality problems often project them onto their counselees, or unconsciously seek help for themselves while trying to counsel others.*

6. *Feeling forgiven.* Many Christians go through life feeling that God has forgiven them. They start each day as it were with a clean slate and are able to function unusually well. However, other born-again believers feel the opposite. They may know what the Bible says about forgiveness, yet they do not feel forgiven themselves. Merely telling such a person to change or reminding him of specific Scriptures regarding forgiveness may not change his attitude. If a person has been raised in a home where he was often shamed or made to feel guilty, it may have left such a strong impact on him that he rarely feels forgiven. *It is difficult for an adult to feel forgiven if, during his first seventeen years, he was continually made to feel guilty.* A process of counseling that recognizes both spiritual and psychological factors is needed.

7. *Making certain of salvation. Some born-again people are sure of their salvation.* But others are plagued by feelings of uncertainty. Many believers feel they have been born again only if things are going well. Uncertain feelings about one's salvation may be traced to a lack of understanding of Scripture. But often, the problem may not relate to biblical understanding as much as it does to his general feelings of insecurity. Insecurity may affect many aspects of life, including the spiritual. Pastors often encounter people who are not sure they are genuinely saved. Such pastors and Bible teachers may have tried to resolve the problem by quoting many Bible verses from both the Old and New Testaments that point to a person's security in Christ. Yet that person may still feel uncertain about his salvation. *When helping a person who is unsure of his relationship with Christ, we should keep in mind the basic causes may be more psychological than spiritual in*

> *When helping a person who is unsure of his relationship with Christ, we should keep in mind the basic causes may be more psychological than spiritual in nature.*

nature. His general feelings of insecurity may be influencing him profoundly, including his assurance of salvation. Such a person needs to carefully examine and resolve the experiences that have turned him into an insecure person. This may suggest Christian professional counseling.

8. *Skillful counseling. Counseling is a process that requires real skill. After all, people are fearfully and wonderfully made.*

   Therapy involves much more than "chewing the rag" with someone you're trying to help. During the foundation's seminars for pastors and missionaries, we have placed emphasis on the dynamics of effective counseling. This has included specific do's and don'ts when seeking to help a person.

9. *Relating better to people.* I presume we would all like to relate better to people, but it is not always easy to do. Relating well to others involves (a) adequate understanding of ourselves, (b) a basic understanding of other humans, (c) specific relational techniques and approaches, and (d) being well-adjusted ourselves. We are all acquainted with people, including some leaders, who are functioning below their potential. They may know the Scriptures well, but their approach to people leaves something to be desired. In our seminars for ministers and missionaries, we have stressed the four aspects above.

10. *Referrals.* Successful people realize the value of networking. Today innumerable sources of insight and help are available. No one has to go it alone. I'm sure there are many Christian leaders who feel it would be a mark of weakness and a definite failure of Scripture if they had to refer a troubled person to someone else. As one man incorrectly said, "If I can't help a person by using the Bible, then there's no reason I should send him on to anyone else; he can't be helped." During our seminars, we have stressed the importance of utilizing appropriate referrals and improving our attitudes toward being a part of an effective team. *One of the marks of competency is the use of available resources, even though they are continually changing.*

11. *More complete understanding.* The understanding of medical and psychological factors does not negate or reduce the power of the Holy Spirit and God's eternal word, the Bible. In fact,

the opposite is true. Some people erroneously believe that if they looked, for example, at the causes of behavior other than spiritual, they would be reducing the powerful impact of the gospel. In truth, the more complete understanding a counselor has of the causes and solutions of problems, the more successful he's likely to be and the more he is appreciated by his counselee. If a person were merely a spirit fluttering around the room, all he would need is spiritual help. But that is not what human beings are. They are complex and respond to spiritual, physiological, and psychological approaches. It is important to understand the relationship of each to the other. All behavior is caused, and the causes are multiple.

******

In addition to the psychological and spiritual content of the daily lectures and counseling, serious attention was given to other aspects of the seminars. Each morning chapel service featured outstanding pastors and other Christian leaders from southern California. These speakers were carefully selected to bring optimum help and inspiration to the conferees. Our daughter Melodie, a Christian dramatist, presented one chapel service at each seminar. It was entitled, "Women of the Bible." She also discussed the use of Christian drama in the church, relating to both evangelism and Christian growth.

During noon and evening meals Ruth provided Christian music on the organ or piano. We also honored the conferees at an evening concert open to the public. We featured talented Christian musicians, including Gloria Bendell of our staff, and Ruth, who played the Swiss bells, vibraharp, and alpenhorn. All in all, we endeavored to make the seminar a memorable lifetime experience. We also utilized the talents of the conferees. Following is an example from one of the "undiscovered poets."

THE JACUZZI

Down at the Jacuzzi our group meets every night
To decide if we're neurotic or our heads are screwed on right,
To talk about our hang-ups, paranoias, and fears;
And in that bubbling water, we've a chance to dry our tears.

There we laugh at Taylor Johnson, our Sten, and M.P.I.
And everyone's accepted; we're assured that tests *do* lie!
We talk out all our tensions and shake out all our kinks,
And agree *we're* well-adjusted, but psychologists are sphinx'!

We decide we're not *all* crazy, then go on to greater things;
We compare the latest preacher jokes, then everybody sings.
We laugh at Weeping Willy, the Mennonites from a choir—
And the tallest tales that are told prove who's the biggest liar.

We argue through the Scriptures when through with other junk—
"Should we immerse" or "pour" or "sprinkle" — or do a "triple dunk"?
We discuss our churches' problems and eschatology;
We compare denominations, and we spout theology.

We're all on the same level; each one has dropped his mask—
Not a subject we can't talk about, not a question you can't ask
While the water soothes your body and the closeness soothes your heart.
No one is feeling lonely; each person feels a part.

Oh, there are group dynamics in that pool without a doubt,
When to our chins in water, we can let it all hang out.
But I think I know a secret and that is this: I'll bet
"Doc" Narramore could teach us more *if only he'd get wet!*
— Margee Dyck

BUSINESS AND PROFESSIONAL SEMINARS

One seminar given several times a year that was open to most people was the one-week seminar for business and professional people. Christian workers were not included, since there was another seminar for them. We did not want to attract people who had serious problems, because we were not set up to offer adequate help for them in a one-week professional seminar. Our seminars were geared to people who were reasonably well-adjusted, but who wanted to improve and be at their best. We were grateful to be able to minister to many from around the world—about forty or sixty at a time.

Of the thousands who took this training, all said it was very beneficial. (1) They had learned specifically about any personality deficits. (2) They had learned what caused these traits. (3) They experienced daily private and group therapy. (4) Now they were seeing improvement. Perhaps one of the best testimonies came from Jim Erwin, who had walked on the moon. At the end of the seminar he said, "This has been the greatest experience of my life!"

SEMINARS FOR EXECUTIVES

Once a year, we offered a seminar for business executives. Most of the attendees held top positions in companies. Many of them had heard about our seminar from another executive who had attended. However, there were some exceptions. One day I asked a man who was attending how he had learned about the seminar.

"Well," he said, "that's interesting. It happened at the athletic club where I'm a member. I went into the sauna, and of all things, I saw a magazine called *Psychology for Living*. I turned to the back and saw an ad about the seminar. So I took the wet magazine home, phoned you, and here I am!" These were his bare facts!

Once when I was in Dallas speaking at a banquet for business people, I mentioned the seminar we offered for executives. After the banquet, a nicely dressed lady asked me if she might qualify to take the seminar.

"What is your profession?" I asked.

"We provide items to beautify the home," she replied.

Then when I asked her how many employees she had, she smiled and said, "Twenty-five thousand!"

I laughed and said, "You must be Mary Crowley, president of Home Interiors." Then I added, "Mary, you cannot only attend our seminar, you can help teach it!"

Executives are sometimes lonely. They may want to consider certain personal issues, but they know it is best not to talk about them to staff members. So where do they go? Our seminar for executives met a special need. And since many of them held responsible positions in their local churches—such as deacons, elders, trustees, and Sunday school superintendents—their influence, upon returning home, was significant.

TEACHER TUNE-UPS

We also offered one-week seminars for teachers. These were given during the summer. Educators in elementary schools, secondary schools, and colleges attended. The curriculum for them was different from other seminars. These conferees were very special because they were directly influencing boys and girls day after day. Having been a teacher at all levels myself, I felt comfortable working with them. Many of our seminar considerations involved curriculum and teaching techniques, but mainly personal adjustment issues.

During the year, it was interesting to note the differences between the groups that came for training. Each seminar group was predictably different from the others. The ministers and missionaries were different from the business people. The executives were different from the educators. Each group needed a somewhat different curriculum and approach. But they all benefited from diagnostic personality testing and counseling therapy. And they all responded to our strong biblical emphases.

Missionary Kids Training.

SEMINARS FOR LAY COUNSELORS

In time, it became evident that we should offer seminars for lay counselors. Men and women with bachelor's and master's degrees were serving in schools, hospitals, correctional institutions, businesses, churches, missions, and other places. Most were not interested in taking several more years of training to become licensed psychologists, but they did want to improve and get additional training that was also Christ-centered. Very few had ever taken a psychology course taught by a Christian. They wanted more than a secular approach. These were intensive ten-day seminars, and many interesting and capable people came for this particular seminar.

One day when Ruth and I were conducting a summer tour to Europe, we had an interesting experience in a city just outside of Rome, Italy. Our tour guide took us to a famous site. As we entered the courtyard, a young lady in another tour group turned, looked at us, and called out, "Dr. Narramore!" Then she ran toward us and asked, "Do you remember me!"

I smiled and said, "Yes, about a year ago you took our seminar for lay counselors."

"That's right," she said. "And it was one of the best things I ever did. After taking the course, I applied in our firm for a better position that required some skill in counseling. I got the promotion and a good raise in salary. That's why I'm here in Italy on vacation."

The seminar for lay counselors enabled the conferees to take tests, look at themselves, and have individual and group counseling. In addition, we focused on techniques of counseling. We also did a lot of role playing as counselors and counselees. Interestingly, some of them went back to university, received their doctorates, and became licensed Christian psychologists!

SEMINARS FOR SONS AND DAUGHTERS OF MISSIONARIES

Each year, hundreds of special young people fly to the shores of the United States. They make no noise, and you see and hear nothing about them on television or radio. Their arrival is not loud or spectacular, and they're not waving flags or heralding special causes. But they are arriving just the same. And as they attend college and prepare for their life's careers, they will make a significant difference in society.

Who are they? They are sons and daughters of American missionaries who are serving in foreign countries. Probably few people stop to think about missionary kids (commonly known as MKs) and what happens to them. People know that missionaries have children, but they don't consider where they go to school during their growing-up years.

My wife and I began to get a deeper understanding of the lives of MKs as we traveled overseas holding seminars for groups of missionaries. The parents nearly always asked us to speak to their teenage sons and daughters, who might be attending a nearby academy. Before long, we better understood their way of life, their concerns, and their experiences living in a boarding school in a foreign country.

Mission organizations have different policies regarding the schooling of MKs. Some parents are able to homeschool their children using courses of study that have been developed professionally. But many more missionaries in foreign countries send their children to special schools, some near and some far away. These are commonly called "academies." Examples are Faith Academy in the Philippines, Morrison Academy in Taiwan, Hillcrest Academy in Nigeria, Rift Valley Academy in Kenya, Black Forest Academy in Germany, Vienna Christian Academy in Austria, and many others around the world.

Ruth and I had traveled to various parts of the world where we talked with missionaries and conducted seminars. We knew they were concerned about sending their sons and daughters to the United States to begin college. They realized that many other MKs had never adjusted well to America, and others had forsaken their Christian upbringing. And since Ruth had been an MK herself, she held a special place in her heart for those wonderful young people.

In 1979, we began to offer a new kind of two-week seminar: for the sons and daughters of missionaries—MKs. We called it the "Reentry Seminar." We have continued this special seminar for over thirty years. About forty to seventy young people have come each year. They are usually around eighteen years of age, having just graduated from high school overseas in Africa, South America, Asia, Europe, the islands of the sea, or elsewhere. One MK even came from Timbuktu in Africa! We now conduct one or two seminars each summer.

Missionary kids tend to be bright and well-educated. Many have been raised apart from their mothers and fathers in boarding schools, seeing their parents only at intervals. Like some American kids, their basic emotional needs may never have been met very well, causing them to have problems that may affect them for a lifetime unless they receive special help. Many, of course, are well-adjusted. They are world travelers and usually speak two or more languages. They tend to think quite differently from the typical American Christian teenager.

We devoted about a year off and on, developing a special curriculum. Through the years, we have made a few modifications, but basically the program has remained much the same. Students live on the campus full time, and their days are filled from 8:30 AM to 8:30 PM with tests, lectures, counseling, discussions, and fun times. They feel especially comfortable with other missionary kids. Some of our faculty have also had experience on the foreign mission field.

MKs are among the most interesting people in the world. They usually come from godly families where both parents are bright and well-educated. Missionary dedication to the Lord's work is such that they are willing to leave Main Street USA, go to a foreign country where they must learn the language, fit into the culture, and become spiritual leaders.

Characteristically, these wonderful families have little money, but their lives are rich with unusual experiences. And so are the MKs themselves. You never know what experiences an MK may have had.

For example, I was in Africa holding a seminar for missionaries when one of them asked me, "Would you like to go with us in the morning to see the kids off?"

I wasn't sure just what he meant, but I thought if missionaries were doing it, it would probably be okay, so I told him I would like to go. The next morning, we drove in the missionary's car out of the little dusty community to a barren field where we saw another car, a missionary couple and two teenagers. They explained that a plane would be arriving to take the kids to a distant place where they would be attending a boarding school for MKs.

A few minutes later, a little plane landed and settled near us. There were two seats in front and two in back. The door was on the side. Since one seat was occupied by the bush pilot, there was room for three youngsters. The two teenagers had gone through this process before, so they said their good-byes quickly, hopped into the back seats, and buckled up.

The missionary couple, whom we'll call the Smiths, said good-bye to their six-year-old son, "Bobby," and the father began lifting him up into the side door of the plane. But the little guy began to fight like a tiger, kicking and screaming, saying he didn't want to leave his mother and daddy. Mr. Smith struggled to shove the boy into the plane, but the youngster spread his legs and arms out and refused to go in. All the time, he screamed and cried that he didn't want to leave home. He begged his parents not to make him go. Finally, the father began to cry and turning, placed the child into the arms of his wife, saying, "You try to get him in."

She struggled with the little boy and told him that by going away, he would get to learn to read and there would be other children to play with.

"I don't want to learn to read, and I don't want to play with anyone but you and Daddy," he cried. After more struggling, Mrs. Smith realized she couldn't handle him, so she turned to me and said, "Dr. Narramore, will you hold him and help me push him in?"

My heart was torn as we held him tight and shoved him into the plane. The pilot put the seat belt around the screaming little boy, closed the door, and the plane took off and disappeared in the sky. The parents stood there hugging each other and crying until they could see the plane no more. Then they went back to their car and we returned to the missionary compound … all with heavy hearts.

I have thought about that episode many times, realizing many MKs have gone through this or some other heart-wrenching episodes; but separation from his parents would only be the beginning of Bobby's unusual, and sometimes unfortunate, experiences during the next twelve years until he graduated from high school overseas.

One summer several years later, Ruth and I had an interesting experience with an eighteen-year-old MK who was taking our Reentry Seminar for two weeks at our California campus. It was about the fifth day of the seminar. We had just finished lunch and were getting ready for our next session. We noticed one of the fellows sitting on the cement steps just outside the dining room. He was slender and about six feet tall. As we drew near, we could see he was bent over with his head in his hands. Then we saw he was crying. Ruth put her hand on his shoulder and said, "That's all right, Steve, you go ahead and cry. It's good for us when we feel that way."

Steve sobbed and said, "But I don't know why I'm crying."

I explained that sometimes MKs, and in fact, any person, may suffer from delayed grief. I reasoned with him along the line of his having left his family, his friends, his language, and his community in Indonesia. Even though it may have been exciting to come to the United States and to the MK seminar, he may now be reacting unknowingly to the severe changes and losses that had recently come into his life. I saw to it that he had individual counseling each day with one of our psychologists. Later on, he told me that what we had done was a real benefit, and that perhaps he would be able to help someone else in the future.

The MK Seminar is rather intensive, conducted by a professionally-trained staff. Much attention is given to orientation to life in the United States. Through personality tests and interviews, each student comes to understand the extent of his personality adjustment. Vocational tests point each person to the best career choices. All of the seminar experiences are designed to help each MK grow spiritually.

Individual and group counseling are available on a daily basis, along with many fun times and recreational activities.

Space here does not allow for a full description of these two-week seminars in which we have seen tremendous growth and change in young people. We challenge and encourage them, and many have gone on to receive their bachelor's, master's, and doctor's degrees. Some are now heading up Christian organizations, and we feel this has been a major contribution to God's kingdom. This is undoubtedly one of America's remarkable ministries, and we feel so privileged to have created and been so involved in it!

In summary, the foregoing in-depth seminars for adults and young people have served more than five thousand around the world.

Ruth and I will always be grateful for the privilege of entering into the lives of these Christian leaders and MKs as they have taken our seminars. We had two meals a day with them and visited with them during the morning and afternoon breaks. We also presented musical concerts in which Christians in the community were invited to come and meet the conferees. There were often some MKs who were musically talented, and we involved them in the program as well. In addition, many came to our home for a time of fun and fellowship.

Unlike a speaker who may not know the people in his audience, we were with our conferees all day, every day, getting to know them intimately. Although much of our ministry is and has been to groups, the one- and two-week seminars have given us the privilege of working one-on-one with these precious people. How richly they have blessed our lives!

CHAPTER TWELVE

IT MADE ME LAUGH!

"To everything there is a season," the Bible says, including a time to laugh. It also tells us that a merry heart does good, like medicine.

I suppose few people see more funny things in life than a psychologist who is traveling extensively and working with people intimately. At any rate, I want to share some humorous episodes that bring a chuckle every time I think about them.

WET PANTS

It happened in northern Italy when Ruth and I were conducting a summer tour. Our group of fifty was having dinner in a lovely restaurant overlooking beautiful Lake Maggiore. Next to Ruth and me was a table of four from our group. One was a lady, whom we'll call Mrs. Jones. She was taking her first trip abroad and seemed not to be aware of some of the subtleties and goings on in foreign restaurants and hotels.

As we sat there, I noticed that their waiter, a little older man, was definitely on the lookout for tips. He was a crafty-looking guy who was scraping and bowing to everyone and lavishly complimenting his customers. Every once in awhile, he would make some gesture that would endear the people to him and that might cause them to give him a large tip. His hand gestures seemed to be asking for a tip. Evidently this was his modus operandi.

Mrs. Jones had asked him for some more water. Immediately, he went to the kitchen and brought a large glass to her and placed it with flair and style near her plate.

At that point, he took his hand and opened up the right front pocket of his pants. He also gave her a little nod and a friendly, ingratiating smile. The lady didn't seem to know just what he wanted. She looked puzzled and then noticed the open pants pocket again. I suppose he felt that if he stood in that position a moment longer, she might "catch on" and slip a dollar bill into his open pocket.

But she still didn't understand and looked perplexed. She started to drink from her glass as he continued to stand there with his front pants pocket held open. To give her a hint, he pointed toward her water. Still puzzled as to what he was getting at, in frustration, she took her water glass and in a flash, poured it all into his front pants pocket! I wish I could describe his expression as he stood there stunned, while water leaked all down the front of his pants to the floor!

Needless to say, he ran to the kitchen and never showed up again for the duration of the meal. Those of us sitting nearby and watching this episode couldn't help but laugh.

I'm sure he never tried that money-getting technique again!

Has the Lord Come?

This next humorous episode took place at the Sandy Cove Bible Conference in Maryland. The Narramore Christian Foundation was conducting a week's seminar for people on the East Coast.

In one of the initial sessions, I was speaking from the platform where there was a large free-standing chalkboard. My lecture that morning was rather intensive, and I noticed a lady on the front row who was listening to every word. Her eyes were glued on the speaker.

During my presentation, I wanted to demonstrate a certain point, so I stepped in back of the chalkboard where I couldn't be seen. But just before I did, the lady on the front row who was watching so intently began to sneeze, putting her head into her handkerchief. Consequently, she didn't see me move in back of the board.

When she finished sneezing, she looked up and I had disappeared! Without thinking, she screamed, "Oh my goodness! Dr. Narramore is gone. Has the Lord returned?"

Needless to say, the entire room roared with laughter. But if she had known her Bible better, she would have expected a "shout" and a "trumpet sound!"

I Can't Get It to Play

As we have moved into the twenty-first century, most adults have been confronted with dozens of technical items and gadgets they did not understand. In fact, children have been teaching their parents and grandparents about computers and other electronic devices.

Changes take place so rapidly that we tend to forget, for example, that only a few years ago even audio cassettes did not exist. Several years ago, I offered a special cassette premium to all who sent gifts to the foundation that month. So we monitored our mail for the next few weeks to see how the cassette offer was being received. A few wrote saying they did not have a cassette player, so they returned it or gave it to a friend.

But one day we received a letter from a lady saying, "I have received your cassette, but I just can't get it to play. I've squeezed it; I've pressed it from the bottom, top and all four sides, and still it won't play! I waited for awhile and then squeezed it again with my hands, but no sound comes out."

Then she continued, "There must be something wrong with it, so I'm returning it to you. But thank you just the same."

Everyone at the office had a little laugh over this. Then we wrote to our friend telling her that in order to hear it, she would need a cassette player and that we were sorry we had not explained that. We were careful not to ridicule her lack of understanding of "new gadgets" because undoubtedly, all of us, even Bill Gates, may be somewhat lagging when it comes to *some* inventions of the twenty-first century!

Sunshine and Shadow

For a number of years, Ruth and I made our daily radio broadcast, *Psychology for Living,* from our home. We placed the Ampex recorder on the corner of our dining table; then Ruth and I would sit side by side and speak into the microphone. Behind us was a cage where we kept our two canaries, Sunshine and Shadow. Each time we made a broadcast, we placed a covering over the cage to keep them quiet.

One night, Ruth and I came home from church and sat down at the table with our recording equipment to make a broadcast. But we made one mistake: we forgot to put the covering over the bird cage.

About two-thirds through the broadcast, the birds began to chirp and sing. My wife smiled, but I became very upset because the broadcast had gone along well up to that point. And now those silly birds were ruining everything! But since we were nearing the end of the program, we completed it.

At the conclusion of the broadcast, I turned to Ruth and said, "Those crazy birds! What on earth happened?"

"Well," she answered, "we forgot to put the cover over the cage."

"Oh," I said, "we're going to have to make that broadcast all over. We can't have those birds on it."

"What's wrong with the birds?" Ruth asked. "Maybe some people will like them. Furthermore, I'm so tired, I can't make another broadcast tonight. Let's just let it go as it is."

"Oh, no," I said, "*Psychology for the Birds!* That will never do."

But it was getting late and we both were tired, so we went to bed. The next day the duplication company made copies of the broadcast and sent them all over the United States to stations that aired our broadcast.

Much to our surprise, people began to write telling us how much they liked the birds. One woman said, "Now we know you're normal!"

Another lady wrote a six-page letter and all she talked about was the birds and how much she liked them. In fact, she had some of her own. Then she added a P.S. "I think you're okay, too!"

So we just left the birds on, and evidently, they cheered people up. Maybe they caused people to relate to psychology even more! In fact, people began to name their own birds Sunshine and Shadow. But from that time on, I never knew whether the listeners liked me or the other birds!

I WANT TO MARRY THAT LADY

One day we received a letter from a woman who was single but who wanted desperately to get married. She had written me hoping that somehow we could help her overcome the hurdles to a happy, successful marriage.

"I'm not bad looking," she said. "In fact, I think you'd say I'm rather pretty. I know how to keep a good house, and I'm a good cook. I'm also a born-again Christian, and I could surely make some man happy."

So Ruth and I decided to use a portion of her letter without giving any identification. Ruth read it beautifully, as she always did on our broadcast.

Evidently a farmer in Iowa turned in to the program just as Ruth was reading the letter, and he became very excited. He thought the lady speaking was the one who was eager to get married. The farmer wrote me immediately saying he wanted to meet the lady on the radio who wanted to get married.

"I liked everything she said," he wrote, "and she also has such a beautiful voice and speaks so well."

Then he went on to say that his wife had died several years before, and he was lonely. Above all, he was eager to get married again. "I have a great deal of money," he said, "and after we are married, we can travel around the world and have a wonderful life together."

I wrote the man and explained that it was my wife who had read from another lady's letter, and that Ruth and I were happily married.

But he wrote back, insisting he had heard the lady with his own ears, and that he could not rest until he met her and claimed her for his bride!

Ruth and I had many laughs about this. And from time to time, she teases me saying, "You'd better be nice to me, because there's a wealthy farmer in Iowa who's looking for a wife!"

Too Much of a Good Thing

I presume that all Christian organizations make a few mistakes. No matter how hard they try, things do happen, and they just have to make the best of them.

This is an embarrassing thing that happened one day at the Narramore Christian Foundation. One of our staff ladies was in charge of addressing all magazines before we mailed them out across America and around the world.

At that time, we used an Elliott addressograph system that worked quite well. The magazines would run swiftly through this machine while little addressograph plates dropped down and imprinted the name and address on the magazine. In this way, we could address hundreds of magazines in just a few minutes.

Our addressograph operator was alert and mechanically inclined, so the department ran along smoothly.

But one morning, while the addressograph was whirring away, printing addresses on the magazines, she went down the hallway to get a drink of water. While there, she met one of her co-workers, and they chatted briefly.

But wouldn't you know, the very moment she left the room, one of the addressograph plates got stuck in the machine and kept printing the same name and address on each succeeding magazine as it rolled through.

The operator didn't know this, because by the time she came back into the room to oversee the work, that particular addressograph plate had become unstuck and was humming along properly. So none of us knew that it had happened.

But about ten days later, we found out. We received a frantic call from a dear lady in Pennsylvania saying, "I don't know what on earth to do. When the postman came this morning, instead of delivering my copy of *Psychology for Living*, I got 156 copies. And what made it all the worse," she continued, "was that in the afternoon the postman came again with 170 more magazines. I'm beside myself and I don't know what has happened."

We had to admit we didn't know either. But when I told our operator about it, she said, "Oh, no! That's when I stepped out of the room!"

"How many magazines did she receive?" she asked.

"More than you'll ever know!" I replied.

P.S. This employee is no longer on our staff!

THEY DIDN'T MEAN IT THAT WAY

Writing, like speaking, is very interesting. Sometimes we write things in a certain way, when we mean the opposite.

For example, one day a woman wrote a letter saying that her husband had died. "I've been doing just fine since my husband's death," she wrote. "With the Lord's help, the new year should be better!"

I think she actually meant to say the Lord had been her strength and comfort since her husband's homegoing. And that with His continued help, she would be able face the new year with confidence, *not* that things had been fine since he died and that the new year should be better without him!

I'm so glad her husband never knew what she had written!

Not long ago, we received another letter with a rather unusual twist. "I've been concerned about my friend," the lady wrote. "I'm sure that if she gets married, she'll be in depression."

I still don't know what she meant. The Bible tells us that a husband should rejoice with the wife of his youth. But rejoicing certainly doesn't sound like depression!

Lost in the Fog

One of the finest Bible conferences in the United States is Word of Life, located on the shores of beautiful Schroon Lake in the Adirondacks in upstate New York. It was Jack Wyrtzen, well-known evangelist, who developed that conference facility and a number of others around the world.

One summer, I was there speaking all week at the adult conference on the mainland. One evening Jack said to me, "Clyde, we need you over at the island in the morning to speak to five hundred teenagers. They're a terrific bunch of kids, and they've come from everywhere. If you'll be down at the dock at seven in the morning, one of our boatmen will meet you and take you to the island, which is about a half mile away."

So I set my alarm, and the next morning I got dressed and stepped out of our cottage. But I could hardly see six feet in front of me because a thick fog had come in and settled over everything.

I finally stumbled my way down to the dock. Then all of a sudden, a teenage boatman appeared and hollered out, "Dr. Narramore, I've come to take you over to the island. Just hop in!"

He maneuvered the boat around, and I asked him how he could possibly find the island or anything else in the terrible fog.

"Just leave it to me," he said. "I can find it without any trouble."

Then I asked him if he had much experience running the boat.

"Oh, yes," he said, "I'm very experienced! I've been here for a whole week."

At that moment I thought to myself, *I guess when you're only seventeen or eighteen years old, one week seems like a long time.*

I asked him how he was going to find the boathouse over on the island.

"It's easy," he said, "I just get going in the same direction this dock is pointed, and in a few minutes we'll be there, and I'll take you right into the boat house. No problem."

Well, we wandered around in the fog for about a half an hour, and the fellow began to admit that he was having some difficulty.

Finally he said, "Oh there's a bush right in front of us. Now let me see, I wonder what bush it is."

After going up and down the shore for a few minutes, he admitted we had made a complete circle and we were back where we had started!

By that time, the meeting where I was to speak to the teenagers was over. But I felt it was my responsibility to assure him that when we encountered disappointments, we shouldn't give up. So I said nothing about how late it was and that we had already missed the meeting.

"Well." He said, "let's try it again. I must not have started out quite right."

So we headed out again, but before long, he realized we were hopelessly lost in the middle of the lake with the dense fog pressing in on us.

A few minutes later, he shouted, "There, I see something, I think it's a tree!" He went a little closer and said, "But I wonder what tree it is."

Finally, after about another hour, we got back to where we had started and called off the whole attempt.

About ten years later, my wife and I were in Portland, Maine, where I spoke one evening at the First Baptist Church of Portland. I wanted to use an illustration of needing a sure compass, which is Christ and the word of God. So I told the story of the teenager ten years before who was unable to navigate me to my destination.

As I concluded the story, people began to laugh. But one tall, slender fellow stood up in the middle of the church, raised his hand, and then said in a clear voice, "I was that boy!"

"Ohhhh," the audience gasped.

While he was standing, I asked, "Sir, what are you doing now?"

And almost embarrassed, he said, "I'm a pilot for a major airline!"

The audience roared with laughter again and when the noise quieted down, I asked him which airline he was with. He told us, and I said to the audience, "Friends, now you know which airline never to take!"

THEY DON'T QUITE GET IT RIGHT

When you're listening to a radio broadcast, you may not catch everything the speaker is saying. You may be rushing through a room, getting ready to change a diaper, or you may be dashing into the kitchen to pick up a ringing phone. Thousands of things can interrupt a perfectly good radio broadcast.

I've found that's true.

I wish time and space permitted me to tell many of the crazy things that have happened as I have maintained a radio broadcast for over fifty years.

+ Naturally, some interesting episodes have centered around the broadcaster's name. For example, not long ago, a lady addressed her letter to me as "Dr. More, Not Less." At least she got the "more" right. I'm glad she didn't say, "Dr. Less!"

+ One day I received a letter from a radio listener in New Jersey. She addressed the letter, "Dear Father, I don't know what else to call you." I don't know what or whom she had in mind.
+ Another person wrote, "I attended your seminar in Dallas. But I couldn't take notes fast enough. You mentioned Five Things about Men That Women Should Know. I know one of them is that they are strange, and another is they are gluttons for compliments. But what are the other three?"
+ Another person wrote saying, "Please send me your material on self-conception." Now that's a new twist!
+ Another man addressed an envelope to "Dr. Nehemiah." At least he put me in good company!
+ Still another man wrote us for Dr. Narramore's booklet on "Demolished Emotions." Maybe that's not such a bad title!
+ One lady wrote saying, "I think it's funny that you're offering a book on Procrastination. Anyone who has this problem would never get around to ordering it." I put off answering her!
+ One lady wrote, "I enjoyed hearing you on the radio telling that your mother loved you so much that she often told you she wished she had forty little boys just like you. So I started telling my young son the same thing. Finally, after about three months, he said, 'Mommy, you're always saying that, but you never get pregnant!'"
+ Another person addressed his envelope to "Dr. Narrowmoore, Ft. Worth, Texas." Somehow someone at the Fort Worth post office must have known me, because he rerouted the letter to our office in California.
+ A man from Detroit addressed his envelope, "Sex Development; Attention Mr. Merry More." I suppose that's better than if he had Spelled Merry with an "a"!
+ Yet another one I got a chuckle out of was from the lady who wrote, "For the longest time I thought you spelled your name 'Merrimore.' But now I have is straight: "Nammore.'" No, not quite right yet!
+ Another person wrote a letter addressed "To the Living." Well, that's better than "To the dead." She wanted to sign up for our magazine, *Psychology for Living.*

✦ But one of the most unusual, I believe, was a letter intended for me, but the envelope was addressed only to "Dr. Nerves, Los Angeles, California."

Well, Los Angeles is a big city with millions of people, and my address was not even Los Angeles, although it was in southern California. When I received the letter in our own mailbox, someone had written on the envelope, "Dr. Narramore, Rosemead, California."

When I read it, I found that, indeed, it was intended for me. The man who had written the letter quoted some things I had said on the radio and mentioned something I was offering that day.

What happened? I'll never know, but I presume someone in the Los Angeles main post office must have known me, so he took a chance on addressing it and forwarding it! Later on I wondered if there was any Freudian significance of his addressing me as Dr. Nerves. Perhaps I was getting on his!

THE HORSERADISH TOUR

Many interesting things happen in restaurants. And considering the thousands of places where we have eaten our meals while conducting summer tours around the world, we have undoubtedly had our share.

For example, one time our tour group was staying in a nice hotel in Rome, Italy.

We were having our evening meal in the hotel's ornate dining room. Several of our people had ordered roast beef. They were just beginning to taste the choice morsel when someone said, "I wonder if they have any horseradish. I'd sure like to have some with this roast beef." Several others joined in with, "Yes, that would be great."

So I summoned the waiter and tried to explain what we wanted. But he didn't speak English, and no one in our group spoke Italian.

In trying to explain it, I couldn't figure out just how to get the idea of "horse" and "radish" across. So our waiter asked three other waiters to come to our table as we tried to explain. But they couldn't understand either.

By this time, we were ready to give up the whole idea. But our waiter felt that if there was something these Americans wanted, they should surely have it. So he asked every other waiter in the restaurant, but to no avail.

Finally, he went into the kitchen and brought out the head chef. Since they had gone to all that trouble, I thought we should try a little longer to get across the idea. So we did everything we knew, but they still didn't understand.

We had said the word, "horseradish" scores of times. Then, with a burst of enthusiasm and accomplishment, the chef said, "I know! You are the Horseradish Tour!" I nodded my head and said, "Si, signore."

Our group burst out laughing and for the rest of our European tour, we called ourselves "The Narramore Horseradish Tour." Even though we never got our horseradish, we did leave the hotel and the city of Rome with a good taste in our mouths!

THIS IS WHAT YOU THINK

Like many others, I have had my share of television interviews.

Talk show hosts are an interesting lot—even those who are Christians. Some of them invite you to discuss a certain topic so they can get across their own point of view, hoping you will agree with them. For example, I remember a fellow who asked me a question, but before I had a chance to discuss it, he gave his point of view. Then he said, "That's what you believe, too, isn't it?" And he hardly knew what to do when I answered, "No, I believe just the opposite."

Other talk show hosts ask questions, but they haven't done their own homework and hardly know what you are talking about.

Then there are those who spiritualize everything. No matter whether you're talking about cutting the grass or cooking noodles, they have what you might call spiritual "tunnel vision." And they attach special spiritual significance to nearly anything and everything.

But Pat Robertson of the *700 Club* is different. He's one of the most knowledgeable talk show hosts I've ever met. He knows so much about theology, law, economics, politics, investments, and other things. It's wonderful to be his guest because he knows what you are talking about, and he tries to draw the best out of you without forcing his own opinion.

HOLD THAT CHALKBOARD!

I've had the joy of speaking on the *700 Club* program on numerous occasions. But one time was especially hilarious.

Pat gave me more than thirty minutes to speak to his vast audience. I asked him if I could use a chalkboard when I was explaining some points.

"You bet," he said. "That would be great. The more action, the better."

So when it came time for me to speak, I stepped over to the large chalkboard, which was mounted on two legs with rollers on the bottom. After looking at the camera, I took some chalk and began to mark certain things on the chalkboard. But "oops!" I found I had a problem. The rollers on the bottom of the two legs had not been locked, so every time I made a mark on the board, the chalkboard moved backward.

So I turned toward the cameras and tried to use the board as little as possible. But eventually I came to a point where I needed to use it again. I was hoping the rollers had turned sideways so it wouldn't move when I touched it.

But no such luck! I glanced at the cameraman, who was making some dramatic facial grimaces, and I knew in a split second that he saw my predicament.

So what did he do? He zoomed the camera in closer so it would just pick up my head and shoulders and the one spot on the chalkboard where I was writing. Since he was doing that, I knew I could wrap my legs around one of the legs of the board, sort of like bulldogging a calf.

That did it. I had stabilized the unstable. In the meantime, Pat, Ben Kenchlow, and the studio audience giggled their heads off.

When I returned home, Ruth asked me how I got along at the *700 Club*, and I was happy to report that I had had "a very *moving* experience!"

I KNOW JUST HOW YOU FEEL!

One morning our family of four was speaking and singing at a church in Honolulu, Hawaii.

Although Ruth was not taking part in the service that morning, we all knew who the good musician was. Ruth has a graduate degree in music from Columbia University and is multi-talented in the field. She is a pianist, organist, singer, trumpet soloist, harpist, alpenhorn player, vibraharpist, cellist, and an arranger of music for choirs and orchestras. The other three of us in the family stand in awe of Mom's musical ability.

On that particular morning, our son, Kevin, sang a solo. Our daughter, Melodie, also sang a solo, partly in English and partly in Hawaiian. Then they sang a duet. They did their songs with a cassette tape accompaniment. Melodie also gave a dramatic presentation of Women of the Bible. Then I brought the message.

Since Ruth did not perform that morning, she sat in the audience. Later that day, she told us what happened at the close of the service. A lady came to her and said, "You're Mrs. Narramore, aren't you?" Then she continued, "Your family is so talented, but since you don't have any talent, you have to sit back and just listen to them."

"Oh, but I enjoy listening," Ruth answered her.

"Even so," the lady went on, "it must be hard. But don't feel bad, I know just how you feel. I don't have any talent either, and I have to do just like you—sit back and listen. Maybe when we get to heaven, both of us will have some talent!"

Isn't it good that God has given us a sense of humor!

MAY I INTRODUCE …

What happens when a speaker walks up to the platform and faces a new audience?

If you've ever done this from state to state and from group to group, you know what I mean.

It may happen during the introduction, or midway through your speech, or even before or after. But you never know.

This is what happened to me when I spoke at the Hotel Astor in New York City. It was a group of women only, and the auditorium was packed. The lady who was to introduce me seemed to be a thin, nervous person who was evidently ill at ease on the platform. Before the meeting I shared the fact with her that I received my doctorate from Columbia University and I was now a *consulting* psychologist for the schools in California.

I don't know what notes she wrote on her little piece of paper but when she got up to introduce me this is what she said. "I now introduce Dr. Narramore who received his Doctor's degree from Columbia University and who is now an *insulting* psychologist from California."

She didn't realize she had said *insulting* rather than *consulting*. But hundreds of women in the audience were roaring with laughter. So when they quieted down I thanked her for such a friendly and accurate introduction!

But such is life. You win some and you lose some.

263
- 176
/87/
263

CHAPTER THIRTEEN

IT ACTUALLY HAPPENED

They say that every profession has its hazards. That may be so. But every profession also has its uniqueness. And that's certainly true of psychology. So I'd like to let you in on a few of my experiences.

THE PAPER BAG

One day I received a phone call from a young man asking if he could talk with me for a minute. He had heard our broadcast and knew our NCF phone number. He then said he wanted to call me at home and asked if my name was in the phone book. So that night he called. I didn't realize how serious his situation was or how long the relationship would last.

"Carlos" was about twenty years old and lived in East Los Angeles. He was extremely withdrawn. He felt he couldn't leave the house where he lived with his mother and two older brothers. That first phone call was just the beginning. After that he called me virtually every evening—often during the dinner hour when he felt I would be home. With each call, he would go into his problem more and more.

One evening one of his brothers grabbed the phone from him and said, "I don't know who you are, but you ought to know that my brother is a nut. He won't leave the house. He thinks he'll die if he leaves the house, so he sits in the corner all day long and *wears a paper bag over his head!*"

"What kind of bag does he wear?" I asked.

"Just a plain brown paper bag," he replied. "He keeps it on his head night and day, and even wears it at night while he sleeps. He has cut holes for his eyes and mouth. A real nut, no?"

The next evening when Carlos called, I asked him about this and he said it was true. He had worn the bag for about three years, and he couldn't take it off his head, because he was afraid he would die if he did.

In our many telephone sessions, Carlos said his brothers had beaten him up many times. They thought there was nothing wrong with him, and that he ought to take the bag off his head, get a job, and make a living like they were doing. He told me his mother didn't know quite what to think, but that she stuck up for him a little bit.

I continued to counsel with him (free of charge, of course) for about four years. Sometimes he would call me twice an evening. Once in a while my family would say, "Why don't you ask him not to call again?" And I replied, "Well, I could but he is extremely troubled, and if he were my own son, I would want someone to help him."

"Do you think you're getting anywhere with him?" they would ask.

"Yes," I replied. "He's bonding with me, and he's gaining insights little by little. He has a severe anxiety disorder, and the emotional baggage he's been carrying around for years is almost unlimited. Besides that, he has a very sensitive nature. So we need to work through on many things."

Carlos was not a believer—he had never trusted Christ as his personal Savior. However, he did feel that perhaps somewhere there was a God.

One evening I asked him, "Well if there is a God, where do you think He is?"

"He's probably a long ways up in the sky somewhere, hiding behind a cloud," he said.

I thought that was very revealing. Then I asked him, "If He sees you, what will He do?"

"Well," Carlos said, "He probably has a big club, and He'll probably clobber me a good one and try to kill me."

So that was his concept of God! And I must say, it is not too different from the opinion of many people who are walking our streets, heading our businesses, or running for public office. Most people who are unsaved (and even some who *are*) have distorted and inaccurate concepts of God, what He is doing, and what His attitudes are. But when Carlos told me about his concept of God, I realized that he was probably talking unknowingly about his dad, who had left the family years earlier. *So many people attribute to God the characteristics of their own fathers.* But these God attributes may be completely inaccurate, causing a person to live by a faulty compass.

I found that Carlos liked music and had a guitar. Once in awhile when everyone was out of the house and we were talking on the phone, he would sing a part of a song. Then he asked me, "Do you play the guitar?"

> *So many people attribute to God the characteristics of their own fathers.*

"Yes," I said, "I play some."

"Would you play something for me?" he asked.

So occasionally I'd play a song, and sometimes, he'd join in with me. I felt he was beginning to bond and feel much closer to me and believe what I said.

People who have been continuously or seriously abused usually find it hard to trust others.

> *People who have been continuously or seriously abused usually find it hard to trust others.*

After nearly four years, he began to listen more to what I said about the gospel. I would take a few minutes in each session and explain what the Bible said about him and the fact that God loved him. Of course, he didn't believe anyone loved him! Or that God could save him.

Finally he began to ask more questions about Scripture, so I sent him a Bible. Then I would ask him to look up verses and read them. Sometimes I would say them to him on the phone and have him repeat them. Surely, God's word was getting through and lodging in his mind.

He was also beginning to get more understanding of his basic psychological problems as well as the severe physical abuse he had sustained for many years as he was growing up. His two older brothers still kicked him around and beat him and told him he should get out and start working.

One particular week, I had stressed the gospel a great deal, and I felt he was beginning to accept it. That Friday night Carlos called me. His voice and attitude seemed more positive. "What," I asked, "has happened to you?"

"Let me get my guitar and sing it to you," he said.

So he got his guitar and sang the chorus,

> *He touched me, O, He touched me,*
> *And O, the joy that floods my soul;*

> *Something happened, and now I know,*
> *He touched me and made me whole.*

It was his way of saying that he had been "born again." I encouraged him and began to give him Scriptures to grow on.

As time went on, I told him, "What you should do now is take the bag off your head at certain times, and if you feel you're going to have to put it back on, you can pray and ask God to help you." So he agreed he'd try that.

After about a month, he said, "Yes, I'm taking the bag off some when no one is in the house." Then he told me there was a little mission church about a block and a half from his house, and they had guitars, and the people sang songs. "I'd like to go down and hear them," he said, "but I couldn't go inside."

So I said, "Why don't you go in the evening? You could either wear your bag or not wear it when walking there on the dark street. Then take it off when you come to a street light, because a policeman may come along and see you with the bag on your head and arrest you. When you arrive at the church, you can take it off, fold it up, and hold it in your hand. Just stand outside the church and listen to them sing." I knew he loved music.

A few days later, he reported that he had done that. And from time to time, he told me he had stood outside the church again. Then I said, "Now, Carlos, the next thing to do is go inside the church."

"Oh, I don't think I could ever go in!" he said.

"I've got an idea how you can do it," I said. "You can keep your bag in your pocket, even keep your hand on it, and then go inside the church and sit on the back row. If you feel you just have to leave, you can get up and go where it's dark and put your bag on your head and go home. But remember, God *loves you and is with you* whether you have a bag on your head or not."

I talked to him a few days later, and he said he had tried our plan. "I went inside," he said, "and there were several other people sitting on the back row, so I sat there, too. But I did get to feeling awful funny, so I got up and left."

In time, he went to church more and more. Finally he reached the point where he could take the bag off his head most of the time.

You can imagine my joy when one day he said, "You know, I don't live more than a few miles from the Narramore Christian Foundation. I've got a friend who will take me over there. He knows that I wear the paper bag part of the time, and it doesn't make any difference to him."

I was thrilled the day he came to the foundation, asked for me, and came into my office. I had never seen him, but I knew immediately it was my friend, "Carlos." As I gave him a hug, I noticed also that the brown bag was bulging in his pocket, but I said nothing about it. We had a nice time, and not long after, he was able to come to our clinic and get help until he was finally well.

I've often thought of the patience it took to work with him for nearly five years. But just think of how patient God has been, and continues to be with you and me.

One day my son who knew about Carlos said, "Dad, in a way, we all have bags on our heads, don't we?"

"Yes, that's true," I said, "but some are much thicker and tighter than others."

Indeed, *Every Person Is Worth Understanding.*

HOLLYWOOD CHRISTIAN GROUP

The ink on my doctoral diploma was hardly dry when I began to receive invitations to speak to various groups. One was the Hollywood Christian Group. Long before hugging was a popular greeting in churches, people in the film industry were warmly expressing their emotions.

We met each one in the group, including two who were known throughout the world: Roy Rogers and Dale Evans. They were as warm and genuine as could be, had a deep love for the Lord, and a desire to learn His Word. I might add at this point that many years later when I was leading a tour group in China, I talked with our two national Communist guides about life in the United States. They both spoke English. One day I asked them, "Have you ever heard about Disneyland?"

They looked at me quizzically, so I put it another way, "Disneyland. Do you know what Disneyland is?"

They shook their heads and said, "No, never heard."

Then I asked them, "Have you ever heard of Roy Rogers?"

Immediately they smiled from ear to ear and said, "Cowboy, cowboy!"

At any rate, we had a fine time that evening with the Hollywood Christian Group. We soon learned that people in the film industry were not all stars. Some were accountants, others were set designers, some were janitors or night watchmen, while others were seamstresses or what have you. I suppose for every one star there are several thousand others in the industry working at related jobs. Few appear before a camera with perfect makeup, exotic hairdos, glamorous clothing, and expensive jewelry.

Some people look at well-known people in sports, films, politics, and other fads, and in a sense almost worship them. But little do admirers know of the unhappiness and futility of those they may be admiring. As in other segments of society, there are believers who are bringing a Christian influence to those whose lives are so empty.

God's eternal word assures us that "godliness with contentment is great gain" (1 Tim. 6:6).

GOLD, FRANKINCENSE, MYRRH, AND LEAD

As we study the Bible and focus on the life of Jesus Christ, several points are poignant. One is how Christ was mistreated.

He was the Son of God who had come from heaven, yet was abused at nearly every point. He was ridiculed, spat upon, falsely accused, reviled, misunderstood, despised—a man of sorrows acquainted with grief. Considering all the good He was doing as He comforted people, raised the dead, caused the blind to see, then died for the sins of mankind, one would expect He would have been treated with more respect. But He wasn't.

Those who are in Christian work realize they will not always be treated fairly either. Although nothing compared to Christ's suffering, sometimes human mistreatment happens because the perpetrator is maladjusted, laden with problems, or unsaved. Occasionally we mistreat each other because we lack understanding. I remember something that happened one Christmas. I received a notice from the post office that a package was waiting for us with postage due. Needless to say, I was very happy. Finances at the Narramore Christian Foundation were unusually low. Few people understood our ministries. We had always observed the guidelines of the American Psychological Association to never mention finances on the radio. And since we never spoke about money, few people even knew we had needs.

I had sent our monthly letter in December describing our ministries and encouraging people to send gifts if the Lord so led. In this particular letter, I briefly described six people who had serious problems we had recently helped.

As I walked to the post office, I kept praying that the package I was about to pick up would mean something significant financially. When I went to the clerk's window, she said, "Yes, there's a package here for you. It has $6.47 postage due."

Since the foundation had no money, I paid it out of my own shallow pocket. I took it back to my office, rejoicing every step, anticipating what might be inside. Perhaps it would be something of unusual value—something we might possibly sell and then use the proceeds in our ministries. So when I returned to my desk. I opened the package and looked inside.

What was it?

A big, heavy piece of lead!

The lead was wrapped in the letter I had sent out that month. Scribbled all across the letter was: *people shouldn't have these problems!*

My first reaction was anger and keen disappointment. After all, we were doing our best to help others. And many of our staff members were sacrificing a lot in an effort to accomplish our work. Also, Ruth and I had gone at times without a salary. Then too, it was Christmas and our hearts were tender.

But as I began to think and pray about it, I felt differently. I was certain that *this man who had sent the lead was, himself, in need of our help.* Who knows what had happened to him all through his childhood. He may have felt like the man who once told me that when he was growing up, he felt like an orphan without an orphanage. Who knows what may have taken place when he was a teenager or a young adult? Or perhaps he had been terribly disillusioned by a Christian leader he had trusted. At any rate, he was another person who needed help.

So I bowed my head and prayed that God would help him, and that, if possible, we might be the ones who some day would minister to him.

Then I thought to myself, *I have known since I was a child that the Bible said Christ Himself was mistreated and misunderstood. And surely what had happened to us that day was nothing at all compared to what Christ had endured.*

But you know how it is; we have great expectations at Christmas time. So disappointments are a little harder at the special "good will to all men" season. We like the gold, frankincense, and myrrh but not the lead.

And upon reflection, I'm glad it was I who had *received* that piece of lead, and not I who had *sent* it!

GRAPHIC NAME

One of the amazing things to a radio broadcaster is learning about and picturing the circumstances under which people listen to a broadcast.

People have told me that they listened to *Psychology for Living* while driving a tractor. Others were cultivating a field or milking cows. Teenagers have said they heard us when they were running away from home. As one delinquent girl said to me, "Back home my mother listened to your broadcast religiously. She tried to get me to listen too, but I never wanted to. Then another girl and I ran away from home the night we graduated from high school. But a couple days later when we had reached another state, we went into a country restaurant and there you were on the radio again. But somehow, you sounded good this time!"

Others have said they listened to the broadcast when they were in the hospital. Still others listened to us while driving their taxis. And so it goes, unbelievable places (some unmentionable) where people were listening to our broadcast. And very few listeners are carrying a notepad and pencil with them. Consequently, they may hear something on the radio, but by the time they get to a place where they can write it down, they may have forgotten a few letters.

One day a lady wrote me, but she didn't get my name quite correct. So when my secretary handed me the letter, it was addressed to Dr. Narrow Head. Then with a smile, my secretary said, "At least the writer understands that you're a shrink!"

WHICH ONE ARE YOU?

For many years I was the only Narramore psychologist who had a doctor's degree, a national radio broadcast, was writing books, and speaking in person around the nation.

But as time went on, my nephew, Dr. Bruce Narramore, received his doctorate in psychology and became a well-known speaker and writer. He also served as Dean of the Rosemead School of Psychology. Nearly everywhere I went, someone would ask me "How's your son, Bruce?" Then I explained that Bruce was my brother's son rather than my son, although we worked closely together.

But the plot began to thicken when my own son, Kevin, received his PhD in psychology and became the author of *Personality on the Job* and also wrote numerous articles for our magazine, *Psychology for Living*. He also spoke to various groups. So I suppose many people became confused about which Narramore was which.

One Sunday at the close of a church worship service, I was coming out of church when a fellow who was a visitor that morning walked up and said, "Excuse me, but you're Dr. Narramore, aren't you?"

"Yes," I said.

Then he looked at me again and asked, "Well, which one are you? Are you the grandfather? Or the son? Or the nephew? Or the uncle?"

At that time I did not have a grandson, so I said, "Well I'm no one's grandfather, but I am a father, a son, and I'm also an uncle and a nephew."

He looked at me strangely, shook his head, and said, "Oh. Thank you very much."

On another occasion, my phone rang and I talked with a lady about a problem. Finally, rather abruptly, she asked, "Are you the *real* one, or are you one of the others?

I laughed and said, "We are all three real— Dr. Bruce, Dr. Kevin, and myself, but I happen to be Dr. Clyde!"

"Well," she said, "I just wanted to be sure!"

One time in Florida, an interesting thing happened when I was speaking at a conference. During an intermission, a young lady walked up and in a dynamic and effervescent manner said, "Oh, thank you so much for writing this book. It has helped to change my life." Then she handed me a copy of Bruce Narramore's book, *Help, I'm a Parent!*

"Will you please autograph it?" she asked. Then I explained that I had not written it, but that Bruce had. But by the look on her face I wondered if she had understood a word I said. Then she said, "You sound just like you do on the radio. Just autograph it on the first page."

So I signed it and as she turned to leave, she smiled and said, "Thank you again for writing it!"

I blinked my eyes and thought to myself, *Well, some people hear but don't listen!*

On another occasion I was walking across the lobby of a hotel in Cairo, Egypt. A couple was walking toward me, and just as we passed each other, the lady turned around and asked, "Excuse me, but is that you?"

I smiled and said, "I am I."

"But," she countered, "do you write books about problems?"

I told her that I did. Then she said, "You must be Dr. Narramore."

I asked her how she knew, and she said, "Last week I was in a Christian bookstore in Beirut, Lebanon, and I saw a book by you with your picture on the back cover."

As we went on our way my wife said, "If you ever did anything wrong you could never get away with it. They'd catch you in five minutes!"

A PREMONITION

November 22, 1963, was a day I'll never forget.

I was at home, shaving, getting ready to go the Los Angeles airport. I had seminars and meetings lined up for several days in Oregon and Washington. It would be a full schedule.

As I stood there, I began to think about President John F. Kennedy going to Dallas that day. As I thought about it, I began to wonder if he would be assassinated. He had lots of friends and many enemies. The more I thought about it, the more definitely it affixed itself to my mind. I thought about it several times as I drove to the airport. I couldn't seem to erase it from my thoughts.

I boarded the plane and flew to San Francisco for a brief stopover. Then we took off for Portland where I was to have a seminar in a couple of hours.

About halfway between San Francisco and Portland, our pilot made a serious announcement: "Ladies and gentlemen, we have just received very sad news. President Kennedy and Vice President Johnson were riding through the streets of Dallas when a gunman shot and killed Vice President Johnson and also slightly injured President Kennedy."

Everyone was shocked. Then I thought, *That isn't the way it came to me at home this morning while I was shaving. It was the president who was killed.*

A few minutes later our pilot came on the loudspeaker again: "Ladies and gentlemen, the first report we gave was incorrect. President Kennedy has been killed, and Vice President Johnson has been slightly injured." Everyone on the plane seemed stunned.

When we landed in Portland, a friend met me at the airport and took me directly to the auditorium where I was to speak. It was filled to capacity, but a strange quietness had settled over the audience. This was going to be a difficult time for me because I would need to talk with the people about the tragedy. But at the same time, it would be necessary to make the seminar lively and interesting. I had planned to use a great deal of humor during the seminar. How much would be appropriate?

I began by sharing what we had all just learned. I also read some suitable Scripture. Then we prayed.

Considering what had happened, we made it through the two-hour seminar very well. That evening I had another speaking engagement. For the next three days, I traveled by bus and car to other seminars. My schedule called for speaking every day and evening. Most of the attendees were born-again Christians, so that made it much easier. I was able to share God's word and bring His comfort.

Through the years, I have thought about that premonition. I'm certainly not a spooky person, and in fact, I'm quite the opposite. I don't know why God permitted me to know this would happen, but I feel that it was because I had such a tight schedule during the next several days and He wanted me to serve Him well. So He prepared me for the tragedy and made it possible for me to go ahead and minister in His name. In the lobbies of the hotels where I stayed, all eyes were glued to the television. Mournful music and the steady beat of drums permeated the airwaves.

But God was with us. As I look back, I realize that I had planned to serve the Lord in one way. But with His help, I was able to minister to people in additional ways—through understanding and comfort. And while ministering to others, God ministered to my own heart as well.

"And we know that all things work together for good to those who love God, to those who are the called according to His purpose" (Rom. 8:28).

ATTORNEY GENERAL'S TASK FORCE

One morning in 1983, I received a phone call from an attorney friend in Washington, DC. He was a long-time associate and advisor to President Ronald Reagan.

"The president and the Attorney General are concerned," he said, "about family violence. So the attorney general is bringing together a committee of nine men and women to study the problem and to make recommendations based upon their findings."

He then asked if I would serve on that committee.

"How long a period of time are we speaking of?" I asked.

"Perhaps a little less than a year," he replied.

He went on to say there would be no other psychologist or psychiatrist on the committee. He explained we would meet every month or so in various cities throughout United States to conduct hearings.

"There'll be no compensation," he said. "But of course, we will cover all travel and hotel expenses."

I agreed to serve, hoping the dates required for this assignment during the next year would not conflict with seminars we were conducting at the Narramore Christian Foundation headquarters in California.

The day came when all nine of us met in Washington, DC to get acquainted and to learn the specifics of the assignment. A federal marshal met me as I stepped off the plane in Washington and took me by car to the hotel where all of us would be staying.

The next morning, we met in a large room at the Justice Department, where we had refreshments and began to get acquainted with each other. One member of the committee, whose name was John Ashcroft, walked up to me and said, "Dr. Narramore, I've heard you on the radio for years, and we really appreciate your ministry."

He then identified himself as a Christian who was the Attorney General for the state of Missouri. "I'm running for office just now," he said, "and hope to be the next Governor of my state." He did become Governor, then a U. S. Senator. Even at that time, John Ashcroft was being mentioned as a possible future Vice President of the United States. Little did we realize that in 2001 he would be our new U. S. Attorney General.

I was certainly impressed with Ashcroft and the other members of the committee. They represented attorneys, social workers, law enforcement personnel, health specialists, and others from across the nation. One of the members was Ursula Meese, wife of the U. S. Attorney General. I came to really appreciate Ursula and her husband during our association the following year.

Our modus operandi was this: our committee would meet in a major city such as New York, Kansas City, Chicago, or Sacramento, and spend about three days there. Long before we arrived in the city for the hearings, a group of specialists would have met in that city and in surrounding states to collect and bring together research about family violence. This involved many individuals and organizations. For example, one of hundreds of research projects might have included a study of all children six years of age and under who had been admitted with broken bones to certain hospitals.

Then research would indicate the nature and cause of the fractures. Were they accidental? Or was there a person in the home who was bruising, beating, and breaking the bones of most of those children?

During the day of the hearings, the nine of us would sit at a long, curved table with high-back "judge-looking" chairs. In front of us was a smaller table where the presenter and one or two witnesses would sit and present their findings. During each presentation, our committee members asked questions that enabled us to better understand the facts being presented. A chief of police who was on our committee would typically raise questions about law enforcement. I, on the other hand, usually focused on questions which were of a psychological nature. In this way, each member brought his expertise to the hearings.

Then, at an appropriate time of the day, our committee of nine would review the findings. We also shared our insights and understanding together as we convened that night at the hotel where we were staying.

Needless to say, this was a tremendous learning experience for me, and I'm sure, for the other committee members. We were presented with summaries of these significant research studies, and before long, we saw patterns of family abuse, whether it took place in New York City; Laramie, Wyoming; Dalton, Georgia; Honolulu, Hawaii; Fairbanks, Alaska; or elsewhere. Several things stood out:

- I was impressed with the other members on the committee. All of them exhibited excellent backgrounds and knowledge, and it was a privilege to work with them.
- I was also impressed with specialists around the nation who appeared before us to present their research. They were exceptionally well-trained and professional in their presentations. It made me feel proud to be an American.
- Family violence, unfortunately, seemed to be in every nook and cranny of the nation. Women were abused. Children were abused. Husbands were abused. Abuse was widespread.
- Another observation that kept coming across to our committee was the relationship of the consumption of liquor and drugs as it related to family violence. It seemed that most cases of severe violence in the home were related to liquor and drugs.
- Our committee also learned that home violence is closely tied in with divorce and unhappy marriages. Almost every report

presented to us mentioned the father's absence, personality deficits, and the extreme unhappiness, abuse, and anger in that home.

♦ Another fact that impressed me was that family abuse was seldom connected with godly, Christian families. As the researchers reported to us, I often followed through with questions about the spirituality of the home, and they seldom reported abuse if the home was a godly one where Christ reigned. This I expected, inasmuch as the person who trusts Christ as his personal Savior is the benefactor of God's peace that passes all understanding.

♦ I'm sure that each member of our committee was struck by the fact that much violence is aimed at young children. The person who is the biggest and strongest is usually the one who inflicts violence on one who is younger, smaller, weaker, and unable to protect oneself. So the innocent victim is often the child or the wife.

♦ We also became acutely aware that the effects of violence tend to continue throughout a person's life. Unless it is resolved through professional or spiritual means, results of violence continue as long as a person lives, often bringing about devastating results, generation after generation. Violence begets violence. A parent who was abused as a child tends to abuse his spouse or children later on unless he gets professional help to resolve this issue.

♦ Another fact that was somewhat surprising had to do with a person's feeling of guilt. Over and over again we heard that people who are abused commonly blame themselves. This is especially true of children. Somehow they feel that if they had acted differently they would not have been beaten, whipped, molested, and mistreated. This attitude prevents a person from telling anyone about his abuse because he feels he probably caused the problem. This is also an important factor when considering the rehabilitation of people who have been severely abused.

♦ Still another factor that came before our committee day after day was the secrecy that surrounds abuse. Those who are inflicting abuse on others tend to live in an area where they can keep their dastardly deeds secret. They don't want neighbors who will suspect that something terribly wrong is going on next door. Also, abusers usually swear those they are abusing to secrecy and threaten the victim if he or she tells anyone. Sometimes a victim doesn't feel free to discuss the abusive treatment until he or she is in her forties or fifties, if ever.

Our committee met at various major cities throughout America where research on abuse had been conducted in adjoining states. For example, in a city such as Chicago, we entertained research and reports from specialists all the way from the Canadian border to the Mexican border. In this way, we became aware of what was going on in virtually every area of the United States.

Toward the termination of our study, which lasted a little over a year, we combined our findings and printed them in a book that was then distributed widely to senators, members of the House of Representatives, college presidents, heads of seminaries, law enforcement agencies, and others. This report made many observations as well as suggestions on how to reduce the problem of violence in the American family.

During that year, we had countless interesting experiences. One that I'll not forget took place in the Kansas City area. We had just completed the hearings in that city with people reporting from about nine states. Most of our committee members were then taken by a federal marshal in a van to the airport, where we would board planes and return home.

As we were riding to the airport, one of our committee members spoke up. "Dr. Narramore," she said, "every time we are introduced, they introduce you as a licensed Christian psychologist. I've been wondering what the difference is between a psychologist and a Christian psychologist."

While everyone listened, I explained the difference. I told them that in order to be a licensed psychologist, one had to have a bachelor's degree in psychology followed by a two-year master's degree in psychology. Then he must have a four- or five-year course of study to receive his doctorate. Before he completes his doctorate, he is required to have a year's internship working alongside a licensed psychologist or psychiatrist in a clinic or psychiatric ward of a hospital, or some other setting to experience working with people with significant problems. I explained that after a person received his doctorate in psychology, he was required to take another year of internship, followed by a state examination that included both oral and written segments. After passing both oral and written exams, he was then awarded a license to practice. Both Christian and non-Christian psychologists must have this training.

"But," I told them, "a Christian psychologist, in contrast to one who is not, recognizes his sinful nature and his need for a Savior. He believes that Christ, God's Son, died on the cross to pay the penalty of each person's sins. Further, he invites Christ into his life and at that moment a miracle takes place: God's Holy Spirit invades his very being and remains there, helping to change and mold him into all that God would have him to be. This brings much change, understanding, and power into his life."

At that point, our van was arriving at the airport. The lady who had asked the question, said, "That has happened to you, hasn't it?" and I humbly said, "Yes, although unworthy, it has been my experience."

A few minutes later, the members of our task force were flying in many directions to our various states and our own homes.

Speaking at the C.I.A.

SPECIAL PEOPLE IN SPECIAL PLACES

After speaking at the Pentagon in Washington, DC, I began to receive invitations to various governmental and educational institutions.

I've had the privilege of speaking several times at the historic U. S. military academy at West Point. This institution for the training of young men (and now women) as career officers in the United States Regular Army is located at West Point, New York. The setting is beautiful, near the Hudson river north of New York City.

The curriculum is both military and academic in nature, designed to provide a liberal education in the humanities, social sciences, natural and physical sciences, and military science. Many of our great military leaders have taken their training at West Point.

On one of my visits there, I was invited by an instructor at West Point to teach his class. When speaking to groups such as this, one becomes acutely aware of the possibility of an opportunity to enrich in some way the life of a future Dwight Eisenhower, Douglas McArthur, or Colin Powell.

After my lecture, I opened the class for questions and discussion. This was especially interesting. The cadets were sharp as could be, in top physical condition, and highly focused and motivated.

At another time, I had the privilege of holding an all-day seminar at the base for officers and their families. In fact, I was invited to stay overnight at the home of one of the high-ranking officers there. What a splendid Christian family!

A number of the young men came to me during these visits to talk about their concerns and issues. I had complete freedom, not only to discuss psychological topics, but also to share spiritual matters.

On other occasions, I especially enjoyed speaking at the U. S. Naval Academy at historic Annapolis, Maryland, a town founded by Puritans. This great naval academy is located on the Severn River near Chesapeake Bay about thirty-two miles northeast of Washington, DC. It is an accredited, federally controlled institution for the education and training of midshipmen to become officers in the U. S. navy or U. S. marine corps. While touring the campus, I was told that their buildings had sixteen miles of hallways!

There I had an opportunity to speak at a chapel service. I also held an evening seminar for officers and their families. Having been a naval officer myself, I could identify with them to some extent.

It was a special experience to have a meal with the midshipmen. The serving of food to the hundreds of hungry young men is a lesson in gastronomical precision!

Upon leaving the campus, I praised God for such a fine institution with high standards. And I was especially grateful that speakers were invited to the campus and that we could have a spiritual impact on those future leaders. This is in great contrast to most other nations.

One year during the month of May, I was invited to speak at the U. S. Army War College at Carlisle, Pennsylvania. This institution is for the academic study of war, especially in the fields of strategy, logistics, and the relation of military to foreign policy. The Army War College is the highest academic institution in the army's educational system. I was told that only top-flight military personnel take this training, which lasts the better part of a year.

It was a beautiful morning, and the spacious campus was highlighted with colorful azaleas and dogwoods. The meeting took place about eleven o'clock, after which we headed to a luncheon with the officers and their ladies.

First we were briefed in protocol instructing us as to where each of us would sit on the platform. Then one of the officials asked me to step into the office of the commandant in charge of the war college. He was a most friendly, cordial, and brilliant man.

"I want you to feel free, Dr. Narramore," he said, "to say anything you wish. Don't feel restricted. Also," he continued, "if you want to say anything of a spiritual nature, feel free to do so."

Then after a pause, he leaned forward in his chair and said, "I want to ask you a personal question. A few months ago, my wife and I had an unusual experience. We were invited to travel to Colorado to meet with Christian officers at a weekend retreat. While there, we heard people talk about being saved and being born again. We had never heard of this before. My wife is a nice lady, and I suppose you would say I'm fairly nice. In fact, my wife teaches a Sunday school class in a church not far from here. But even she had not heard about a person turning his heart to the Lord and being saved."

"What did you do about it?" I asked.

"Well," he said, "both of us confessed our sins and asked Christ to come into our lives and save us. Since then, life has been much more rewarding and we've never been happier. Now to come to the point," he continued, "when I'm walking across this campus or even driving my car, I tend to shoot up little prayers to God throughout the day." Then he slowly asked, "Is this normal?"

I smiled and said, "Yes, it's not only normal, it's desirable. Now that you're born again, you are God's child, and He is your heavenly Father. He wants to speak to you as you read your Bible, and He is eager to hear from you and me as we talk to Him in prayer. Since we have an open line to God, we can speak to Him any time all through the day or night. This is what God wants."

The time was getting short, so we shook hands and went into the hall, where I was introduced and spoke for forty-five minutes. I was building up to challenge the men and their wives to commit their lives to Christ toward the end of my presentation. When I asked for a show of hands, eleven indicated that they were surrendering their hearts to Jesus Christ!

As my associate and staff member, Dr. Ken Markley, and I left the campus to go to our next assignment, he said, "Wow, that was good."

I rejoiced in the fact that the superintendent of that strategic organization was alert to the spiritual as well as all other aspects of a person's life.

On another occasion I was invited to speak at the Central Intelligence Agency (CIA) near Washington, DC. The CIA's primary mission is to collect, evaluate, and disseminate foreign intelligence to assist the president and senior U. S. government policymakers in making decisions to national security.

As we approached the campus, a security guard questioned us and checked us out. In addition, we went through three additional checkpoints after we got inside the main building. Since I was to be the main speaker that day, and since many were invited to attend, I was certain they must have done a background check on my grandmother, great-grandmother, and anyone else connected with me. I had a good feeling as I realized that I was "squeaky clean." And I had evidently passed all their scrutiny!

As well as being photographed, every word I said was recorded. As I remember, my topic for the occasion was "Coping with Pressure." (I spoke from experience!)

I opened the session by thanking the personnel for their dedicated service to our wonderful country. Then I suggested we begin with a period of questions and answers. I realized this would give me an opportunity to better understand the people I was addressing, what their interests were, and how free they felt to express themselves.

By beginning this way, it also gave them an opportunity to get to know me, my point of view, and my method of thinking about problems. I knew if they enjoyed the question-and-answer period, they would attach more credence to what I would say in my main lecture.

We had a great session. At the end, I challenged people to surrender their lives to Christ. As I remember, twenty raised their hands, indicating they were inviting Jesus Christ into their lives.

After the meeting, we had a delightful lunch. As we left the campus, the security guard checked us out and sent us on our way. Dr. Markley and I praised God that again we had been able to minister to these special people in these special places!

DAD AND DAUGHTER AND SON

Two of the happiest days of our lives were when our son and daughter were born. Ruth and I thoroughly enjoyed raising our children. In fact, every day was special. With one son and one daughter, our foursome often traveled together.

But children grow up, and times change. Our daughter, Melodie, a few years older than her brother, Kevin, finished college first. She graduated from Biola University in southern California, then went on to receive her master's degree at California State University in Los Angeles. Next, she joined the faculty at Biola University as a drama and communications teacher. Later she became chair of the communication arts department at California Baptist University at Riverside, California. Kevin, with many interests, went on to receive his PhD in organizational psychology, with a minor in communications.

Since Melodie was a Christian dramatist and singer, and still single, we were often invited together to conferences. One was the National Sunday School Association Conference held each year at Cobo Hall in Detroit. Sunday school teachers, pastors, Christian educator directors, and others throughout the nation converged there for several days. I spoke at the general sessions to an audience of about ten thousand, then along with other speakers, conducted workshops.

Melodie sang and presented dramatic presentations of Women of the Bible at the general sessions, then later conducted workshops on the use of drama in the Sunday school and church and for Christian outreach.

These were wonderful days for us as we would board a plane in Los Angeles, fly to Detroit, and meet with each other throughout the day and evening during the convention. Along with scores of other Christian organizations, the Narramore Christian Foundation had a booth in the exhibition hall. So between sessions, Melodie and I would meet at the booth, where we had the privilege of greeting people.

One day, a humorous thing happened. Melodie was conducting a workshop on the use of drama in the Sunday school and church. In another room, I was scheduled to conduct a session on counseling. About ten minutes after my session had commenced, I noticed that about a hundred more people suddenly poured into the room.

Later, as Melodie and I were having lunch, I told her about it. She laughed and said, "I'll tell you, Dad, what happened. When I came to the platform in my room, I saw the place was packed, and many were even standing. So I asked them if any had been confused and had come to the wrong workshop. They probably had seen the name Narramore and took for granted that you would be the speaker. I explained I was your daughter and would be speaking on drama, and if people had come to my workshop by mistake, they could leave and go to your session. At that time, about half of the group got up and walked out!"

I asked her how she felt about that.

"Fine," she said. "I planned to give demonstrations of drama using people from the audience, and I still had over a hundred!"

We traveled together for several years, and I was becoming known as "Dr. Narramore—Melodie's father."

Several years later, our son, Kevin, and I had great experiences traveling together. He was both a speaker and a singer. But I learned something special on one trip. Dr. Ken Markley, psychologist and East Coast representative for the Narramore Christian Foundation, met Kevin and me at the Baltimore airport. At that time, Kevin was about twenty. For a couple of days we held meetings in Pennsylvania.

Late one Sunday afternoon, we arrived at the Hawthorne Gospel Tabernacle, a beautiful new church in New Jersey, not far from New York

City. We met with the assistant pastor and talked about arrangements for the evening service. Kevin was to sing a solo, and I was to speak.

Then came time for the service. The platform was very wide. Dr. Markley and I sat with the pastor on the extreme left side of the platform, and Kevin sat on the extreme right, near the director of music and the large grand piano.

After a few congregational hymns, Kevin sang a solo, which was well received. A little later, the offering was taken while a pianist played a special arrangement of a hymn. As he began to play, Dr. Markley sitting next to me, leaned over and asked, "Is that Kevin playing the piano solo?"

"Oh no, I don't think so," I replied. "He plays a little, but not that well. That guy who's playing is terrific."

"Well," Dr. Markley said again. "I'm sure it's Kevin."

So I looked again, and much to my amazement, it *was*.

After the service, the three of us got in our car and headed for Manhattan. "Kevin," I said, "you amazed me when you played that piano solo during the offering."

He smiled and said, "I knew I could do it so I told the director of music I could play the offertory if he would like, and he said that would be just fine. So I did."

When we returned to California, I told my wife about it. "Well," she said, "we both know he's gifted musically, and although he only plays snatches of this and that at home, he can do a lot more. And you know Kevin; he's the essence of creativity, and we've always encouraged this. So I don't suppose we should be surprised when he does these spontaneous things!"

Now, years later, we look back at those experiences as some of the most fun times of our lives. We praise God that as parents and daughter, or parents and son, we had the privilege of traveling and ministering together as adults. The growing-up days with our children were wonderful, but later, as adults ministering together was different, but just as precious!

Rosemead Commencement

CHAPTER FOURTEEN

ROSEMEAD GRADUATE SCHOOL OF PSYCHOLOGY

"Do you know of any Christian psychologist in our area?"
"Is there a Christian psychologist in our state?"
"Where is the nearest Christian psychologist to us?"
"Where do I have to go to see a Christian psychologist?"

From the time I became a licensed Christian psychologist in 1949, questions like these have been asked thousands of times. People have written letters wanting the name, address, and phone of a Christian psychologist near them. Our phones have rung countless times asking for the same information. In fact, people arriving in person at our home have rung the doorbell seeking help with their problems.

Unfortunately until recent years, there were few, if any, licensed Christian psychologists in America who had private practices.

AN UNMET NEED

Clearly, there was a great need. I also felt badly about evangelical Christians having to take their problems to unregenerate counselors who had no insight about spiritual matters and who often gave advice contrary to the plain teachings of the word of God. This really bothered me.

For years, I prayed earnestly that God would raise up someone who would create a Christian graduate school of psychology offering a doctor's degree, especially in counseling. I waited, but little happened.

Finally, it became evident that perhaps I was the one to do it. But my responsibilities with the Narramore Christian Foundation where we were offering help through radio, literature, phone, seminars, counseling clinic, and public meetings were already too heavy, let alone to take on the giant task of creating and funding a graduate school of psychology.

But about that time my nephew, Bruce Narramore, had received his doctorate in psychology, joined our staff, and was especially interested in the field of counseling. His strong academic background was just what we needed to form a team and create a graduate school. So we began to seriously consider future plans.

AN EARLY PERSPECTIVE

Recently I asked Bruce to look back about thirty or so years and give us his assessment of conditions when we launched the Rosemead Graduate School of Psychology. Here are his remarks:

> By the mid 1960s, we were receiving thousands of letters and phone calls from individuals and families throughout the United States and many countries around the world. These calls and letters described a variety of personal, family, and emotional problems. Many came from pastors and missionaries. And thousands of them asked if we knew of any Christian psychologists in their area to whom they could go for counseling.
>
> Unfortunately, at that time there were very few fully trained and licensed Christian clinical psychologists in America. We had only a handful of referrals. In city after city across the United States, we could not find even one committed Christian psychologist who was licensed for clinical practice. Frequently, people drove many miles to our counseling center in southern California, and many even flew in and lived in nearby motels for several weeks in order to receive intensive Christian counseling. I had one client, a businessman from San Francisco, for example, who flew to Los Angeles nearly every week for over a year because he could not find a Christian psychologist in his area. Other times, entire families would travel to our Narramore Christian Foundation headquarters in Southern California.

Initially, we tried to fill this critical need by starting small clinics in Phoenix, Arizona, and Harrisburg, Pennsylvania. But we faced the same dilemma. We could not find enough fully trained Christian psychologists to adequately staff these clinics. We also began an internship program for psychologists with their master's or doctoral degrees, but we could only train a few each year.

So the board of directors of the Narramore Christian Foundation authorized us to do a feasibility study about the possibility of founding a Christian graduate school of psychology. At that time there were no free-standing schools of psychology apart from a larger educational institution. So we had to consult with our regional accrediting agency to see if they would potentially accredit this specialized type of Christian training program. And we had to determine if we could find sufficient faculty to develop a strong doctoral training program for Christians in clinical psychology.

We knew there were hundreds, if not thousands, of Christian students who would love to receive their graduate training in psychology in a Christian school. But we needed faculty to help them integrate their Christian faith and biblical understanding with their psychological studies and their eventual counseling ministries.

When we concluded our feasibility study, it seemed clear that God wanted us to move ahead. So in 1968, the directors of the NCF voted unanimously to found the Rosemead Graduate School of Psychology. Our goal was to equip outstanding Christian young men and women who viewed their calling to become Christian psychologists as sacred a call as to the ministry or to the mission field. These young people would be committed to meeting the deepest spiritual and emotional needs of their counselees. They would participate in Jesus' ministry of "binding up the broken hearted, proclaiming freedom for captives, and comforting those who mourn" (Isa. 61:1–3).

—Bruce Narramore

ACCEPTING THE CHALLENGE

So with Bruce as our dean, we took the first big step to create such a graduate school. In the beginning it was a part of the Narramore Christian Foundation. Shortly after, we made it a separate institution. The board suggested we name it after Bruce and me. But we felt it would be better to name it "Rosemead" after the city where the graduate school and the Narramore Christian Foundation were located in southern California.

It was easy to determine the emphasis of the school. Since there was a great need for Christian psychologists who would become counselors, we focused the school in that direction.

For several years previously, the foundation had conducted a large Christian counseling center. People from throughout the world came for help. Little by little, we attracted psychologists and counselors for our counseling center staff, and we provided in-house professional training for them. Consequently, we knew what we wanted to include in a doctoral curriculum.

The foundation's staff of psychologists became the nucleus of the graduate school faculty. We gradually added to this until we had an adequate faculty and staff.

As we started the school, I felt that the most difficult part would probably be the assembling of an adequate faculty. I knew we would have plenty of students because there were so few places where they could receive Christ-centered psychological training. In our first class in 1970, we were looking for twelve or fourteen students who would work at a master's or doctoral level. But before long, nearly thirteen hundred had written, inquiring about entering the program! From these, we carefully selected thirteen men and women. Some had been deans or faculty members of colleges.

In developing the curriculum, we studied the offerings of various universities throughout America. This research, combined with our own practical experience, enabled us to develop what we felt was a desirable curriculum. One basic requirement of all students was the taking of fifty hours of private counseling for themselves. This would enable them to resolve any issues of their own before they began counseling others. Some students were required to take as many as one hundred hours of private counseling. This also enabled them to participate in the actual process of therapy. Later on, they could call upon this experience as they received their doctorates and established counseling practices of their own.

Since we had very few funds, we could not offer scholarships. However, we were able to attract outstanding graduate students. It wasn't long until we realized that one of our greatest challenges was to raise money for such a school.

In order to achieve accreditation by the Western Association of Schools and Colleges, we were required to meet certain standards regarding library, faculty, student recruitment, curriculum, administration, finances, and other factors.

Each month, we wrote a mailing list of Christians asking them to help us get the school financed. But few people were interested, and fewer still would send gifts. So we struggled week by week and month by month as the United States was experiencing a recession. But we kept going while maintaining high ethical, spiritual, and academic standards. Finally, we reached the end of the first year, and we were still afloat. In fact, God had blessed in many ways. Even though we were definitely under-financed, we had made great progress, and we knew the Lord was with us.

Each September, we enrolled additional students in our five-year program. And at the end of our fourth year, we awarded our first doctorates.

Success

Fortunately, we were able to erect the Reese education building on the campus of the Narramore Christian Foundation, and students were impressed as they arrived to begin their four or five years of intensive, full-time training. The enthusiasm among the students and faculty was great.

The graduate school continued to grow, with outstanding students entering each year. Finally, by the end of the sixth year, we had received full accreditation from the Western Association of Schools and Colleges. *We had provided the Christian world with a top-rate graduate school of psychology plus a number of graduates with their doctor's degree.*

At the end of the seventh year, we made the decision to transfer the school from the campus of the Narramore Christian Foundation to Biola University, which was about twenty-five miles away in La Mirada, California. In time, Dr. Bruce Narramore, who had been our co-founder and dean, continued with the Rosemead School of Psychology and helped to develop it with a national reputation.

By the year 2001, about seven hundred men and women had received their doctor's degree. By 2010, nearly one thousand had received their doctorates and were serving the Lord throughout the nation, as well as in some foreign countries.

To gain just a glimpse of the impact of the graduates, you can estimate that if six hundred of them are conducting a minimum of four counseling sessions a day, then twenty-four hundred counseling hours are provided every day!

But of course, that is just a part of the picture. Some are teaching in Christian colleges, others are working with missionaries overseas. Some are writing books and holding seminars, and others are establishing counseling centers in America and in foreign countries.

We are continually receiving letters and phone calls from people who have received counseling from our graduates. We are deeply grateful for God's leading in establishing and developing this tremendous ministry. It was a major step forward in the Christian psychology movement, both in the United States and around the world!

"The enemy of
my enemy's
my friend"

— Chinese proverb

CHAPTER FIFTEEN

AROUND THE WORLD

10/26/12

One day I received a letter from a radio listener in Pennsylvania who wrote, "My husband and I have always wanted to go to the Holy Land, and we'd like to go with you and your wife. Could you take a tour group?"

We laughed about the suggestion. But after some reflection, Ruth said, "Maybe that would be a good idea." So in time we announced the tour, took a group to the Holy Land, Egypt, and Europe, and we've conducted tours for twenty-one years. In addition, at times I traveled overseas alone, or with another person, ministering to missionaries.

We continued these two-week tours, usually held in August. They did not conflict with the seminars we conducted at our California headquarters during June, July, and the first part of August. Our son and daughter accompanied us until they became young adults and had other responsibilities. These trips gave our family of four a splendid opportunity to serve the Lord together and enjoy sights around the world. We worked as a team to make the tour as delightful as possible.

Our groups of forty or fifty came from many states and ranged in age from six to eighty-plus. After arriving in a country, we traveled by bus, train, plane, or ship. Our family was kept busy hour by hour attending to the needs of the group. But it was still a two-week vacation, and we were ministering!

Almost every evening, we had a special devotional hour for our group in the hotel. In each nation, we invited local missionaries or other Christian leaders to speak, sing, and answer questions about their country. I usually concluded with a question and answer period about everyday problems.

Our devotions in Fiji were rather different. Upon arriving at our hotel in the afternoon, I phoned a local evangelical pastor and invited him to speak at our evening devotion to be held outside, near the swimming pool. A few hours later, he showed up with his entire choir! All the men were decked out with traditional knee-length skirts, ties, and bare feet! What music and testimonies! Upon returning to the United States, many tour members would say, "We enjoyed the countries we visited, but the highlights of the tour were the evening devotionals and discussion of problems."

We became quite well acquainted with many missionary organizations and overseas ministries. In addition, I held evening and Sunday meetings in some of the foreign countries we visited. We even had a few surprise meetings. For example, one day in Queensland, New Zealand, a lady from our tour group said, "Today I was at the hairdresser and I read in the newspaper that you were speaking at one of the local churches tonight."

That was a surprise to me, so I phoned the pastor of the church to get clarification. "Yes," he said, "I heard you were coming, so I wrote you a letter inviting you to speak tonight. But I guess you didn't get the letter."

I laughed and said, "That's perfectly okay. I'll be there, along with my wife and family and forty-five tour members!" We had a packed church and a great time. They seemed to especially enjoy the discussion period when I handled everyday problems. After the meeting several local people said, "We've never had discussions like we did tonight."

So the annual tours and visits overseas that began in the late 1950s were not only vacations; they were times of ministry and Christian fellowship. Christian psychology was being introduced in numerous foreign countries.

ALASKA

Young psychologists often ask, "As a pioneer Christian psychologist, how did you get started? Where did you go? Who invited you? What did you speak about? Who paid your way? How well were you received?"

The following report, which I wrote upon returning from a ministry trip in April 1960, will answer some of these questions. As to finances, I borrowed money and paid my own way. I never asked for a fee, but some groups gave an offering.

Who invited me? People who had read my books, heard our broadcast, or who had heard me speak in New Hampshire, Alabama, California, Montana, or some other place. When making plans to go to a place like Alaska, I suggested I would like to speak to many different groups, such as business people, teenagers, parents, pastors, educators, and church congregations. As a pioneer Christian psychologist, I wanted to reach as many segments of a community as possible.

Who attended the meetings? Those who wanted to learn and enrich their lives. Some came out of curiosity. Since most people have problems, many came looking for solutions.

Acceptance? It has been excellent. I've tried to be positive and respectful, not talking against others or other organizations. And I have always tried to honor and adhere to the word of God. In addition, *I have sought to explain what little I knew in clear, understandable terms. And since I believed in what I was saying, I probably came across in a somewhat definite manner.* One more factor: practicality. On the ranch where I was raised, we always said, "If it doesn't work, forget it." So I've endeavored to say things that were practical and applied to everyday living.

Here, then, is a report I wrote in 1960 upon returning from my five-day trip to Alaska:

————

ALASKA REPORT: 1960

Recently I flew to Alaska for a number of speaking engagements. The trip was thrilling, and I would like to give you some of my impressions.

> My friend, Ben Weiss, an educator, and I flew directly by jet from Los Angeles to Seattle and then stayed overnight in a motel near the airport. The next morning, we flew non-stop from Seattle to Anchorage. The flight required (two time zones away) our watches read two hours earlier. The plane followed the shoreline much of the time. Below, we could see the mighty Canadian Rockies in all their pristine brilliance. On our return trip, the sun was setting and the thousands of snowy peaks were now tinted with a rosy hue. Their jagged points reminded me of delicate pink frosting on an enormous cake.
>
> The spring temperature ranged from about forty-five to sixty-five degrees. The days were long because the sun rose

about 3:00 AM and set about 9:30 PM. Spring had finally come, and every bud on the white birches was about to burst.

I stayed in the home of a gracious Christian man, Earl Stenejem. As I looked out from the front window of his home, Mt. McKinley, that great Arctic giant and the highest mountain in North America demanded our attention, even though it was nearly one hundred miles away!

Homesteading is still a reality in Alaska. By clearing twenty acres, sowing seed, building a home, and living on a homestead for seven consecutive months out of one year (three years for non-veterans), a person can have 160 acres of land.

One night after a meeting, I attended a homesteading party where about twenty-five Christian friends gathered in a private home to send off a couple to their wilderness homestead. Everyone was dressed in homestead clothes and brought homestead gifts. This man and his wife and three children were eager to go into the "bush" to claim their homestead. It was thrilling to hear this couple tell about their experiences and anticipation as they left their comfortable home to pioneer in this wild and rugged country.

One of the ladies led a song she had just composed. She called it, "Alaska, My Homeland." I can imagine the feelings of each one as he began to sing this "homeland" song. Some were thrilled to be pioneers. Others probably felt ashamed that they had been so homesick for the "lower forty-eight." Some undoubtedly held resentment at finding themselves in such an isolated, cold place. What an unusual and heartwarming experience!

During my stay in Anchorage, I had the privilege of speaking ten times. The first meeting was at a Christian Business Men's Committee (CBMC) banquet the evening I arrived. My topic was "Why A Psychologist Believes the Bible." We had blessed fellowship with these seventy Christian men and women and their unsaved guests. A number gave their hearts to Christ.

The next day, I was taken to a local church, where we held a citywide seminar for Sunday school teachers and Christian workers. Here I spoke on "The Psychology of Teaching." The long, sunny days allowed activity well into the night. Besides the parents and teachers, I was impressed with the teenagers who were attending the meeting. Most of them had been born elsewhere but had lived in Alaska for several years. Now, it was their home.

The next day we held a memorable morning meeting twelve miles south of Anchorage on the Seward highway. Rev. Rex Lindquist, pastor of the Chapel by the Sea, was our gracious host. The pastors and missionaries came from as far as 150 miles. They said it was the largest gathering of evangelical leaders in the history of Alaska. It was a humbling experience to speak and reason with these outstanding men and women of God. I shared with them for over an hour on the topic, "The Marks of a Mature Minister." After a short break, my educator friend, Mr. Ben Weiss, challenged the men with their responsibility for individual soul-winning.

While the group had refreshments, I returned to Anchorage for an afternoon television interview. The TV host emphasized the fact that I was a Christian psychologist, and that it was his first experience meeting such a person! During this interview, I had the opportunity to witness for Christ and to deal with everyday problems as people phoned in.

That night I spoke again at another citywide meeting for parents and business people. My focus was on the Christian home. Interestingly, the teenage crowd was there again. They seemed to be following me around. We soon became good friends. I chatted with a number of them after the service and asked them if they would like to go back to the "lower forty-eight" to live. Their answer was an emphatic, "No! There's so much to do here and we have such a good time that we would never want to leave Alaska. There's not much to do in the lower forty-eight!"

The next day, we held an all-day seminar on professional counseling. I discussed the "Do's and Don'ts of Counseling." This was attended by nearly one hundred pastors, health care professionals, and educators—most of whom traveled quite a distance to get there. I was impressed with the outstanding caliber of those who came for this day of professional growth.

That night I had an opportunity to speak at an auditorium in Anchorage for a citywide meeting of teenagers. I brought a message on "What Makes a Good Marriage," followed by a period of questions and answers. A large number of these young people made decisions to trust Christ and for life dedication. The service, under the leadership of Lloyd Mattson, a pastor in Anchorage, was quite similar to Saturday night Youth for Christ rallies held in the lower forty-eight states. I was impressed with the excellent music the young people presented.

Pastors and other Christian leaders in Alaska face many difficulties: a mobile population, a short-term clergy, lack of finances, cold, dark winters, and few established ministries. Anchorage desperately needs a full-time Christian radio station that can reach thousands who live in remote areas.

On Sunday, my last day there, I spoke at three churches—two in the morning and one at night. Again, we saw a number of decisions for Christ. I always encourage people to be saved because it is the most important decision in life, and it affects a person for all eternity.

At the conclusion of all these meetings, I was about "spoken out." I left immediately for the airport, boarded a plane, and started the flight back to California. As we flew through the sky, my heart was filled with praise and gratitude for the privilege of serving the King of kings, for many opportunities to enter the lives of people, and for the unusual blessings I had received in Alaska, our largest wilderness state.

I might add that as I flew home, I tried not to focus on having to be at work the next morning at nine o'clock!

————————

Now, years later, I'll try to summarize what I think happened during this five-day trip to Alaska:

1. A number of people surrendered their lives to Christ.
2. Christians were encouraged in their walk with the Lord. It is one thing for a pastor to talk about spiritual matters, but in some ways it is different when a licensed psychologist does the same thing. One is not more important than the other, but I believe the impact may be different.
3. People undoubtedly received insights and solutions for their lives.
4. Some expanded their understanding of the causes of problems. At all meetings, I stressed the physiological causes, spiritual causes, and the emotional (psychological) causes.
5. People were encouraged to seek professional counseling when needed. *Many people need counseling but hesitate to get it, so they respond to a definite nudge.*
6. Listeners were encouraged to attend psychological seminars where they could gain more insight and understanding.

> *Many people need counseling but hesitate to get it, so they respond to a definite nudge.*

We knew this happened in Alaska because many people from that area later came to the Narramore Christian Foundation in southern California to attend one-week or two-week seminars.

7. People were encouraged to read printed materials of a psychological nature to better understand themselves and others.

8. Young people were challenged to consider psychology as a profession.

This trip to Alaska and its impact was similar to hundreds of other trips I've made to most of the larger population areas in the United States and many foreign countries. Through radio, literature, cassettes, videos, books, booklets, the *Psychology for Living* magazine, seminars, television appearances, telephone counseling, and in-person speaking engagements, people began to understand the benefits of Christian psychological services. These paved the way for other Christian psychologists in the future to minister more readily and easily.

GREECE AND THE GREEK ISLANDS

"You really ought to see the Greek Islands," friends kept telling us. So one summer our family conducted a tour for Christians to Greece, including the nearby islands. We were looking forward to seeing Mars Hill in Athens where Paul spoke and many other places.

You can imagine our excitement when we boarded the beautiful liner in Athens to begin our cruise. As we stepped aboard the ship, we were handed a specially printed greeting that read:

> Sail away! Break away! Forget all your worries, and the ship will carry you through the temples of magic and mystery— to the islands of freedom! Days of pleasure, fun, relaxation, and excitement! Savor the beauty. Experience enchantment, eloquence, and paradise! You'll breathe tantalizing scents. It's a true escape to Eden! Days that can change your outlook on life!

My, I thought, *this is going to do more for me than I expected! I should have come years ago!*

So we sailed from one interesting island to the other. Our first port of call was the picturesque island of Mykenos with its unique windmills and white houses on the hillsides. Next, we docked at the Island of Rhodes with its enormous and famous Colossus.

From there we sailed to the ruins of Ephesus, a historic city in Turkey. When Paul preached at Ephesus, it was evidently an extraordinary, thriving seaport. But today it is in ruins, with pieces of white marble, broken columns, and sections of ancient walls here and there. But stranger yet is the fact that the ruins of Ephesus are located five miles from the sea. When we asked our Turkish guide what happened, he said, "Through the years, the winds, rains, and rivers have brought silt down from the nearby mountains, pushing the sea back several miles from Ephesus."

Consequently, today the remains of the once-lively port city are lying silent on a dusty, dry plain. As our family looked at the desolate ruins of Ephesus and later Corinth, this Scripture came to mind: "Heaven and earth will pass away, but My words will by no means pass away" (Matt. 24:35).

As we took our final look at the ruins, I wondered how many people listened to Paul and trusted Christ as their Savior. Or did they go their own way and walk into a terrible eternity without the Lord?

We went on to the Island of Patmos where John was exiled and where he was inspired of God to write the book of Revelation. As I stood on the hill where John lived, I was impressed by the sea. Everywhere I looked I saw the sea. I was reminded of the tremendous portion of Scripture, Revelation 21:1, "And I saw a new heaven and a new earth, for the first heaven and the first earth had passed away. Also, there was no more sea."

No more sea! There on the Island of Patmos, I saw how beautiful the sea was, especially as I looked at the coast. But I'm sure John thought about and longed for other things when he looked out across the water. To him the sea was a jail. He was exiled, and the sea stood between him and freedom. The sea kept him from seeing family and longtime friends. It prevented him from going city to city and preaching! And the sea, no doubt, kept him from receiving many gifts and messages from his family. Little wonder, then, that in Revelation 21:1 when John was talking about the future new heaven and new earth, he finished by telling us, "Also, there was no more sea!"

On we sailed to other destinations. Often the ports were too small to accommodate our large ship, so we anchored a short distance off shore, then climbed into small boats to taxi back and forth between our ship and the island. It was indeed a super cruise, and our Christian group of forty-five provided wonderful fellowship.

One evening, Ruth and I were invited to dine at the captain's table. The captain's wife was sitting next to Ruth. Since we were from the Narramore *Christian* Foundation, she wanted to know how to become a Christian. We shared fully, and she was most interested. She was spending much of her life sailing around the Greek islands and many other places. But she felt that surely there must be more to life. She was hungry for something that satisfied. So we were happy to share Christ with her and give her appropriate Christian literature. She also attended a special on-ship Sunday morning service, which I conducted.

Everyone needs a new nature. The Bible says, "The heart is deceitful above all things, and desperately wicked; who can know it?" (Jer. 17:9). Without this new nature, even the good things we do are unacceptable to Him. Isaiah 64:6 reminds us, "All our righteousnesses are like filthy rags."

We can do nothing on our own to change our sinful nature. "For by grace you have been saved through faith, and that not of yourselves; it is the gift of God, not of works, lest anyone should boast" (Eph. 2:8–9). No matter how much we work and struggle, our efforts to change our natures are in vain. Salvation is an "inside job" that can only be done by our Creator.

The solution to so much of man's need is readily available, but people don't realize it. Not long ago, a radio talk host from a secular radio station phoned me for an interview about a person with a particular problem. After discussing it for a few minutes, the talk show host asked, "Dr. Narramore, just what *does* this guy need?"

I think I shocked him when I answered, "He needs a new nature."

He stuttered for a moment and said, "A new nature?"

"That's right," I said, "that would really fix him up."

"But," he asked, "how can a person get a new nature?" Then I had the opportunity to explain to him (and all who were listening) that Christ came into the world to save sinners, and that this could be accomplished as a person admits his sinful condition, asks Christ to come into his heart, and then the Holy Spirit enters and gives that person a new nature.

An Old Testament prophet illustrated the truth this way: "Can the Ethiopian change his skin or the leopard its spots? Then may you also do good who are accustomed to do evil" (Jer. 13:23). It simply is not possible for anyone to eliminate the roots of his own sinful nature.

OFF TO CHINA

In 1982, we took our first tour to China. There were about forty in our group. Since Ruth had been raised her early years in China (daughter of missionaries), we were eager to go there even though it was Communist.

We flew from Los Angeles to Hong Kong, where we stayed for a few days before flying on to mainland China. In addition to seeing that area, we were eager to follow God's admonition to "go into all the world and preach the gospel." We realized that God's command to spread the gospel would not always be easy. We knew Satan would sometimes put up tough roadblocks.

In Hong Kong, we met with a Christian organization that provided us with scores of Chinese language Bibles, Bible study books, and small hymnals. We explained to our tour members that among other things, local Chinese Christians had made private arrangements for us to give these books to a Christian believer in one or two of the major cities in China. About two-thirds of our group said they would be happy to take eight or ten books and scatter them in their luggage. No one, of course, was required to do so.

CLEARING CUSTOMS

Our port of entry was Shanghai. We knew that when we entered customs they would ask questions and have us fill out forms. We also felt certain they would require us to open our suitcases so they could examine them carefully. We realized that if the books were found, they could be taken. That was okay with us. But we also knew that when we left China, they were supposedly obliged to return the books to us.

As we stepped off of the plane at the Shanghai airport, I suggested that Ruth be the first of our group to walk into customs, because she still remembered some Chinese, which was actually her first language.

We approached a long counter, where an English-speaking officer questioned us. Ruth told him how happy she was to be "back home again," since she had lived there as a child and Chinese was her first language. "It's a privilege to be back to the country of my sister's birth and burial," Ruth continued. "My sister died here and is buried in China, so this country is very special to me."

The customs officer seemed impressed and nodded thoughtfully. He gave us forms to fill out and then told us to move on to the next counter. There each of us was asked to identify his own luggage. This second officer and his assistant lifted the suitcases onto the counter, and we were sure they would open and rummage through our belongings. But before doing so, he lined us up and asked if anyone had any special friend or acquaintance in China. I spoke up and said, "Yes, I have a friend here, and in fact, every member of our group has a friend here." He blinked his eyes, raised his eyebrows in surprise, and asked, "Who is your friend?"

"You, sir," I replied. "You are our friend."

He processed that thought for a second, smiled warmly, clasped his hands, and bowed courteously as he repeated, "Thank you, thank you!"

Then he told us to take our (unopened) bags and put them on the bus, and go. We all breathed a sigh of relief as we loaded our uninspected luggage and boarded the bus. Then we burst out singing, "Praise God from Whom All Blessings Flow!" We headed for a hotel a few miles away that had been chosen for us. Indeed, we had arrived safely in China, and we felt that our luggage would probably not be examined until we left the country.

Two Communist guides (women in their thirties) were assigned to our tour group. Their job was to stay with us day and night for two weeks until we left China. We weren't sure whether they were English-speaking "guides" or "spies"—probably both!

A Witness to All Nations

Early morning on the first day of our visit to China, Ruth and I, our son and daughter, Kevin and Melodie, left the group and went to a pre-arranged restaurant located in another hotel, a few miles from where our tour group was staying. There we had an early morning breakfast.

According to arrangements made in Hong Kong, a Chinese Christian man would meet us at this restaurant, identify himself, go with us to our hotel, and take many of our Bible books. The password involved our looking at a map and his asking a certain question.

After an hour of slowly eating our breakfast, sipping our coffee, and looking at a map, no one had shown up. We talked quietly and tried not to be noticed. Finally, our son Kevin said, "Dad, what do you think we should do?"

"Well," I said, "in a Communist country like this, I suppose a hundred different things could slow down our contact who is to meet us. But I think we ought to stay a little longer and see if he shows up."

"But Dad," Melodie said, "I can't eat any more, and what if they begin to wonder why four Americans are taking two hours to eat breakfast? Beside, why would we spend two hours looking at a map?"

Since we were two parents and two children sitting together, I felt we looked fairly normal and innocent, so we sat a little longer fingering our cups and nibbling on the toast. Finally, we gave up, left and returned to our hotel, where we thought about a second contact since the first didn't work out.

A few days later in another city we arranged for a Britisher to come to our hotel room and very discretely take many of the Bibles and other books. That was a clever accomplishment in itself! We made sure that he left our room when the two lady guides across the hall from us were evidently taking showers. We could hear the water running! So our British contact with two suitcases left unnoticed and took the Bibles and books to a secret Bible study group that distributed them to others. After he left, we discovered we still had a few more Bibles and study books.

SOWING THE SEMINARY

A day or two later, our group was taken by bus to Nanjing to visit a government seminary. It was actually supervised by the Communists, and only a limited number of students were attending. Our tour group sat quietly in the room adjacent to the library listening to the guide talk about that particular seminary we were visiting. Most of our tour members became a little restless listening to this Communist drone on and on about their great country. We were eager to get moving because our pockets were loaded with Chinese Bibles and study books, and we wanted to sow them around the seminary, if possible.

Finally, the lecture ended, and the lady guide asked us to follow her as she led us through the library, which was neither well-lit nor well-stocked. Fortunately, she walked in front of the group, so we strung out some distance behind her in single file and quietly scattered our books among the stacks of shelves. In a real sense, we were sowing the seminary with Bibles!

A half-hour later, we were on the bus traveling to other parts of the city while other tour groups came to the seminary and took their turn getting the "library lecture."

I have often wondered when the students discovered the books—and what they thought. Perhaps some of the born-again students began to find them and told other Christian students about their great spiritual gold mine!

LET'S ALL SING!

While touring China, we usually traveled as a group in one bus. Our two federal guides were omnipresent. They stuck with us throughout China.

These ladies spoke English fairly well and had eagle eyes. They seemed to observe everything we were doing. Each morning as we rode along in the bus, our tour members took Narramore Christian Foundation song sheets out of their pockets and sang gospel songs. The purpose in bringing the song sheets was to have songs we could sing and enjoy as we traveled along and viewed the countryside.

Little did we realize, however, that God would do something else. By the third or fourth day, our two lady "spies" were reading their song sheets and learning the songs quite well. And as we traveled, I took the microphone and asked the group what song they would like to sing next. One of the guides called out, "Let's sing number fourteen, 'For God So Loved the World.'"

"Oh," I said, "that's a good one. You pick the best ones, don't you?" So we sang her choice. Then the other guide asked for number twenty-three, "Since Jesus Came into My Heart." And they sang along with us. My, what singing day after day as we rode from one community to another. We could have been called the "Hymn and Rice Choral Group."

By the time we left China, these two ladies memorized every song on our song sheets! Undoubtedly, this was one of the best ways to plant the gospel solidly into their hearts and minds. During the last few days of traveling together, I privately explained to each of the ladies how she could be saved. They were both receptive and grateful. I realized that as bright as they were and speaking English so well, they would have special influence wherever they were employed in the years ahead.

Now, whenever I read the Scripture, "Go into all the world and preach the Gospel to every creature," I think of how God allowed us to do just that—including our two guide gals!

Our two tours to China were four years apart. During that intervening time, we saw many changes. Hotels were new, and uniformed soldiers were less visible. People had discarded their black and white clothes and were wearing brighter colors. But beneath it all was a communistic government.

SEARCHING FOR HER CHILDHOOD ROOTS

On our second tour, Ruth and our son, Kevin, left the tour group in Beijing for one day and traveled about ninety miles southeast to Tientsin (now Tianjin) where Ruth grew up as a young child. The effort to get there was almost unbelievable. But they finally made it. An entire book could be written about this visit. In short, they did make it to the very spot where she had spent her early childhood. She also talked with a Chinese woman who had known Ruth's parents!

"This was one of the most memorable days of my life," Ruth said.

Hotel Hostess

At the Great Wall Hotel in Beijing, we became acquainted with a lovely lady who was the assistant manager of the hotel. During our three-day stay, we gave her a copy of our magazine, *Psychology for Living*, of which Ruth was the editor. She was overjoyed to get it, so we asked if she would like us to send it to her each month. "Oh yes," she said, "that would be so nice." Then she added, "But I have no way to pay for it."

We assured her that our magazine would be a gift. As soon as we arrived back in California, we made arrangements for her to receive it and other pieces of our literature each month. Of course, we never knew if she ever received it because of the Communist rules and regulations. But at Christmas we received a letter from her saying she was receiving the magazine each month. Then she added, "I have now invited Christ into my heart!" Needless to say, that thrilled our hearts and made our Christmas very special!

How He Get There?

One day our tour group was taken to the beautiful, large Sun Yat Sen memorial park that contained a number of unusual statues and gardens. The local Chinese there, like elsewhere, were quiet and polite. But after being around them for a few minutes, one or more would approach one of us and ask, "Can I speak English with you?" They all wanted to learn English.

This very thing happened to me that day at the park. I was standing alone near one of the statues when a young man about thirty walked up and asked if he could speak English with me. I told him that would be fine. We then began to talk, and I tried to speak slowly and distinctly. After becoming "friends," I told him I would like to ask him a question.

"Oh yes," he replied.

So I asked, "Do you believe there is a God?"

This new Communist friend looked rather puzzled, then pointing a finger toward the sky, asked, "Up in sky?"

"Yes," I said, "the God who is up in heaven. Do you believe He is there?"

Then in a sad voice, he haltingly said, "I do—not—know. You believe?"

I smiled and said, "Yes, I'm sure there is a God."

"How you be sure?" he asked.

"Because," I said, pointing to my chest, "He lives in my heart."

Then the inquiring young man asked the million-dollar question, "How He get there?"

So I quietly and slowly explained how a person comes to know Christ and experiences eternal salvation. I also placed a Chinese tract in his hand.

He was eager to learn, and he seemed to accept what I said. When we left, I thought, *I've visited many parks around the world, but this is one of the best times I've ever had in one!*

CHINA IMPRESSIONS

There's no place in all the world like China. You may have traveled far and wide, but until you've seen China, you have much yet to experience!

The country is so big—great plains, rivers, mountain ranges, valleys, coast lines, and deserts. And it seems that no matter how far you go in China, you've just begun to see it all.

Another lasting impression is the multitudes of people. Wall to wall people! Whether you travel by bus or train, you keep thinking you'll eventually get out of town into the country. But people seem to be everywhere. Oh yes, there are unending rice fields and farms of tea plants, but there are still people.

As you see the people go about their work or play, you get the feeling that they are doing things in groups, that they are comfortable working together as a unit. Whether the delicate-looking little children are holding hands, walking outside school, or adults working on ice cream-colored carpets, they seem to function as teams.

When you visit China, you are almost overwhelmed by the numbers of bicycles swarming down the streets in unison. They look like a quiet, polite army of two-wheelers obeying the traffic lights and police. When you see them parked—all black and all the same—you wonder how a person can ever find his or her own bike!

Compared to people in other parts of the world, the Chinese seem rather quiet and self-controlled. You get the feeling, too, that they have an inner sense of politeness. Their soft speaking, nodding of heads, and polite bowing, come across as "politer and smoother!"

A must see in China is the Great Wall. The first time we were there, not many people were looking around, but a few years later, a visit to the Great Wall was something like a commercialized county fair. In certain areas where visitors are allowed to see, feel, and walk the wall, little stands and booths are crowded together to sell almost every souvenir imaginable. If you can think it, they've probably made it and have it ready for you to buy and carry home in your suitcase!

No visit to China would be complete without seeing the Great Wall. Our tour groups saw it at a point not many miles from Beijing. More than two thousand years old, the Great Wall is one of the true wonders of the world, its engineering feat rarely matched in the twenty-two centuries since its construction began. It stretches forty-five hundred miles, from the mountains of Korea to the Gobi Desert.

Why such a wall? It was first built to protect the ancient Chinese empire from the marauding tribes out of the north. But today it is something more—a boon to trade and prosperity and of course a symbol of Chinese ingenuity, persistence, and available manpower.

The Great Wall is actually a series of walls built and rebuilt by different dynasties over one thousand years. Now that all nations have airplanes, the Great Wall really does no good, even though thousands were killed and entombed in the wall while it was being constructed. However, it is an emblem of China's development throughout the centuries.

The top of the wall is wide enough for eight or ten people to walk abreast as it snakes its way up and down the mountains and valleys. When you look at it, you wonder what could have been accomplished if these same millions of builders had been serving the Lord and helping mankind.

Another incredible sight is located in Xian, China. It is an underground army of terra cotta life-size, uniformed men and life-size horses!

When you walk into this enormous viewing building, you are almost shocked to look down a few feet lower than where you are standing to see this mind-boggling sight. Row after row of men and horses just as if they were alive! *This can't be*, you say to yourself.

What's more, the government is still digging (since the 1970s) and unearthing more regiments of soldiers and horses. One wonders when it will end!

These soldiers are carefully uniformed, and the horses are decked out with all their harness and trappings. Each man's face is different from the others. It is said that each soldier represents a man who was living at the time the terra cottas were formed.

In the early spring of 1974, a number of peasants accidentally discovered some ancient bronze weapons and pieces of the broken terra cotta armored warrior while digging a well. This was at the northern foot of Mt. Lishan, thirty-five km from Xian, the famous cultural city in China's history.

No one ever expected that this accidental discovery would prove to be one of the most significant modern archeological finds. But this added greater understanding to China's history and at the same time unfolded a unique and majestic spectacle for the world to see. It's a most spectacular and important place to visit. Just think, a twenty-two hundred-year old colored terra cotta army of more than eight thousand soldiers and horses. Some say that the purpose of these soldiers and horses was to "protect" the tomb of the first Qin Emperor. Our guide explained it this way: the Emperor believed that he would go to heaven and that his army would go with him.

What a futile preparation for heaven! Little did he know God's truth as given in the Bible: "Eye has not seen, nor ear heard, nor have entered into the heart of man the things which God has prepared for those who love Him" (1 Cor. 2:9).

SCANDINAVIA

Is Scandinavia (specially Norway) the most beautiful place on earth? Some travelers would feel so, or at least a runner up, especially during the summer.

The great, curving expanse of Norway occupies the western half of the Scandinavian peninsula. Off its spectacular western coast lies the Norwegian Sea and the Atlantic Ocean, and to the north is the Barents Sea and the Arctic. With an area of about 155,000 square miles, Norway is roughly the size of California. It is long and mountainous, with more than 30 percent of its land covered by forests, rivers, and lakes. In the summer, the fjords, inlets, and countryside defy description.

Bergen on the west coast of Norway is called "The City between Seven Mountains," and the gateway to the fjords. Beautiful Bergen with its picturesque churches and mountains was the home of Edvard Grieg, Norway's greatest composer.

ONE TOO MANY

On one occasion, we were leaving England and boarding the plane to fly north to Norway with our tour group of seventy-one. We had settled down and fastened our seat belts when a flight attendant came to my seat and said, "Sir, you have one too many in your group."

"One too many?" I asked. "What do you mean?"

"Well," he continued, "we have seats for seventy. This teenage boy (who was last in line) will have to stay here. As I said before," he persisted, "we only have seating for seventy."

"But the plane accommodates more than seventy," I said. "Furthermore, we bought and paid for seventy-one seats on this flight, and the last thing I would do is fly on ahead and leave one teenage boy behind. He's never been overseas, and he knows almost nothing about traveling."

Then the flight attendant brought another airline employee who tried to assure me that they would try to get this young boy on another plane sometime soon.

"Oh no," I said, "we have a tight schedule and we'll be flying from city to city, staying at various hotels and taking daily sightseeing tours. Who knows when this boy might catch up with us—if ever."

Then I said, "You'll take all of us, or none at all. If you don't arrange to have a seat for him, we'll all get off the plane together. The choice is yours. You can have seventy-one paying passengers, or you can have none."

I suppose I sounded determined, so a few minutes later a supervisor came to my seat and said, "We'll make room for the boy."

"All right," I said, although I was still rather peeved about their wanting to leave our teenage boy behind. So the plane took off, and we all stayed together for the entire tour.

A few months after returning to the United States, the mother of the teenager came to see me. "You remember," she said, "when they tried to put our son off the plane. But you insisted that we all fly together or all get off the plane together!"

We talked about it for awhile, and then she said something very interesting. "Our son has talked about that a number of times since we've come home. He said that particular episode meant a lot to him. He had been a Christian for awhile, but was definitely not committed to the Lord as he should have been. But when he saw you, another Christian, sticking up for him the way you did, it caused him to want to be a strong believer also. And we've noticed a real interest in spiritual things ever since!"

Later, as I thought about it, I was reminded of the Scripture, Proverbs 18:24: "... There is a friend who sticks closer than a brother." We need to help each other. But regardless, our Savior will never leave us nor forsake us.

SAILING BY TRAIN

One day while traveling in Scandinavia, our tour group had a really unusual experience. In reviewing our itinerary and the map, I was puzzled. They had scheduled us to go by train from one city to another. But the only way to get there was over a large body of water. There was no way to go around. We were crossing from Copenhagen, Denmark, to Stockholm, Sweden. But a portion of the North Sea separated the two.

How would we get across the sea? The mystery began to unfold as our train approached the body of water. As we got very near, we could see an enormous ferry with a rail track running down the middle from one end to the other. So our train edged up to the ferry, locked onto its rails, and ran right onto the giant ferry! When every car of the train was safely on, the ferry pulled away from the shore and sailed out on the sea. As we ferried across, we got off the train, walked around, and then got back on. When we arrived on the other side, the train rolled onto the permanent tracks, and away we went across the countryside!

Our tour members were all impressed because regardless of the depth of our spirituality, not one of us had ever walked on water or crossed a sea by train!

WHY DID HE RESIGN?

The date was August 8, 1974, and Ruth and I were leading a tour group in Sweden. In fact, we were staying at a hotel in Stockholm. When we went downstairs for breakfast, the newspaper headlines screamed at us,

"President Nixon Resigns!" Immediately strangers began walking up to us asking, "Why is President Nixon resigning?"

When we took a few minutes to try to explain the Watergate situation, they said, "So what? That's not so bad! European leaders do that all the time. We liked him; we thought he was one of the best presidents you've had!" President Nixon was well liked there, and they felt his leaving office must have been the result of "bad politics"!

Our group was embarrassed and saddened. But as we prayed in our evening devotions, God gave us peace. We knew that God was in charge and that He knew the beginning from the end. Praise God, our future is in His hands!

Maasai Tribesmen

AFRICA

Africa—an enormous continent of many nations, climates, natural resources, and interesting people. I've had the privilege of taking several trips there and visiting certain countries from the fabulous pyramids of Cairo, Egypt, in the north, to historic Capetown in the south.

On one occasion, our tour group of fifty took the famous Blue Train overnight from Johannesburg down to Capetown at the southern tip of

South Africa. What an unusual experience as we saw villages, mountains, and farmland pass by our windows!

There were also times when I went to Africa without a tour group. I traveled from one major population area to another, holding five-day seminars for missionaries from different denominations and mission organizations. The purpose was to bring encouragement and instruction to these remarkable, dedicated servants of God. I'm sure I learned more than they did.

Many overseas missionaries live in groups near a village or a larger population area. For example, several mission organizations may occupy several acres called their "center" or "headquarters" or "compound." They often use a common dining room, meeting room, auditorium, and clinic. Located at or near that center may be a publishing facility or an academy for MKs. They may also maintain a hospital open to the public. The missionaries can then spend all or part time working at the center, or they may carry on their work some miles away, returning at intervals to the headquarters. An individual missionary may handle several jobs, such as teaching, nursing, writing, cooking, mechanics, practicing medicine, translating, accounting, preaching, and the like. I'm always impressed with the remarkable talents found within any group of missionaries. If it needs to be done, they can usually do it!

In the early years, various groups inviting me to work with them overseas provided room and board. But it was up to me to finance the trip, including the round-trip airfare. I gladly borrowed the money and then repaid it as the months went by. I realized that a ministry by a Christian psychologist was new to them, and if they benefited from it, they would undoubtedly begin to budget money to invite me or some other Christian psychologist in the future. In other words, I was more or less a pioneer icebreaker!

When I was first asked to go overseas to hold seminars, the invitations were not very specific. When I corresponded with them about what they wanted me to do, they never seemed to know just what to say. So I often suggested a daily schedule including lectures, discussions, private counseling sessions, and small group counseling. I also suggested topics. I found that the administrators usually wanted to discuss personnel and other private matters as well. After serving at a place for a couple of days, additional needs became evident. Occasionally I was asked to meet individually with a native pastor or a person in his church. All of this added up to twelve-hour days and a host of new experiences for me. When I returned to my home in California, I felt deeply grateful to the Lord for making this unique ministry possible. We were plowing new ground.

DIVINE APPOINTMENT

Sometimes we made travel plans and focused our attention on places to visit. But after returning home, we realized that some of the most memorable experiences occurred either on our way to or from our destinations.

On one occasion I was invited by several mission organizations to come to Africa to hold seminars for groups of missionaries. My wife's brother, Dr. Gordon Elliott, a pastor and Bible teacher, was to be my traveling companion and the devotional leader. I planned to meet Gordon (who was flying up from Florida) at the Kennedy airport in New York City. So far, all was okay.

I arrived in New York from Los Angeles and went to the departure gate of the airlines where I was to meet Gordon, and we were to board the plane together. But after a few minutes I received a phone call from his wife saying his plane left Florida late, so he would be arriving late in New York. I immediately began praying. Fortunately, we still had about thirty minutes before our plane was to take off.

Soon everyone had boarded the plane except my tardy brother-in-law and myself. I walked up to the airline employee in charge at the gate and told him I was waiting for my brother-in-law and hoped the plane wouldn't leave before he arrived.

After speaking to him for a minute he said, "You know, Sir, your voice is very familiar."

"Oh, is that so?" I said.

Looking intently at me he said, "You sound just like a man I hear every day on the radio. He's a psychologist, and he talks about problems."

I smiled and asked, "Do you like him?"

"Oh yes," he chuckled, "and I'm wondering if you're that very person— Dr. Narramore?"

"I'm guilty," I said.

Then he leaned a little closer over the counter and said, "I have a serious problem that I'd like to ask you about."

Two thoughts flashed through my mind. One was that I'd like to help him if possible, and the second was that the longer we talked about his problem, the more time it would give Gordon to arrive.

He took a moment to share his problem. Then I cut through the red tape and said, "There are a number of factors we should consider about your problem. But since the time has already come for this plane to take off, and I'll have to board it without my brother-in-law, I'll make a basic observation."

"Sure," he said. "What is that?"

"It seems clear to me," I said, "that your greatest need is a new nature."

"A new nature?" he said. "How do you get that?"

Then I explained briefly that he was a sinner and needed a Savior that God had given His Son, Jesus Christ, to die on the cross for him, and that if he would confess his sins and invite Him into his heart, God's Holy Spirit would invade his very being and give him a new nature. I mentioned several important changes that would come as a result and shared 2 Corinthians 5:17, "Therefore, if anyone is in Christ, he is a new creation; old things have passed away; behold, all things have become new."

I put a Scripture booklet into his hands and said, "I suggest you take this and read it several times. When you feel the Lord tugging at your heart, surrender your life to Him. Write me when this happens. My address is at the end of the booklet."

He thanked me, and as I turned, I saw Gordon running full blast toward our gate carrying a little briefcase. We jumped on the plane, took the two remaining seats, and in a few minutes we were slicing the sky toward Africa!

"Where are your clothes?" I asked Gordon.

"I haven't the least idea," he said. "They put my suitcase on the conveyor belt in Jacksonville, so I suppose it's somewhere between Florida and New York. But at least I'm here!"

We arrived in Nigeria, and since we were somewhat similar in size, I shared my clothing with Gordon until his suitcase caught up with him about ten days later.

After several weeks of intensive and wonderful ministry with groups of missionaries in major population areas of Nigeria, Kenya, and South Africa, we flew back to the States. About three weeks later, I received a letter from New York City. And wouldn't you know—it was from the airline employee with whom I had talked at the departure gate just as we left for Africa!

"You'll be interested to know," he wrote, "that last week while driving through the Lincoln Tunnel here in New York City, I gave my heart to Christ. When I prayed to God, I wasn't able to close my eyes because I was driving and didn't want to cause an accident. But let me assure you, I was genuinely saved. I got me a Bible, and I'm now reading the New Testament. I'm amazed at how much I understand as I go from one chapter to the next. Thank you for sharing with me at the airport!"

As time went by, I looked at the photos we had taken in Africa. I recounted with joy the many places where we had ministered, the people we had helped, and the great blessings which had come to us. But undoubtedly, one of the highlights of that particular trip was the divine appointment at the Kennedy International Airport in New York City that resulted in rejoicing in heaven. "I say to you that likewise there will be more joy in heaven over one sinner who repents than over ninety-nine just persons who need no repentance" (Luke 15:7).

LOST: BRIDE AND CHICKENS

Professional counselors hear many things from their clients—some happy, some sad, some amazing, and some tragic. And about the time you think you've heard everything, you get a real surprise.

That's what happened to me one day on another visit to Africa. A missionary friend in Nairobi asked me if I could make time for a counseling session with a young local pastor. I made arrangements to do so, and I found it to be a heartwarming but sad experience.

The local pastor, twenty-five years of age, had been shepherding a small church for only about a year. I found him to be a devoted, consecrated man of God with a great love for the Lord and a strong desire to help others. He had an eighth-grade education but in recent years had studied the Bible at a local Bible institute.

About two years earlier, he had met a girl who became a Christian and who was now attending his church. He said they had fallen in love and decided to get married. The girl's parents had died, and she was now, at seventeen, living with her uncle and aunt, neither of whom knew the Lord.

According to local customs, the pastor had agreed to pay the girl's uncle for the privilege of marrying his niece. So the pastor met several times with the uncle, and they agreed on a price for his future bride—one cow, six goats, and twenty chickens. That was practically all the pastor owned. As the wedding date approached, the pastor gave the cow, goats, and chickens to the uncle, who took them and sold them and kept the money. But about two weeks before the upcoming wedding, the uncle told his niece that she could not marry the pastor. In fact, he set his foot down and insisted that she cancel her plans. The pastor asked the girl what was wrong. She said her uncle had talked to her several times and had insisted that she would never be happy married to a pastor. When she asked why, he kept saying that preachers were no fun and she would never be happy married to a man like that.

Finally, the girl, with no place to go, acquiesced to her uncle's demands and broke off their engagement and plans for marriage.

"I'm broken-hearted," he said as he began to cry during our counseling session. "I love her so much, but now she refuses to marry me. What makes it worse," he continued, "is that I gave all I had for my intended wife. Now I don't know what to do. It will take me years to acquire all of those animals again. I'll have to leave the ministry, get a job, and drop my church."

This dejected young pastor then said, "I hate that man—my girlfriend's uncle—for doing this terrible thing! I thought he was honest, but now I know he's a thief. He doesn't even let his niece come to my church anymore, and he forbids me to see her. He says he'll kill me if I try to see her."

This was the first time I'd ever been called upon to counsel anyone about losing both his bride and his bride price. But my heart went out to this dear man, and I sympathized with his loss. I suggested we talk about it fully.

We had one more counseling session, and I asked him about other losses he had experienced. Tragically, he had lost his mother when he was nine years old, and his father had died when he was only twelve. I helped him understand the relationship between these two traumatic losses and the current loss of his intended bride and bride price. *Our adult feelings of fear, guilt, anger, and insecurity are often tied in with childhood trauma.* Such insight and discussion helps to bring relief.

> *Our adult feelings of fear, guilt, anger and insecurity are often tied in with childhood trauma.*

"I was too embarrassed," he said, "to share it with anyone. But when my missionary friend told me you were visiting my village, I wanted to see you. Thank you so much for coming to Africa."

During our counseling sessions we discussed several basic principles:

- God knows and understands exactly what we are going through. Others may not, but He does. He even knows when a little sparrow falls.

- In our personal relationships, it's not our responsibility to get even with those who have done us wrong. That is God's prerogative. He clearly says in His Word, "Beloved, do not avenge yourselves, but rather give place to wrath; for it is written, 'Vengeance is Mine, I will repay,' says the Lord" (Rom. 12:19). *We don't have to punish people who have caused us grief and pain. We can leave that up to the Lord.* We have happier and more productive things to do.

> *We don't have to punish people who have caused us grief and pain. We can leave that up to the Lord.*

- God loves us unreservedly, and as our Friend, He wants the best for us. He's on our side. When we draw close to Him, He draws close to us.

- God can take our disappointments and turn them into future happiness. While going through a period of grief or disappointment we may feel that we will never recover. But He who holds the future in His hands can turn that disappointment into a future greater good.

As I look back on those brief counseling sessions, I trust the young pastor will incorporate those truths in his life so he can benefit personally in the years ahead and so he can also share them with others with whom he counsels!

DID YOU HEAR ANYTHING?

I had been ministering in Africa to a group of thirty-five missionaries for several days when the director said to me privately, "We have a missionary lady on our staff who works out in the bush. She's a pleasant person, well-trained, and has a real heart for the people. But lately it has come to my attention that she has told another missionary she's hearing voices which the second missionary doesn't believe actually exist. I haven't talked with her about it because it has just come to my attention, and I've found no appropriate opportunity to bring up the subject. If you could see her for a session or two, perhaps you could give me some guidance."

The next day this lady and I happened to be talking in the fellowship hall. I suggested we get together and that I would like to know more about her work. She was glad to do so. We met the following morning in a quiet place just off the fellowship hall. She was about fifty years of age, tall, slender, nice appearing, and well-dressed. She was intelligent and talked with ease about her work.

During our first session, I detected nothing out of the ordinary. Not having psychological tests to give her, I was dependent on observation and what she told me. At the end of the first session, I suggested we get together again.

"I'd be glad to," she said. "It's great to find someone who will listen. Even back in the States in my own church, which supports me, not many people seem to be really interested in my work here. I guess they all have their own agendas."

The next day as we talked, I said, "I suppose that working out in the bush as you do, among people who have very different customs, you have a few experiences that are hard for even your missionary friends to understand."

"That's right," she said. "Every once in awhile I have those experiences."

"For example?" I asked.

"Well," she said, "one has to do with things I hear. I usually don't mention them because I don't think anyone will believe me. But when I do, they seem to turn a deaf ear."

I asked her more about what she was hearing, including who said them, the circumstances, and what the subjects were. Before long, she shared a great deal and I saw that she *was* having the problem of hearing non-existent voices.

At that point, I remembered something one of my psychology professors at Columbia University had said to us, "People's ears play more tricks on them than do their eyes or other senses. Hearing voices, for example, is not terribly uncommon."

Near the end of our last counseling session, she asked if there was any way she could come to the Narramore Christian Foundation in California and have some counseling.

"Oh, yes," I assured her. "We conduct seminars throughout the year for various groups. Three of these two-week seminars are for ministers and missionaries, and you would surely be welcome."

"Would I have to tell anyone here at the headquarters why I was coming?" she asked.

I laughed and said, "Just tell them you're going to take one of the most wonderful professional seminars in all the world at the Narramore Christian Foundation in California!"

She laughed and said, "That sounds good to me!"

The next day, I told the director I had talked with the missionary.

"Do you think," he asked, "that she really hears voices?"

"She thinks she does," I said. "They are real to her at this point."

"Can she be helped?" he asked.

"Yes, I believe so," I answered. "She has so much good going for her. If she can have professional diagnosis and therapy, I believe her problem will subside and probably disappear."

Several months later, this fine lady arrived at our California campus for an intensive two-week seminar for ministers and missionaries. During that time, we assigned her to one of our most capable psychologists for daily therapy. Then she decided to stay on after the seminar and have daily counseling for a couple of months.

> It's true that God usually uses people to help other people.

About a year later, she wrote me from the mission field saying she no longer had the problem and that she was deeply grateful for the help she had received.

Praise God that He gives people gifts, including counseling, and then enables them to receive professional training to skillfully work through problems to a good solution! It's true that God usually uses people to help other people.

DOUBLE DELIGHT

It's amazing to consider all that God provides for our enjoyment. Just think of the myriad of colors we enjoy each day. Sometimes we see something that is so beautiful and impressive that it defies description. But it is satisfying, and we incorporate it into our total life experience.

This happened to me one Sunday morning in Africa. I had ministered non-stop at a mission headquarters, spending nearly every waking hour with missionaries we were serving there. One day the director said, "I have you scheduled to speak at a local national church on Sunday. It's a wonderful congregation of native people, and I'm sure you'll enjoy it."

That sounded exciting to me, and I was happy to go to his church, which was located about fifteen miles from the headquarters. When we arrived, I found it was crowded with about two hundred people. The pastor invited me to sit with him on the platform about six feet behind the pulpit.

Just before he introduced me, a special musical number was announced. As the pianist began to play softly, six tall, slender ladies walked gracefully to the platform. Each one wore a bright cloth headdress, which towered about one foot above her head. They were elegant as they walked up to the front. The first lady wore a rich gold turban. The next wore one of chartreuse. The third had a Christmas-red headdress, and the fourth wore orange. The next lady had a white turban, and the sixth wore one of vivid blue.

Their long dresses cascaded to the floor, each one contrasting in color with her headdress. *I've never seen anything like these tall, elegant women,* I thought. With their headdresses, they must have stood about six-and-a-half or seven feet tall, and their long, slender robes made them appear even taller and more queenly.

But that was only half of the spectacle. As the six ladies turned and faced the audience, I saw that each one had a baby strapped on her back, facing the pastor and me! The infants were dressed in their finest as well! The women sextet sang an arrangement of a lovely old hymn.

Can you imagine the pastor and me sitting there with grandstand seats just about four feet behind them! The mothers didn't know it, but as they sang I began to wink at the six babies, who soon responded with big smiles.

The only name I could think of for this experience was "Double Delight!"

I do praise God for the many wonderful experiences He gives us. Even though we cannot fully describe them, they are rich in our minds, and those memories delight our hearts all of our lives!

THIS IS HOW I'M SUPPOSED TO DO IT

The Bible says, "…of making many books there is no end…" (Eccles. 12:13). And that's so true. Being an author myself, I plead guilty to being a part of this phenomenon.

Each time I've written a book, I've wished for more time to spend on it. I'm sure that would improve it considerably. But on the other hand, if a person had nothing to do but sit around and write books, I presume few people would be interested in what he had to say.

Most Christian book writers are extremely busy people whose best writings seem to ooze out of their daily ministries. I was once asked if I could tell while writing a book if it would likely become a best seller. I had to admit that I really never knew how well it would be received. In fact, if an author has a heavy daily work load and is writing "on the side," on weekends and at night, he gets tired and sometimes begins to wonder if it will be the world's best or the world's worst!

I got a little feedback on one of my books while ministering in Kenya, Africa. A local missionary organization had arranged for me to speak at two services at a large church near downtown Nairobi. It was packed out twice. Our family was asked to bring special music. Our son, Kevin, was still quite young, so my wife Ruth, and our daughter, Melodie, joined me in a trio. A few minutes later, the pastor introduced me as the "preacher of the morning." He began by telling the audience a little about my ministry.

"This man," the pastor said, "writes books about counseling and problems. In fact, when I was studying at the seminary, I was required to read two of his books on counseling. One was called *The Psychology of Counseling*, and the other was *Encyclopedia of Psychological Problems*." The pastor continued, "Everything I know about counseling, I learned from Dr. Narramore."

Much to my surprise, he began to tell the people what he had learned about counseling. "When I counsel with you," he explained, "this is what I'm supposed to do." Then he listed ten or twelve points.

I was amazed how he remembered them all. Then he took a few steps away from the pulpit, and raising his left hand, he said, "However, there are several things I'm *not* supposed to do when I counsel with you, and I want to tell you what they are." At that point he started his list of what he had learned *not* to do when counseling.

Returning to the pulpit, he said with a loud, clear voice, "Now, dear brothers and sisters, you have it. When you come to me for counseling, you can check me out to see if I'm doing it right."

Then turning to me with both hands outstretched, he said, "Dr. Narramore, welcome to our pulpit and thank you for teaching me everything I know about counseling!"

I stood there, thinking back to the times I wrote those books. You see, both of them took a lot of work, and I wrote them at a time when the demands of the Narramore Christian Foundation were extremely heavy. So I was really burdened as I wrote each one. I remember so well putting on the finishing chapters of each, wondering if it would be my best or my worst. But that morning at the church in Nairobi, I was humbled to know that this pastor, and perhaps many others like him around the world, was blessed and strengthened in his ministry because of my faltering attempts at writing. I'll always cherish that service!

Come See the Lions!

When you think of Africa, you probably conjure up visions of herds of giant elephants, towering giraffes, and magnificent lions. Ever since I was a child, I had wanted to go to Africa and see the wild animals in their natural settings. Finally this dream came true. In fact, I've been able to go to several wild game reserves during our trips to Africa.

On this particular occasion, my brother-in-law, Gordon Elliott, was with me. We left Nairobi, Kenya, and traveled by car for about an hour to the Great Rift Valley. There two local missionaries joined us. Both of these men had worked for years in that area and knew the country well. The four of us then got in our automobile and headed south through the Rift Valley; our destination was a wild game reserve. The dirt road was relatively level, and since there was no rain, we made pretty good time. After traveling along on this flat, dusty plain highlighted by an occasional lonely, skinny tree, we saw a small herd of cattle meandering down the road heading toward us with a couple of men herding them. When we got about one hundred yards from them, the herdsmen stepped into the middle of the road and stopped us. They were tall, slender, dark-skinned Masai tribesmen, probably in their late teens or early twenties, each wearing a cloth over one shoulder and waist. They had reddish-brown paint on their shaven heads, as well as on most of their bodies. Each carried a round, wooden spear about five feet long.

We got out of the car to see what was up. Fortunately, one of the missionaries knew their language, so they exchanged a few words. The missionary turned to me and said, "They want sweets." Unfortunately, we didn't have any candy with us, but we gave them a few sticks of gum. As they accepted it, the second missionary quietly snapped a picture of us. The two Masai tribesmen then continued on with their little herd of cattle. We got back into the car and drove ahead as the missionaries told us a lot about the Masai, their customs, and recent successful efforts to evangelize them.

Late in the afternoon, we arrived at a lodge where we were to have our meals. Situated in a clearing, it was a rough-hewn log building with a rustic dining room. Just before we had supper, one of the lodge's armed guides took us to our room in a separate cabin about sixty yards from the main building.

"Be very careful walking between your cabin and the lodge," warned the guard. "Wild animals around here could sneak up and kill you in a minute." Then he added, "Two weeks ago, one of the young women who worked here at the lodge wasn't careful. She walked out of her cabin without looking around, and about halfway to the lodge, a lion jumped her and tore her to pieces."

Needless to say, that was all the warning we needed! We returned to the lodge where a few people were eating. After supper, our guide, carrying his rifle, said, "Perhaps I should go back to your cabin with you now, and I hope you can get some sleep. I'll be ringing a bell and knocking at your door at three o'clock in the morning. Then I'll drive you out to where we'll likely see the migration of herds of wild animals."

So with a gun and a large lantern in hand, the guide walked us back to our cabin. The next morning at three o'clock, a bell began to ring, followed by a knock on our door. We jumped up, got dressed, crawled into his van, and then headed out to see what we could find. In some places, there were little dirt roads. But mostly, it was just open space. After about an hour, we came to a place where we saw enormous numbers of wild animals migrating. Herds of elephants lumbered along, knocking down and chewing on small trees, then trodding ahead. As groups of giraffes came to a tree, they nibbled from the treetop and then continued on their way. Enormous herds of water buffalo passed by only a short distance from where we were sitting in the van. We also saw countless springbok—swift and graceful southern African gazelles noted for their habit of springing lightly and suddenly into the air. They looked like they were ready to outrun anything.

After this astonishing parade of thousands of wild animals, our guide said, "Well, I think most of them are gone." So we drove out to a few other locations where our guide thought we might see lions. But no such luck.

At about 8:00 AM, we headed back to the lodge and sat down for a big, hearty breakfast. About halfway through, our native guide with his rifle ran in excitedly saying, "*Come see the lions!* They're out there, and I think we'll be able to see them! There's been a kill, so they're nearby!"

We jumped into the van again and headed out to find the big cats. A few miles later, we neared a small, dry ravine with scrubby trees growing alongside. Our guide told us he thought they'd be there. But unfortunately, we couldn't find them, so we headed in another direction where we saw buzzards circling in the air.

"Oh," he said, "lots of buzzards. Now I think we'll find them."

We drove a little further and saw the carcass of a water buffalo. "Now," said our guide, "I'm sure we can find the lions, because after a kill, they go to a nearby ravine to rest under the scrubby trees. They'll be absolutely gorged."

Sure enough, a few minutes later we drove within about twelve feet of two giant lions resting in the shade of some small shaggy trees.

"I doubt if they'll move," the guide said, "because they're so full."

I quietly asked the guide, "Can I roll down this window enough to get my camera lens through it to get their picture?"

"Sure," he said. "This is a good time, and the sun's just right."

As I rolled down the window, a thought crossed my mind. A few months before, I had asked my college-aged son (who was good at photography) something about my camera. "Dad," he said, "I don't think you have the background in photography to use this camera. It's complex."

So with that encouragement, I thought, *I'll show him who's the best photographer!* I took a picture of the lions, turned a gadget on my camera a little to the left and took more, then to the right to be sure I got a good one. When I got home and had the pictures developed, several were perfect! I had one developed into a beautiful, big enlargement, and then I had it framed. And guess where I hung it—in my son's room!

As we left the lions, the guide explained several things. He said perhaps one of the reasons why there was no young lion with these two adults was because they may have starved to death. When lions come in for a kill, the male lion eats first. Then he backs off a bit and the female lion eats. But the cubs don't get anything unless there's something left over.

It reminded me of the Bible verse, "The young lions lack and suffer hunger; but those who seek the Lord shall not lack any good thing" (Ps. 34:10).

We left the game reserve that afternoon and started our drive to Nairobi, where we ministered for a few days.

Since then, I've often thought of when I was a boy on an Arizona ranch looking at pictures of lions in Africa, wishing I could see some in their natural habitat. That dream came true and proved to be more than I had imagined!

SAFELY IN THE ARK

Today, archeologists worldwide are studying the effects of the Great Flood. Genesis—the first book of the Bible—tells about this flood and how God directed Noah to build an ark for himself, his family, and for animals. This ark has inspired men through the ages to write songs, books, poetry, and stories, and to risk their lives in expeditions.

One of the most interesting depictions of the ark is in Kenya, Africa. With our son and daughter and a group of forty tourists, we went to this world-famous Ark to see the wild animals.

We were excited as we drove up to this park where we parked our bus. Then each of us took one small, overnight case and walked across a drawbridge to the entrance of a huge building designed like, and named after, Noah's Ark. We didn't know what we were going to see, but world travelers had told us it was terrific. As we stepped inside, we found it was much like a rustic hotel with three decks from which numerous balconies and lounges provided superb vantage points for viewing wild game. In addition, a ground-level bunker gave excellent photographic opportunities and took us closer to the animals than we believed possible. We were assigned to our rather small, rustic rooms. Each person was handed folders that described the activities.

The Ark had sixty cabin-styled rooms with private bathrooms and shower. All were comfortably furnished with a view of the forest waterholes. Set in the heart of the Aberdare National Park, this unique game lodge overlooks a floodlit waterhole and salt lick that attracts a host of wildlife—elephant, rhino, leopard, bushbuck, and occasionally an elusive bongo or giant forest hog.

Shortly after arriving, we were called to the main dining room where our tour group had our evening meal. After dinner while still seated around the tables, a staff member explained what we were in for. We were told we would see scores of wild animals and possibly some of the world's most unique and rare ones.

We hurried to these vantage points and saw a flat water area outside the ark about the size of a football field. There we viewed shallow watering holes where wild beasts came to drink. Even the officials never knew just which animals would come out of the nearby woods to drink at the watering holes. The area was lit by floodlights mounted on tall poles and on the Ark.

There were four main game-viewing areas from which to observe the ever-present wildlife. A ground-level slit in the cement wall made it possible to come almost face to face with some inquisitive animals.

We were told the signals for viewing the rare animals would sound anytime during the night. One short buzz in our room meant a fairly rare animal could be seen at the watering hole. Two brief ones would indicate a rarer animal was approaching the area, and three buzzes meant that a very rare animal had arrived and that we should make every effort to jump out of bed and run to a viewing area.

Just before sundown, we began our wild-animal watching. It was thrilling to see each one, or each small group of elephants, zebras, giraffes, and herds of water buffalo. There was also a variety of smaller animals, such as bushbuck that came out of the forest, looked around, and then cautiously approached the watering holes.

Boy, were we excited! We didn't want to go to bed because we might miss something. So we chose comfortable chairs at one of the viewing areas and watched the animals come out of the nearby forest, go to the watering holes, get a drink, then leave. A wild animal specialist watched with us and quietly explained over the speaker system what animal we were seeing, how frequently he had seen it, and what its characteristics were. This was a tremendous help.

I noticed that when several elephants came to the watering hole, their big feet would sink into the muddy area. Then as they left, the water would trickle in, filling those foot-deep holes. At that point smaller animals came and drank from the holes left by the elephants' huge footprints.

We watched until late at night, then went to bed, praying that the Lord would bring some really rare animals to the watering hole. At about 2:00 AM, the buzzer in our room went off, so we jumped up and ran to the viewing area. There we saw something unusual—a pair of bongos, a large African antelope known as the forest eland. They were red, with about twelve vertical stripes on each side. Each stood about four feet high at the shoulder. Both sexes had sharp horns, bent slightly forward and varied in length from twenty to thirty-six inches. We were told herds of bongos live in dense, wet forests and deep jungle country and feed on the leaves and twigs of shrubs and herbs. The bongos stayed at the watering hole for a few minutes and then disappeared in the nearby wooded area.

We went back to bed, and at 4:30 AM, the buzzer went off again, signaling an unusual animal at the watering hole. We shook ourselves awake, threw on our robes, and headed for the viewing area again. What an experience! This time as we returned to bed, I said to my wife, "I don't care how unusual the next one is, I'm going to sleep through it all!"

After breakfast the next morning we watched a little longer, then walked out of the Ark across the drawbridge to the parking lot and boarded our bus.

Our next stop was at the Rift Valley Academy about thirty-five miles west of Nairobi. We enjoyed meeting students, mostly MKs, the faculty, and visitors. It was Ruth's birthday, so they gave our tour group a special dinner, as well as a birthday cake for Ruth. But we kept thinking about the wild animals we had just seen.

The experience at the Ark reminded me of God's great creative ability in forming each animal, and in the case of the bongo, it seemed like perfection. This gave new meaning to Genesis 1:25: "And God made the beast of the earth according to its kind, cattle according to its kind, and everything that creeps on the earth according to its kind. And God saw that it was good."

After each visit to Africa, we marveled at the unusual sights on that continent. But what stood out most were the wonderful people. Nearly everywhere we went we met precious believers in Christ who were an inspiration to us. Indeed, we came away with a greater appreciation for the dedicated Christian leaders both among the nationals and missionaries.

RUSSIA

Several years before the Berlin Wall crumbled and the Soviet Union fell apart, Ruth and I took a tour group of over seventy to Russia. They came from various parts of the United States. We spent about ten days there and saw communism in its ugliness, as it had strangled the people for many years.

OUR ENTRANCE—SURPRISE, SURPRISE!

Our point of entry was through Finland. We arrived at the Russian border by bus in mid-afternoon. The countryside was rather flat, with forests here and there. We were all excited as our bus pulled up to the checkpoint. A huge metal gate extended across the two-lane asphalt road. A high wire fence ran to the left and right across the countryside as far as we could see. Mounted on lookout towers about fifteen feet high were two soldiers on the right and two on the left. Ferocious-looking German Shepherd dogs were "milling around."

When we drove up to the gate, three Russian officers in uniform boarded our bus and talked briefly with our driver, who spoke Russian. Two grim-faced officers walked up and down the aisle of our bus with one German shepherd each. The third man was checking on the other two. Most of us smiled broadly as they looked us over and as the dogs sniffed each seat. But the officers didn't dare crack a smile. Then we had to fill out forms declaring what we were bringing in. Finally they left the bus and motioned the driver to proceed through the gate. Now we were on Russian soil.

One member of our tour group was a fourteen-year-old girl accompanied by her parents. Unknown to me, she was planning to try out for cheerleader at her high school in New Jersey. As a part of her routine, she used a sword nearly three feet long. Little did I know that she had packed it away in her long suitcase. Except for our little carry-on luggage, all of our bags were stored on the bus in the large compartment below.

As the sour-faced officers began to take our suitcases from the bus and place them on a table for inspection, the teenage girl stepped back to my seat and said, "Dr. Narramore, I forgot to tell you. I'm trying out as a cheerleader back home, and we have one drill that requires all of us to use a sword. I wasn't sure I'd be able to make the team, so I brought the sword along to practice, and it's in my suitcase!" She looked at the officers and then back at me and asked, "What do you think they'll do when they find it? Am I in trouble?"

"They'll probably faint just like I'm getting ready to do right now!" I said.

Russia's arch enemy, the United States, trying to enter with a three-foot sword! So you can just imagine how we watched when the grim, leather-faced, uniformed guard opened the teenager's luggage. He pressed his hands down on the girl's clothes which were lying on top. His fingers felt something hard and stiff like a piece of metal. Then out from under the panties and bras he pulled a long, shiny sword! What a picture as he stood there blinking his eyes in amazement!

He called his higher-ranking officer, who motioned for three other officers to come, and they all stood in a circle trying to decide what to do. Fortunately, one woman from our tour group spoke Russian. So she did her best to try to explain why we were carrying a sword. Eventually, after ransacking all our luggage, they let us go. I've often wondered if the officer in charge may have had a "crazy" teenager in his own family!

We traveled east toward St. Petersburg. The farms and shacks looked pitiful. Their equipment was old and worn. Fields were being furrowed by antiquated hand-plows. You wondered how those people could possibly make a living.

We were riding along when Ruth turned suddenly toward me and said, "Say, I forgot to declare all those hymn arrangements I brought along."

And in response I said, "And wouldn't you know it, I forgot to declare all those little books I've written on everyday problems."

"How many are there?" she asked.

"I think there are about fifteen," I said.

"I wonder what they'll say when we leave the country?" Ruth asked.

"I don't know," was my reply. "We'll just have to pray and ask God to help us."

SAINT PETERSBURG

In time we arrived in Saint Petersburg, a city of more than five million, beautifully situated on the Neya River. Construction of Saint Petersburg (a center for education and scientific research) began in 1703 under Peter I, who employed Italian and French architects. The city's landmarks include the Royal Winter Palace and the Hermitage museum. From 1712 to 1918, the city replaced Moscow as the capital. It has been immortalized by such writers as Pushkin and Tolstoy. In 1914, it was renamed Petrograd. On Lenin's death in 1924, it was changed to Leningrad. Many thousands of its citizens died during World War II when the people heroically withstood the prolonged German siege (1941–44). Then the city's original name was restored in 1991.

From the outside, the hotel that was assigned to us after we arrived looked fine. But inside it was basically a shell. As I stood in our room, I could stretch my arms out and touch both sides of it. A sour-faced hostess (spy) sat at a desk just outside the elevator on each floor. We surrendered our room keys each time we left the floor. They knew our every move.

We enjoyed touring the city, especially taking a Hovercraft ride a few miles away to the Winter Palace where past czars lived in luxury. The beautiful artifacts inside the palace contrasted strongly with what we saw outside. Russian women with their heads wrapped in babushkas and dressed in old clothes crawled on their knees trimming the lawn with hand clippers, as they had no lawnmowers.

MOSCOW

As we left Leningrad, we boarded a plane and flew to Moscow. The airport was virtually forsaken, with only one or two cars and just a few people. As we boarded a bus and went into downtown Moscow to our hotel, we didn't see even one restaurant. We soon learned that the Russian citizens were not allowed to go into the hotels. However, two young people in our group were approached on the street by a couple of young Russians who offered to buy their jeans!

The woman who was assigned to watch our particular hotel floor seemed rather kind and thoughtful. I made it a point to leave one or two gospel tracts around that were printed in Russian. On the last day we were in that hotel, I came by her desk and with her hand she pointed up to heaven, then placed her hand over her heart and quietly said, "Jesus." She did this several times, and I'm sure she was saying that she, too, was a believer in Jesus Christ!

The tour included three meals a day, so we were assigned seats at a long table in the drab dining room. The food was fair, including daily cabbage soup. One pat of butter was placed at each plate, and no one was permitted to ask for more of anything.

People looked depressed and downtrodden, and we seldom saw even one person smile. When Ruth and I visited Moscow's main department store, we felt sad to see what few shoddy clothes were available for sale. At one section in the store some dresses had just arrived. Suddenly a number of women dashed to the table where they were about to be displayed, and they fought like children to get their hands on a dress. Two women would grab a dress and pull until you thought it would tear in two. They took off the dresses they were wearing right in front of the crowd and tried on any new ones they could get their hands on. It caused us to reflect, in contrast, on the great abundance of food, clothing, and everything available to shoppers in the United States.

One Communist woman guide was assigned to our bus from the time we arrived in Moscow until we left. About the third day, we asked her if she would direct our bus driver to the location of the Baptist Church, the one main church that was still open in Moscow.

"There's no such place," she said firmly.

"Oh yes, there is," we insisted. "We've heard and read about it, and we'd like to go there." She kept insisting there was no such place. Then after talking with her supervisor she told us there was such a place, but that the streets were too narrow to take our bus.

When we threatened to walk, she changed her tune and finally agreed to try to make arrangements for us to go that evening.

THE MOSCOW BAPTIST CHURCH

When we took our bus over to the church, we saw that the street was lined with row houses connected to each other. We were surprised when we got out of the bus because no church building was in sight. But at that point our guide opened one of the "house" doors from the sidewalk and we entered what was the main church in the city. The lower floor of the auditorium accommodated about two hundred people. It was rather long and narrow, and every seat was filled. We were escorted to the balcony not far from the choir and the organ, which were located across the back.

Our hearts began to melt as we heard the plainly dressed people sing in Russian, the old hymn, "There Is Sunshine in My Soul Today." The next song was "What Can Wash Away My Sin? Nothing but the Blood of Jesus."

Three men sat on the platform up front, behind the pulpit. We were told later that one was a communist overseer of the church, but the other two were true believers. I was sitting next to the aisle when suddenly a man in his forties came and squatted beside me and said, "You're Dr. Narramore, aren't you?"

Surprised, I answered, "Yes, I am."

"Well," he said, "I attended an all-day seminar you conducted in Newark, New Jersey, several years ago, so I recognized you right away."

I asked him what he was doing in Moscow. "I'm a U. S. citizen," he said, "but I'm here for a few days visiting close relatives."

I told him that we had a group of about seventy from across the United States and that I would be glad to come to the pulpit and bring brief greetings from Christians across America.

"I'll see what I can do," he said. "Your group's being here tonight is a real surprise. I'll write a note and get it to the pastor, and we'll see if they'll let you do this."

He left, and a few minutes later returned to tell me they had replied to his note saying my bringing greetings would not be permitted. "However," he continued, "they did say that if you want to write out a special greeting, I could bring it to the platform and they would read it."

"That's great," I said. So I wrote a greeting saying we were born-again Christians from many parts of the United States, that we loved Jesus Christ, and that we also loved each one of them. My new friend took it and I noticed that he handed it to one of the pastors on the platform. Then my friend returned saying, "They have read your greeting out loud exactly as you wrote it."

Our people were happy that we had this opportunity for a testimony.

At the end of the service, our New Jersey friend said, "You can't stay very long because the KGB is here watching everything. They'll suspect something if they see you lingering or talking to anyone."

As we left the church, many of these dear people wanted to hug us. Some were weeping. Walking in front of Ruth was the lady in our tour group who understood Russian. Turning to Ruth she said, "They are asking if we have any Bibles for them."

It hurt Ruth to have to answer that we had not been permitted to bring in any Bibles other than our own and that we would be checked when we left to be sure we hadn't left it behind. To disregard this mandate would be to jeopardize our whole tour group.

"Could you just tear out one or two pages from your Bible for us to have?"

Suddenly, Ruth remembered the hymn arrangements she had forgotten to declare. "They are in English," Ruth said, "but I'll be glad to give them to you."

Our friend talked to the choir director about the arrangements and he almost wept. "We haven't had any new music for almost eleven years," he said.

Plans were made for two of their people to walk outside of the hotel an hour later and get the arrangements.

"But there's one thing," I said. "Inside my light topcoat right now I have fifteen small books that discuss and give solutions to various common problems. I wonder if the pastor speaks English and if I could slip them to him."

At that moment, the pastor walked by us in the balcony and entered his little office. His name was George Vina (who later was imprisoned in Siberia). I quickly followed him into his office, closed the door, and showed him a couple of the books.

"Do you understand what psychology is?" I asked.

"Yes," he answered. "It's about how your brain and emotions work."

I quickly gave him all fifteen books, and he hid them in his desk. He cried as we shook hands and told me how deeply grateful he was.

As I came out of his office, my New Jersey friend said, "Let's move fast—the KGB is getting upset."

So we hurried down the steps and left the church. All along the street, those dear Christian Russians stood to wave at us as we left. Our hearts were heavy for their suffering.

About an hour later, Ruth gave the hymn arrangements to a Russian-speaking man and woman in our group who carried them under their coats wrapped in a Moscow newspaper. They walked up and down the sidewalk outside the hotel until a man and a woman approached them and said, "We've come for music." So as the four walked closely together, the musical arrangements were surreptitiously passed to the Russians, who carried them under their coats.

After returning to the United States, I read in the newspaper that the pastor of that church, George Vina, had been arrested and sent to Siberia. Several years later, we heard on television that he had finally been released.

We saw many interesting things in Moscow, including a state circus that was remarkable. But in summary, our major impressions were:

1) This is an enormous country with tremendous potential.
2) A democratic government led by men of God would make all the difference in the world.
3) If people were free to trust in Christ as their Savior and live for Him, it would influence the entire population.
4) We could easily see how Russia might fit perfectly into the biblical prophecy of some day going south to the Holy Land in an effort to eradicate Israel.

The restrictions we saw and sensed were almost unbelievable. In fact, when we boarded our plane, fastened our seat belts, and took off, the people spontaneously began to cheer and clap! We were so glad to be heading back to the United States!

THE EUROPEAN WINDSTAR TRIP

In the latter part of the year 2000, Ruth and I were given a trip to Europe, so I began to schedule meetings and evening seminars in Austria, Germany, Switzerland, and Spain.

Accompanying us were Ruth's brother and his wife, Dr. and Mrs. Gordon Elliott. He had been a pastor and had also served as a missionary at large in foreign countries.

As we were working with our travel agent to set up the itinerary, he phoned us excitedly and said, "I've been able to book you on a cruise for the last few days of your tour. It will fit in perfectly with your plans. The ship is one of the world's outstanding large sailing vessels called *The WindStar*." He went on to say that there were only two staterooms left and he could book us for half price if we took them right away. So I told him to grab them.

Later in the day, I phoned my son and told him about the cruise on the sailing vessel. He broke into the conversation to say, "Dad, the name of that ship is *The WindStar*."

"That's right," I said. "How did you know?"

"Oh," he said, "people all over the world know about that sail ship. It's the best of them all." Then he added, "But Dad, that's for rich people."

"Well," I said, "that's just what we are—very rich in happiness and in our love for the Lord! Besides, we can get our tickets for half-price!"

So with that special cruise feature to finish out our itinerary, we looked forward even more keenly to our trip to Europe. The opportunity to conclude it by sailing around the Iberian Peninsula visiting six different ports in Spain and Portugal was like the icing on a cake.

VIENNA, AUSTRIA

Our first stop in Europe was Vienna, known for its classical music and magnificent architecture. Arrangements had been made for me to speak to a group of parents and teachers and to hold an evening seminar at the Vienna Christian Academy.

Like Hillcrest Academy for missionary kids in Nigeria, Rift Valley Academy in Kenya, and Morrison Academy in Taiwan, the Vienna Academy is the center for many activities of American missionaries and the central point for various evangelical Christian organizations.

Upon arriving at the Vienna Christian Academy, we walked up three flights of stairs to the offices and classrooms where the boys and girls from kindergarten through high school were studying. One of the first faculty members we met said, "Oh my! You sound just like you do over the radio in Guam."

"Have you lived in Guam?" I asked.

"Yes," she said. "My husband and I were missionaries there for many years, and we heard you each day over Christian radio. In fact, we raised our children on you!"

Since I didn't have the nerve to ask how they turned out, I nudged the conversation to a different topic!

Our morning meeting, "How to Shape a Child's Life," with the teachers and parents was a real thrill for me. That evening we returned for a two-hour seminar where others were invited. Our topic was "Understanding Yourself and Others."

Then we opened the meetings for questions and discussion. Like other places, people gained insights and shared freely (many for the first time) about their problems. One man said he had never realized what a high level of anger he had. Then he began to share how this anger started in early childhood because of the way he was treated. "And now today," he said, "I'm terribly handicapped with my poor relationships with my wife, my children, with other staff members, and with the people I'm trying to reach here on the mission field." Then with tears he asked, "Can I ever change?"

I assured him that he could. "In fact," I said, "you've already taken the first step. You've identified the problem, and you're seeking solutions."

Then I asked him when and where he would be returning to the United States for furlough. "In six months," he replied.

"I know a remarkably fine Christian psychologist in the area where you'll be staying," I said. "When you return, just phone the Narramore Christian Foundation and we'll furnish you his name. As you work through this problem, you'll see a great improvement in your life that will help you as long as you live."

After the seminar, another interesting thing happened. A high school senior, eighteen, walked up to me and asked how he could get training in the United States to become a Christian psychologist. In the midst of our conversation, two women joined us. One was the boy's mother, the other their friend.

"He'll be a wonderful psychologist," they both said. "He likes people, and they like him. He's thoughtful and makes good decisions, and he loves the Lord."

So I suggested where he, a foreign student, might get a college scholarship in the United States and what training was required.

As we left the seminar and returned to our hotel, I thought about the potential of this young man. He could become a leading Christian psychologist in Europe.

I also prayed that everyone at the seminar was impressed with the importance of identifying his or her problems and seeking help for them. As I left, I said to Ruth, "I don't know how our time on *The WindStar* will be three weeks from now, but I'm sure it won't compare to this: ministering to fellow Christians!"

BLACK FOREST, GERMANY

A few days later, we held an evening seminar at the Black Forest Academy in southern Germany, near the Swiss border; the adults who attended represented various Christian organizations in that beautiful area. Some upperclassmen from the academy also joined us.

The discussion period following the seminar brought to light many individual issues. Some weeks later, a local leader wrote, "We are still talking about the content of the seminar."

After the seminar, one student, about seventeen, talked to me personally about her feelings of guilt. "Tonight," she said, "you talked about physical problems, especially neurological impairments. As you gave the symptoms, I wrote them down, and I could see that my younger brother had nearly all of them."

Then she went on to say that her parents were missionaries in another country and that her ten-year-old brother was living with them. "I only get to go home once or twice a year," she said. "Unknown to me, my parents have been taking my brother to a neurologist. But I've just found out about it. They say he has a neurological problem and can't be expected to achieve like other kids."

With tears she said, "I've always treated him like a pest because he's been such a brat. But now I'm so ashamed and I feel guilty. I'm a Christian, and I should have been kinder to him. Is there any way I can make up for my meanness toward him? I feel so bad."

We quietly talked it over, and I shared insights and Scripture with her. She was grateful and said it was a great help. Later that evening, I thought about the millions of people who are burdened with guilt. Praise God for His eternal word, which assures us, "For you, Lord, are good, and ready to forgive, and abundant in mercy to all those who call upon You" (Ps. 86:5).

The Black Forest area of Germany is unusually beautiful. Its gentle hills, forests, lakes, pasture lands, and mountains combine to make it one of the lovely spots on earth.

We visited for five days in this area because our relatives, Joy and Martin Erdmann, had just moved there. We stayed at a country inn a few blocks from them. Interestingly, this three-story country hotel had no lobby. When we entered the front door, we were in the restaurant. From there we climbed steps to the third floor where the view from our room was breathtaking. Almost everywhere we looked was perfection.

We visited and had several meals with our relatives. One thing was missing from their new home: the kitchen! (In Germany, people take their kitchens with them when they move to another house.) Since theirs had not yet arrived, they had no sink, stove, refrigerator, cupboards or kitchen furniture—just an empty room. Imagine feeding a family of four, plus four adult guests and one kitten. When asked why the German people did that, they said they didn't know, but it was the custom and they didn't suppose it was going to change.

BASEL, SWITZERLAND

In Basel, Switzerland, I was invited to speak briefly to the faculty and student body of a solid evangelical seminary. Dr. Martin Erdmann, Ruth's nephew, was head of the New Testament department there. The seminary doesn't have dormitories, so international students who are working on their master's and doctor's degrees live in the community and either walk or ride bikes to classes.

The evangelical Christian life is much different in Europe than in the United States. Here we have thousands of evangelical churches—many of them very large—hundreds of Christian radio stations, many Christian colleges and universities, large Christian publishers, and many fine Bible teachers and evangelists. But in Europe such is not the case. In most countries, evangelicals are considered members of a sect!

Yet many young people in Europe are growing up, getting married, living their lives, and then passing into eternity without knowing Christ personally. So my heart goes out to people in those countries.

I spoke to the seminary student body of about seventy graduate students. These outstanding young men and women will someday be pastoring churches or heading up Christian organizations in the German-speaking world.

MADRID, SPAIN

Several weeks before leaving the United States, our Madrid missionary hosts, Mr. and Mrs. Tom Baker, told me on the phone, "Christian groups working in this area have never cooperated much. Each one does its own thing. But now we're making a major effort to foster cooperation and present the Gospel in a concerted way. Your seminar will be one of the first meetings in this effort." Our evening seminar was held at a church in Madrid, and I was delighted that Christians representing twenty or more organizations attended.

My interpreter was tops! Whenever I raised my hand, he did the same. When I sprang out of my chair, he jumped out of his! It was like an exercise in mental gymnastics for me. I was thinking what to say, how to say it clearly so all could understand, and say it in short sentences so my interpreter could get it all! At the same time, I was listening to the interpreter (since I spoke some Spanish myself) to see if he was saying it correctly, or if I should add another sentence to clarify the thought. It all went along fine, with every eye glued on us. But at one point I forgot. In Spanish, I clarified his interpretation. Immediately, the crowd burst out laughing because they had not realized that I spoke Spanish too! But since the entire crowd spoke either English or Spanish, and quite a bit of both, most of them got our presentation twice.

The discussion period afterward was especially interesting. Many leaders were getting acquainted with each other. One young lady, about thirty-two years of age, ran up to Ruth and me and asked, "Do you remember me? I'm one of your girls. I took your training for MKs about fourteen years ago, and it absolutely changed my life! My husband and I are missionaries now, and we have two young children." She kept hugging Ruth, telling her how much she appreciated our MK training.

Another man said, "Three of our children have taken your MK training, and we're so grateful!" We left the seminar knowing two major dynamics had taken place: (1) people had learned about themselves, and (2) leaders from various ministries had related closely to each other.

In each city, we took a half-day city tour. Our missionary hosts also took us to many places of interest. Our time with these servants of God was precious. Guides who are missionaries usually know so much more than secular guides who are focusing on ancient buildings and empty cathedrals.

BARCELONA, SPAIN

Our last speaking engagement before boarding the *WindStar* was in Barcelona, an interesting city with unique architecture. This is the city of Picasso's birthplace, and his influence shone through. On Sunday morning, I brought greetings and spoke briefly at an evangelical church where five hundred regular members and visitors were in attendance.

One of the highlights of our time in Barcelona was our meeting with a Christian psychologist. We had much to talk about: client load, counseling techniques, fees, advanced training, spiritual emphases, relations with the local church, and a host of other matters. But the most significant topic was the spiritual aspects of professional counseling. He was eager to know more about "Christian" counseling. I soon realized that there were no other professionals in Barcelona with whom he could talk about Christ, the Bible, and Christian living. Consequently, our time together was most profitable! I was reminded again that all around us are believers who need spiritual encouragement to live unreservedly for Him and to make their witness known at their places of work.

SHIP AHOY!

It was mid-afternoon the first week of October when we arrived at the Barcelona port. Great ships from around the world were anchored side by side, but our eyes immediately fell upon a special ship—a very special sailing ship—the *WindStar!*

Since she was anchored in port, her sails were not raised. However, her size and shape were impressive. As we got out of our van, the ship's personnel took our luggage to our staterooms. At the end of the gangplank, the tall, uniformed captain and several of his crew welcomed us aboard and invited us into the lobby, where we filled out forms and met other passengers. We were surprised to learn that many of them had been sailing on the *WindStar* for a week and were continuing their voyage with us around Spain to the west, to Lisbon, Portugal.

The moment came to set sail and begin our cruise. The ship's sound system played a magnificent, stirring instrumental number—perhaps one of the grandest we had ever heard! The 175 passengers applauded as the sails were raised electronically. Soon the proud, white sails were touching the blue skies! The weather was clear and balmy. We were praising God for the prospect of visiting intriguing ports of call—and getting some rest!

We usually sailed at night and went ashore at an interesting island or a Spanish Riviera port during the day. When at sea, we watched the mighty waves and were reminded of God's creation and great power.

One of the most interesting ports of call was Tangier, Morocco, located on the north shores of the African continent. It seemed worlds apart from the cities in Spain, which were only a short distance across the Straits of Gibraltar. As we pulled into this exotic port, we looked down from our third deck and saw men standing and walking around on the dock. They were dressed in long, plain robes from neck to foot; on their heads were turban-like head coverings. They were waiting for the passengers to disembark. Each man wanted to be our guide and take us on a three-hour tour of Tangier. Their English was rather broken, but we could communicate easily. One of these men, Ali, walked up to our party of four and said, "I'll be your guide and take you in my car to see the sights of Tangier. I am seventy-eight years old, and I am the best guide you can get!"

After talking with him for a moment, we decided to go with him. Ali drove us around the city explaining what we were seeing. When we stopped, we got out of his car and went with him through the narrow cobblestone streets of the old city, which had plenty of potholes. Stalls lined both sides of the streets where local merchants tried to sell almost everything from safety pins to camels! The handicapped and beggars were asking for money. At one point, our guide opened a door along the street, and as we stepped inside, we saw several beautiful rooms with marble floors and walls. Immediately we realized this was a carpet store where they wanted to sell us fine rugs. Six or so salesmen stood stoically around the room ready to bring out additional rugs if the "captain" so signaled. When I asked them about a small, round rug, the merchant said, "We have just the perfect one for you, and we sell it for three thousand U. S. dollars—but because you are our first customer of the day (by then it was eleven AM), you can have it for only two thousand." When I offered him $200, he and his associates almost fainted! But they soon regained their poise and began to lower their price. At that point our guide, Ali, said with a wry smile, "Here in Tangier we do not bargain—but we do negotiate!"

After looking around for a short time, we left without any rug. A few weeks later in California, we bought just what we needed for $69!

As we visited the ports each day, we made sure we came back to the *WindStar* for our meals. We didn't want to take a chance on becoming sick. At each place we saw beautiful leather goods, dishes, clothes, tablecloths, and a host of other merchandise. We were reminded again that God gives people around the world creative talents and ability to make beautiful and artistic things.

Lisbon, Portugal

Our final destination on the *WindStar* was Lisbon. As we toured the city, we were impressed that although Portugal is a small country on the Atlantic, it has sent its navigators and explorers throughout the world. Even though I could not speak Portuguese, I talked with the people slowly in Spanish and most of them understood.

On our way to the airport after leaving our hotel in Lisbon, we talked with our driver, who was about thirty-five. I asked him if he went to church, and he replied in broken English, "No, we try to stay away from those things."

The four of us raised our eyebrows and wondered if he meant to say that or something else. Then I thought, that's not much different from the United States. With our wonderful churches in every community in America, a person almost has to make a definite effort *not* to magnify Christ and attend a house of God.

We boarded our Lufthansa plane and flew nonstop from Frankfurt above the Arctic Circle to Los Angeles. When we arrived home, our son had posted a big sign on the front door, "*Welcome Home, Mom and Dad!*"

We walked inside the front door, gave each other a big hug, and almost in unison said, "This is the best part of our European/*WindStar* tour!

My Beloved

CHAPTER 16

MY BELOVED

Just about the time this book was going to press, a severe loss came to us. My precious wife, Ruth, went home to be with the Lord. As she and I were writing and editing this book, we never dreamed that she would go to Heaven and not see this completed volume. But of course she is now seeing wondrous things which our human minds cannot even imagine. But, oh what a tragic loss to our family and friends.

When Ruth walked down the aisle at our wedding in New York City, and we said our vows, little did we know how the Lord would lead us the next 64 years.

During our dating days, it was apparent that she was bright, friendly, attractive and multi-talented. Such things as music, long distance swimming, speaking, writing and art seemed to be done with little effort. But most important was her spiritual commitment. She believed and had a good knowledge of the Bible and she loved the Lord. This affected almost every decision and action during the rest of her life.

Along with her spiritual commitment was her devotion to our marriage. She loved me deeply, and of course it was mutual! This permeated our lives until the day she went home to be with the Lord.

Ruth was encouraging to me and to others. She cared for people and focused on their good points. Hardly a day passed without her encouraging me. When I traveled alone to speak in Boston or New York or elsewhere, I would find little love notes scattered throughout the suitcase. I always felt loved and encouraged and I looked forward to returning home.

From the time I met her, Ruth loved beauty. She enjoyed God's creation and was always doing little things to make our home an attractive place of restoration and enjoyment.

A few years after marriage, our two children came along and I marveled at Ruth's ability to talk quietly with them, listen to them, pray about matters and move along with much love for each other. I couldn't imagine a better mother.

As our unique national ministries began to develop, we learned the importance of a sacrificial attitude. For example, when we launched our Psychology for Living radio broadcast, we were determined to follow the policies and requirements of the American Psychological Association. That meant we could never mention finances on the radio. Because this ministry was so desperately needed, people by the thousands wrote and phoned us for help. This required a larger staff, offices, equipment and the like. And it meant we often had to choose between getting or doing some nice things for ourselves or invest in the ministries. Ruth had a very sacrificial attitude and never complained. She loved to serve and give to others.

Ruth liked humor. She laughed a lot and told funny stories. This created a good environment both at home and as we worked together in our ministries. Because of the heavy responsibilities of our ministry, including taking phone calls all hours of the day at home, we could have felt much stress and pressure. But Ruth took it all in stride and her ability to laugh and see the humorous side of things helped us to keep a good balance in our lives.

One thing I especially appreciated about Ruth was her strength of character. No matter what came up I could depend upon her to quietly look at a situation, think it through, look to the Lord, then move ahead with resolve.

This was so evident not long ago when our beautiful and gifted daughter, Melodie, passed away. Melodie was an accomplished artist, speaker, singer, Christian dramatist and Most Distinguished Professor at California Baptist University. But more than this she was a sweet, humble, Christian and consistent soul-winner.

Losing a child is so painful, and the grief lingers on. But even during this devastating time, Ruth's sterling character and devotion to Christ shown through.

Another of Ruth's attributes was her desire to try new things and accept a challenge. One day we bought a beautiful harp which she soon learned to play at home and later for various concerts. Before long we secured a complete set of Swiss bells which she mastered and played around the nation. In time we purchased a 12 feet long Alpenhorn which she played with an orchestral tape background. And not long ago she published a book of 70 poems entitled "Come Share My Joy". Whether it was swimming across a lake, climbing a steep mountain trail, or mastering a new musical instrument, she was always ready for a new experience or challenge.

When couples get married, they bring along a world of thoughts and feelings and actions – some good and some devastating. As a result they may struggle with personality deficits such as a high level of anger, insecurity, paranoia and the like. I am grateful that Ruth grew up in a loving and encouraging Christian home and that she was free from these types of personality maladjustments. She loved people and they loved her.

In describing my sweetheart, Ruth, I would use the word, OTHERS. In nearly everything she did she was thinking of how her effort could be a blessing to others. Our home was open to friends and relatives for periods of weeks or a year. Even just a few hours before she went to be with the Lord, she asked about a personal friend who had injured her foot. Her "other" attitude was expressed mostly in her continual desire to lead others to Christ.

Our family is now in the initial stages of bereavement. But we praise God for His comforting Word. "Precious in the sight of the Lord is the death of His saints" (Psalm 116:15). My beloved is with Melodie, and I look forward to joining them.

We are now looking forward to many years of great ministry as my nephew, Dr. Bruce Narramore assumes leadership of the Narramore Christian Foundation. He and his wife Kathy are remarkably suited for this responsibility.

CPSIA information can be obtained at www.ICGtesting.com
Printed in the USA
LVOW051151210912

299620LV00002B/135/P